After Liberalism

*

NEW FORUM BOOKS

Robert P. George, Series Editor

A list of titles

in the series appears

at the back of

the book

After Liberalism

MASS DEMOCRACY IN THE
MANAGERIAL STATE

*

PAUL EDWARD GOTTFRIED

PRINCETON UNIVERSITY PRESS

PRINCETON, NEW JERSEY

Library of Congress Cataloging-in-Publication Data
Gottfried, Paul Edward
After liberalism : Mass democracy in the
managerial state / Paul Edward Gottfried.
p.   cm.—(New forum books)
Includes bibliographical references and index.
ISBN 0-691-05983-7 (cl : alk. paper)
1. Welfare state. 2. Public administration. 3. Social engineering.
4. Liberalism. 5. Democracy. 6. Pluralism (Social sciences) 7. Populism.
I. Title. II. Series.
JC479.G67   1998
351—DC21   98-9623   CIP

Acknowledgment is due to the following periodicals for graciously
granting permission to republish parts of chapters 1, 2, and 3 of
the present work that originally appeared in their pages: *Society*
(vol. 32, no. 6, September–October 1995, pp. 39–51); *The Journal of
Libertarian Studies* (vol. 12, no. 2, Fall 1996, pp. 231–51); and *Telos*
(vol. 104, Summer 1995, pp. 27–50).

This book has been composed in New Baskerville

Princeton University Press books are
printed on acid-free paper and meet the guidelines
for permanence and durability of the Committee
on Production Guidelines for Book Longevity
of the Council on Library Resources

http://pup.princeton.edu

Printed in the United States of America

1   3   5   7   9   10   8   6   4   2

✳ *Contents* ✳

Introduction   vii

CHAPTER ONE
In Search of a Liberal Essence   3

CHAPTER TWO
Liberalism vs. Democracy   30

CHAPTER THREE
Public Administration and Liberal Democracy   49

CHAPTER FOUR
Pluralism and Liberal Democracy   72

CHAPTER FIVE
Mass Democracy and the Populist Alternative   110

CONCLUSION   135

Notes   143

Index   177

✳ *Introduction* ✳

T HE 1996 U.S. election confirmed, if further substantiation was
needed, the centrality of entitlement programs in American politics. The
charge leveled repeatedly and effectively by President Bill Clinton was
that his Republican rival Robert Dole would slash Medicare and other
government allowances. Despite overwhelming public sentiment in favor
of balancing budgets and shrinking government, as Gallup Polls revealed
in Spring 1996, 53 percent of Americans opposed the cutting of social
programs and 54 percent were against a significant reduction in military
spending (this being a critical source of social entitlements and public
sector jobs).[1] The efforts made by Dole and other Republicans to present
themselves as fiscally responsible guardians of the welfare state had only
limited success. Though Republicans held on to Congress, Dole could
not save his presidential bid, nor, as columnist Charles Krauthammer
points out, did even heroic efforts keep Republican congressmen from
losing badly in Florida, Arizona, and in other states with large geriatric
populations.[2] By the spring the president's attacks on the opposition as
the enemies of Medicare (for suggesting a need to raise premiums and
to restrict some medical services) were finding their target. Among those
sixty-five and over, Clinton led Dole consistently by 15 to 20 points in all
major national polls.[3]

Whether Clinton and his strategists were engaging in demagoguery,
as Krauthammer, Paul Craig Roberts, and other Republican journalists
insist, is for this study beside the point.[4] More relevant, Medicare and
entitlements in general became the salient electoral issue, and the increasingly vague appeal to "family values," which had belonged to the
Republican rhetorical arsenal in the past, now worked to Clinton's advantage. Family values came to signify the Family Leave bill and other social
measures that the president had pushed through Congress. And though
the majority of Americans stood to the right of Clinton on, among other
moral issues, partial-birth abortion, the identification with a *caring* state
enhanced his image as an upholder of family life.

This obviously accounts for much of Clinton's appeal among women
voters, as columnist Maggie Gallagher argued in the wake of the 1996

elections. Women, Gallagher says, are as likely to vote for pro-life candidates as they are for pro-choice ones and have been active on both sides of the abortion issue. If they are now voting in ever larger numbers for Clinton and other left-of-center Democrats, Gallagher explains, it is because Democrats are perceived as "pro- family." The gender gap in voting, which is now at about 10 to 12 percent, indicates the material concerns of single women, particularly those heading single-parent families. In view of their trials, such women are looking to the Democrats as supporters of an entitlement-based welfare state. But this trend, continues Gallagher, should not be misread as an espousal of social liberalism. Unmarried women vote overwhelmingly for candidates of the Left because they think it aids them materially, not because most of them embrace a liberal ideology.[5]

Although this distinction is correct, it may also be academic. Gallagher's observations simply prove that Clinton's advisors calculated correctly: by associating family values with social programs, they won over the vast majority of single women, including those who appear to be ideologically to their right. They also further pushed the Republicans into awkwardly mimicking ambivalent polls, which showed that the majority of Americans want to reduce "big government" while protecting its results. Dole and other Republicans called for renouncing the collectivist Devil and his works but pledged to keep entitlement programs intact. They and Clinton found a symbolic way of ending the "welfare state as we know it" by signing a bill to reduce the cost of *underclass* welfare.

It is not surprising that entitlements in the United States have come to trump other political issues, all things being equal. The same thing has happened in Europe, where parties of the Right must steadily assure voters that they stand behind entitlements. In France the right-wing populist Front National has moved from advocating free enterprise to being an impassioned defender of working-class pensions and other government benefits. In Austria the regionalist and formerly pro-free-market Freiheitliche Partei has traveled a similar path, less successfully. In 1995 the party lost seats in the Austrian parliament because it failed to move fast enough to express support for existing entitlements. While European parties of the Right have taken the popular side in favoring immigration restrictions, they have often done so for reasons that to many seem less then compelling. They have made *cultural* arguments for their stand on immigration, when the popular reasons for support are chiefly physical and economic. Voters fear non-European alien residents, who are or who are thought to be associated with rising crime rates. Those in vulnerable work situations are concerned about foreigners taking their jobs, and national populations are becoming anxious about the entitlement net being stretched too far.

Throughout this century but most noticeably in the last fifty years, this book argues, democratic practice has entailed less and less vigorous self-government, while becoming progressively dissociated from any specific cultural or ethnic heritage. Democratic citizenship has come to mean eligibility for social services and welfare benefits. It also imposes varying degrees of loyalty to what Jürgen Habermas calls "constitutional patriotism": the acceptance of legal procedures and of democratic socialization, presumably to be carried out by social experts. Liberalism has also lost any meaningful connection to what it once signified. By now it is hard to find in contemporary liberal thinking much of what it stood for at the beginning of the century, save for talk about expressive and "lifestyle" freedoms (freedoms that nineteenth-century liberals might have had trouble in any case recognizing as rights). Our own liberal statements are no longer centered on the merits of distributed powers, the need to protect traditional civil society from an encroaching state, or bourgeois moral standards.

Today's liberal democracies express and accommodate other political concerns, from the need for entitlements to the combating of prejudice and the privileging by courts of lifestyle rights and designated minorities. In Europe, Canada, Australia, and New Zealand, governments have performed these tasks even more energetically than in the United States. There public administrations control incomes more directly, tax more heavily, and, together with courts, impose criminal punishments on those whose speech or writing offends ethnic minorities. Though this form of "democratic" governing leaves little to popular consent, it has enjoyed continuing popular support: whence the vexing problem for traditionalist and populist opponents of the current welfare state. They simply cannot convince a majority of people that those who provide, however ineptly, for their material needs are the enemies of democratic self-rule or are interfering unduly in family life. If people care little about such matters and are devoted to the present centralized system of social services, traditionalist and old-fashioned liberal or democratic arguments will not win the day. In this respect the political debate may already be over, despite the echo of populist rumblings in Europe.

This may be the case even if one agrees with the picture of overreaching government and moral decay depicted by an eminent Harvard professor of law, Mary Ann Glendon. Glendon is struck by how dependent most Americans are on "big business and government" and how thoroughly the two are now intertwined. Furthermore, she observes that "when regime-threatening questions come to mind, the oligarchs have authorized a modern form of bread and circuses, an array of new sexual freedoms to compensate for the loss of the most basic right of all, the right of self-government."[6] Glendon's strictures about the "democratization of vice" and "tyranny by a minority" coincide with critical observations made in this book, with one notable difference. What she and like-minded moral traditionalists derisively call the "regime" is here treated as precisely that, a way of governing a particular society that in this case rests on periodically given consent. If, as Glendon maintains, Americans and other Westerners have gone from being "citizens to subjects," they have done so in the absence of physical force. They have given away what they value less, the responsibility of self-government for themselves and their polity, in return for what they value more, sexual and expressive freedoms of a certain kind and the apparent guarantee of entitlements. It would not be stretching terms to call this a "democratic" choice, despite the resulting loss of what Glendon might consider as essential to human dignity.

While Glendon may exaggerate (though not by much) the steady pursuit of control by managerial-judicial government, others have erred more grievously, by treating the present regime as a broker among interests or as the plaything of competing factions. This view of modern liberal democracy has found a wide range of exponents, from European Catholic conservatives Carl Schmitt and Thomas Molnar to social democrats Robert A. Dahl, Norberto Bobbio, and Theodore J. Lowi. A Norwegian political theorist, Sigmund Knag, sums up this view in a critical observation about present-day Western democracies:

> The danger to democracy is that the spirit of deal making dominates the entire sphere of government . . . to the extent that all groups receive consideration, even groups who care little about the rules needed to sustain society, even groups of spongers, wreckers and whiners. Every corporate objection is welcomed with a diplomatic smile and a show of goodwill; every angry protester is someone who must be appeased in the name of consensus by being tossed at least a tidbit. In the world of corporate pluralism, no rascal is ever thrown out on his ear.[7]

If there is any idea that this book will vigorously dispute, it is the one expressed above. Knag presents the studiously cultivated image of welfare-state democracies and their administrative guardians as those trying to pursue the general good while being buffeted by special interests and by the demands of liberal pluralism. The most that can be said for this view is that it does contain a partial truth. Political parties must attract support and funding to stay afloat, and even administrative states need minimal consensus to prevent the turn of events that brought down the Soviet empire. Moreover, welfare-state democracies succeed to the extent that they provide for material needs, and inasmuch as different groups with different material interests will be required by such governments to maintain minimal consensus, it follows that elected leaders will try to satisfy enough interest blocs to stay in their positions.

But this does not explain the ideological direction taken by what Knag refers to as the "political culture of corporate pluralism." This direction, it will be argued, is determined by the regime itself, both by its interest in destroying the remnants of an earlier civil society resistant to its power and by an evolving project of social reconstruction. Though most Americans in nationwide polls favor restrictions on abortions beyond the first trimester, the federal government has charted its own course here, by guaranteeing a right to ninth-month (partial-birth) abortions. In the last two years, moreover, courts have stepped in to thwart the results of state-wide referenda in California and Colorado dealing with immigration, governmentally-enforced minority quotas, and gay rights. In view of these and other related developments, it is no longer plausible to depict the American national government as first and foremost an earnest or bumbling balancer of interests. More likely, it is becoming the instrument of a political class marked by common access to power and a shared vision of change. Seizing opportunities to transform society, this class has used entitlements to gain leverage over citizens. But it also conceals its power and designs by presenting itself as perpetually caught between interest groups. Unlike the national monarchs in early modern Europe, today's Western rulers hide rather than flaunt the power they exercise. This, however, does not render their power any less real, though it is not individuals but a class of "experts" who speak out against inequality and monopolize this rule.

The first chapter of this book looks at the frenzied quest for a coherent liberal tradition in the context of managerial government and the rise of social engineering. Although pieces of an older liberalism have been tacked on to the self-image of the present regime, the continuity assumed is, for the most part, contrived. Those who assume it ignore a patricide, namely, the slaying of nineteenth-century liberalism by twentieth-century "liberal" social planners. This act was made possible, explain the first two chapters, by the advent of mass democracy: the bourgeoisie's being overtaken by the lower classes and the ensuing "democratization" of government and social institutions. Unlike older republican traditions, twentieth-century Western democracy did not long remain within a fixed cultural or national context. It became the legitimation for public administration, seen as globally applicable, a form of rule that took over not only economic planning but also the task of socializing citizens. While public administrators, moreover, claimed to be pursuing "scientific" reorganization, their true goal was to combat bourgeois modernity, i.e., the political and moral culture that came out of the nineteenth-century Western world. But this goal of public administration, as chapter 2 indicates, was not apparent to most nineteenth-century liberal critics. What such critics feared were "democratic" social violence and the kind of political disorder associated with the French Revolution.

Chapter 3 sketches the evolution of public administration in a way that highlights its critical phases. Nineteenth-century liberals believed in the need for public servants and limited public education; nonetheless, they did not believe that administrators should work to change social classes or social values. They defended public administration as a means of maintaining order and of dealing with abject poverty. Administrators turned into social reformers with political power only after the welfare state came along in the present century. Then there occurred a quantitative leap in state control that eventually became qualitative. The state acquired control over education and began to formulate and apply family policy. Both were achieved in Sweden as early as in the twenties and came in other Western countries in the following four decades. As chapters 3 and 4 emphasize, these extensions of social planning were not deviations from what the welfare state intended to do. The reconstruction of group identity was an aim that social democratic reformers had embraced by the late-nineteenth century. By the mid-twentieth century, this project involved the use of social psychology and successive crusades against "prejudice." However intrusive these policies have become, public administrators have enjoyed the unswerving support of journalists and intellectuals. They had been able to count on those in the verbal professions who share their goals of advancing "tolerance" and "sensitivity."

In chapter 5 consideration is given to recent challenges faced by the managerial state. Unpopular immigration policies, bureaucratic and judicial interference in communal practices, and the suppressing of dissent as "hate crimes" have all aroused opposition to the powers that be. This opposition has expressed itself typically in populist movements, of which the most electorally significant have arisen in Catholic societies. There strong family and other institutional ties have created particularly stubborn resistance to government-directed social policy and to insulated party politics. In the United States a similar oppositional movement is now evident, and during the presidential primaries in 1996 it became temporarily linked to the fortunes and utterances of Patrick J. Buchanan. In a dramatic but not entirely consistent fashion, Buchanan decried the federal administrative state as the enemy of family values and democratic controls. He identified that regime and its media backers with a radical rejection of Judeo-Christian morality and, to minimize arbitrary and unaccountable powers, called for the use of referenda and the placing of term limits on elected officials.

A clear weakness of American counterrevolutionary populism, however, is its inability to find moral or cultural consensus. Contrary to what populism's advocates, particularly on the religious Right, claim, most Americans no longer exhibit either fixed moral habits or deep communal loyalties. They are footloose, perpetually acquisitive, and in varying states of transition from nineteenth-century familial patterns. They do not, by and large, fit the culture which is now conducive to European populism. What resonates among Americans is not the identitarian democracy featured by European populist movements. It is, rather, a stripped-down populism, which captures concerns about physical safety and the standard of living. Both California governor Pete Wilson and Canadian Reform Party leader Preston Manning exemplify the electoral appeal of this populism. They express the concerns of a mass democracy with less and less cultural unity but with an intensifying dislike for administration that seems oblivious to popular fears. Term limits, crime, indiscriminate immigration, and the effects of affirmative action are all issues that animate this populism, one that is giving a new edge to the rhetoric of the two major American parties.

It is entirely possible that this populist wave will be absorbed and neutralized. Also conceivably the managerial state in its present therapeutic phase will continue well into the next millennium. Its material and mass communications assets remain formidable, and while budgetary problems have arisen in terms of financing entitlement programs, the dismantling of the welfare state does not seem likely in societies where most inhabitants live off as well as support the state. At a time of unparalleled population movement, multinational economies, and massive public sectors, administered democracies operate in a favorable social context. What must be questioned, however, is whether this order is truly liberal.[8]

Does it recognize an inviolable sphere of social freedom from which public administrators are to be kept from meddling? Or, do administrators and judges define as social freedom whatever they wish to privilege at a given time? Moreover, is being administered and socialized by a custodial class the defining aspect of democracy? Though this may be the closest that our own society can come to self-rule, nonetheless one may be justified in asking whether administrators should be the prime actors in a democratic society. It may be the case that most people have little interest in ruling themselves or in practicing liberties that are unacceptable to a political elite. All this may be true, but it does not gainsay the need to question the claims being made about a "liberal democratic" regime that may in fact contain less and less of either characteristic. The very raising of these critical and by now unseasonable questions, can be described as an exercise in honesty. And *honestum*, as Cicero explained in *De Officiis*, is more than an intellectual virtue: it is equally a civic duty, especially for those who wish to occupy themselves with public affairs.

After Liberalism

*

CHAPTER ONE

In Search of a Liberal Essence

LIBERALISM AS A SEMANTIC PROBLEM

T HE history of liberalism in the twentieth century has been one of growing semantic confusion. This has resulted from two interrelated problems. First, liberalism has not been allowed to keep any fixed and specific meaning. It has signified dramatically different and even opposed things at different times and places in the course of this century, from a defense of free-market economics and of government based on distributed powers to a justification of exactly the opposite positions. Self-described liberals in the Western world during the last seventy-five years have been nationalists, internationalists, socialists, libertarians, localists, bureaucratic centralizers, upholders of Christian morality, and advocates of alternative lifestyles. They have treated these identities not as random individual choices but as true expressions of their *liberal* convictions.

Second, the term "liberal" has by now assumed a polemical sense, with the result that its antithesis "antiliberal" has come to overshadow any positive definition it may have had. Particularly during the Second World War and its cultural aftermath, a practice came to prevail among journalists and academicians to brand their opponents as antiliberal. Special measures were seen as necessary to curb antiliberal politics and statements, lest they lead to the illiberalism of imperial Germany or, worse yet, Nazism. And as early as 1937, the *American Political Science Review* devoted fifty pages to a monitory essay by Karl Loewenstein, "Militant Democracy and Fundamental Rights." Loewenstein, taking up a theme that would be further developed by David Reisman in the *Columbia Law Review* in 1942, called for the creation of a "militant democratic" America that would counter antiliberal forces by being affirmative about its "values."[1]

By the 1930s liberals were themselves engaged in disputes about the direction in which liberalism should be moved. There was heated disagreement between the Progressive educator John Dewey and the sociologist Lewis Mumford about the role of absolutes in a liberal society. In *The Failure of Independent Liberalism, 1930–41*, R. Alan Lawson shows that liberals became increasingly divided in the thirties between pragmatists and the advocates of "absolute values."[2] The emergence of an antiliberal enemy in the form of fascism therefore provided feuding liberals with a welcome source of unity. "Militant democracy," which would be propagated in postwar Germany as "die wehrhafte Demokratie" by the occupying forces, was an embattled liberalism as defined by an absolute enemy, antiliberal fascism. Social psychological texts, such as Theodor Adorno's and Max Horkheimer's *The Authoritarian Personality* (1950), became important for liberal educators and policymakers bent on protecting their fellow citizens and rallying fellow liberals against reactionary attitudes. The intractability of such attitudes was seen to reflect both the force of traditional religion and faulty child-rearing. Such cultural influences offered a challenge to liberal reformers, one that demanded the adoption of a vigorous social policy.[3] In this therapeutic literature the discussions centered on attitudes and values and on the need for proper socialization. Without such planning, traditional "authoritarian" attitudes, it was feared, would persist and lead to the kind of repressive society which had existed under European fascists.

Such *argumenta ad Hitlerum* have characterized the charge of antiliberalism brandished by liberal advocates since the forties. Invariably this line of attack relies on some form of the slippery slope, by which any serious assault on liberal social planning is condemned as a plunge into the rightist past. This tactic of debate, for example, was favored by prominent liberal intellectuals responding to *The Bell Curve*, a study of the genetic sources of intelligence, in the October 31, 1994, issue of the *New Republic. The Bell Curve*'s authors, Charles Murray and (the late) Richard Herrnstein, argue in excruciating detail that there are "intractable differences in I.Q. that cannot be accounted for entirely by environment." They suggest that social policies intended to remove these cognitive disparities will fail in the end and that American society in the future will likely organize itself hierarchically and multiculturally, along lines of intelligence.[4] Whatever the merits of these debatable propositions, nowhere do Herrnstein and Murray call for the eugenic planning that their liberal respondents ascribe to them. One critic, Michael Lind, traces their research to a "brave new right" that favors "Nazi eugenic policies."[5] Another respondent, *New Republic* senior editor John Judis, offers the opinion that the unwillingness to bring up hereditarian causes of intelligence is "not a taboo against unflinching scientific inquiry but against pseudo-scientific racism. Of all the world's taboos, it is most deserving of retention."[6]

Judis, Lind, and the other respondents do not demonstrate that *The Bell Curve* is "pseudo-scientific." Rather, they perform a kind of liberal exorcism by attempting to drive their debating partners out of the community of respectable scholars. The *New Republic* also published a highly revealing response by the Harvard sociologist Nathan Glazer on the danger of inquiry to a liberal culture. After the agonized admission that Herrnstein and Murray might be right in their conclusions, Glazer goes on to say that there may be higher value in telling noble lies than unsettling facts: "Some truths may not be worth knowing. Our society, our polity, our elites, according to Herrnstein and Murray, live with an untruth. I ask myself whether this untruth is not better for American society than the truth."[7] This truth, we are told, is that "smarter people get more and properly deserve more" and though there is nothing in this view that might offend a free-market or meritocratic liberal, it does not fit together with the current liberal emphasis on social engineering.

This recommendation of teaching through concealment that turns up in the *New Republic*'s defense of liberalism comes from a desperate inherited situation. Liberalism is increasingly adrift. Having gone over to social planning earlier in the century, it had to jettison its nineteenth-century heritage in return for humanitarian and "scientific" goals. Liberalism now survives as a series of social programs informed by a vague egalitarian spirit, and it maintains its power by pointing its finger accusingly at antiliberals. The depiction of sinister enemies has enabled liberals to hold on to those who may be wavering in their faith. In the *Anatomy of Antiliberalism* (1993), for example, Princeton political theorist Stephen Holmes goes after a string of "antiliberal thinkers" on the left as well as on the right who have been communitarian critics of liberal individualism. All of them, from Joseph de Maistre to Christopher Lasch, from Catholic counterrevolutionaries to socialists formerly on the New Left, are thought to resemble "fascist philosophers whose rhetoric is often indistinguishable from their own."[8] Holmes does respond thoughtfully to some of the accusations raised against the Enlightenment by nineteenth-century conservatives, and he is especially effective in pointing to the real absence of individual autonomy that John Locke and the French *philosophes* criticized.

What he fails to prove is that the *same* liberal tradition has been around for centuries. He ignores the changing character of liberal doctrine when he scolds Christopher Lasch for having antiliberal reservations about fair housing laws and for preferring ethnic enclaves to racial integration. Holmes considers those positions as being at odds with the "liberal universalism" that he traces back to his liberal heroes. But contrary to what he suggests, many past liberals, starting with David Hume and Thomas Jefferson, were not racial egalitarians. It is also hard to find examples of pre-twentieth-century liberals who worried more about racial integration than about property rights. In the *History of European Liberalism* (1927), Guido Ruggiero, a self-described Italian liberal, shows the persistent regard of his numerous subjects for private property and constitutional liberty; yet none seemed driven by any concern to integrate social and ethnic groups residentially or educationally.[9] In a glaringly anachronistic spirit, Holmes takes Locke's maxim "No man in civil society can be exempted from the laws of it" to mean what Locke never intended. This statement is made to reflect a "liberal universalism" that goes from teaching that "each citizen must play by rules that apply equally to all" to a variety of modern democratic practices, from state-subsidized universal education to universal suffrage.[10] What is never made clear is how the "disallowance of self-exemption for citizens from the law," which Locke did stress, mandates those measures Holmes would like to enforce. The term "universal," for Holmes, takes on an aura. It is not merely coextensive with authorized citizens but made to envelope humanity in general.

Locke himself was explicit about why civil society was created and repeats the same rationale several times in *The Second Treatise of Government*. In chapter 9 he asserts, after what is taken to be a sufficient demonstration of his argument, that "the greatest and chief end, therefore, of men's uniting into a commonwealth and putting themselves under government is the preservation of their property." The commonwealth, we then learn in chapter 11, need not be "a democracy or any form of government but any independent community," providing, as Locke states repeatedly in chapter 11, it manages to protect property.[11] In Holmes's improved version of Locke, "the enjoyment of property in peace and safety" takes a backseat to twentieth-century democratic rights, all of which are inferred from Locke's alleged attachment to liberal universalism. Holmes goes as far as attributing to Locke the thoroughly modern view that everyone in a country should have the right to vote, regardless of race, gender, or religious persuasion.[12] Such a position was not the one that Locke had in mind when he argued for the equality of legal obligations for all citizens. He was making this judgment about a particular and quite limited group, those who were recognized as citizens by the community in which they resided. His judgment did not apply to those who were not recognized citizens, even though in the state of nature all people were presumed to claim the same rights to life, liberty, and property.[13]

Contemporary liberals, such as Holmes, who undertake the task of devising a usable liberal heritage from John Locke on, have their work cut out for them. Often they begin by imagining that their position has a venerable pedigree, but as they look around for its presence in other times and places, they are drawn into a search that is eventually abandoned. Without an authentic and cohesive heritage, these liberals turn to a contrived one that, we are told, is the real essence of liberalism. We are bidden to focus our attention on this essence or spirit to make sense of an otherwise disjointed patrimony. This essence, we are told, is ample enough to embrace a varied company, from English Old Whigs and French aristocratic opponents of monarchical absolutism to the American civil rights movement and feminist spokeswomen. In one particularly frenzied attempt at liberal comprehensiveness, J. Salwyn Schapiro, in his anthology *Liberalism: Its Meaning and History* (1958), compiles, in defense of his own liberal faith, excerpts from Socrates, Erasmus, Peter Abelard, the German nationalist historian Heinrich Treitschke, Iron Chancellor Otto von Bismarck, Voltaire, Adam Smith, and labor union advocate Louis Brandeis. All of these anthologized figures supposedly share one or more of several defining liberal characteristics, starting with secularism and rationalism.[14] Since Treitschke and Voltaire both despised the Catholic Church and since Bismarck and Brandeis both advocated state support for the working class, all of them are made to illustrate Schapiro's liberal typology. Significantly, free-market liberals are excluded from it, if they had the misfortune of living and working after the rise of the welfare state. In all of this moving about of historical settings, the same persistent concern is evident: All liberalism must be shown to hang together. Otherwise two suspicions may be confirmed: that liberalism lacks a univocal meaning and that it should be replaced by a timelier term of reference.

The need for semantic clarification that this chapter seeks to underline is brought home to me on each successive visit to the Canadian city of Toronto. Public vehicles there exhibit signs with the message "Homophobia is a disease!" The provincial government of Ontario has made it a criminal act to publish statements offensive to racial and ethnic groups, and under the New Democratic Party provincial administration of Premier Bob Rae, which fell in 1995, initiatives were taken to "educate" the public about Canadian multinationalism. Extensive social services operate for which Torontonians and other Canadians pay with almost half their yearly earnings. When asked to characterize their municipal and provincial governments, however, most educated Torontonians of my acquaintance will usually answer "liberal" or "liberal democratic."

Behind this new multicultural and bureaucratically administered Canadian society stands an older one, which is still evident in Toronto. It is the Canada that points back to an English imperial past. Its heritage is kept alive by parks, monuments, and various landmarks. Examples of Victorian and Edwardian architecture abound in downtown Toronto, and the public celebration of the birthdays of Queen Victoria, Prince Albert, and other figures out of the Canadian-English past preserves the connection between sight and memory. Some of those for whom Toronto's streets and landmarks have been named were English statesmen, and most of them, like William Gladstone, Robert Peel, and Henry John Temple Palmerston, were associated with nineteenth-century liberal politics, even if their formal affiliations were Tory. These politicians opposed the sacrifice of widows on their husbands' funeral pyres in British India, the imposition of tariffs on imported grains, and other practices that they believed interfered with personal freedom. But they did not believe in political equality and considered the quest for social equality incompatible with both liberty and the integrity of the family. They were also proudly and resolutely patriotic. They found nothing wrong, as Lord Palmerston bluntly told his people in the mid-nineteenth century, with pursuing *English* interests abroad.[15]

The question that keeps returning to me in observing the two Torontos, one ascendant and the other vestigial, is: what connection is there between their political worlds? Both are thought to be, in some sense, "liberal," but it is hard to discern the common ground between these political worlds. Would Palmerston (1784–1865), for whom the street was named where my late wife grew up and where my children still own property, recognize himself in those self-described liberals living on Toronto's Palmerston Boulevard? Would he and they share some kind of worldview despite their obvious differences? Palmerston was, after all, a proper Victorian, free-marketeer, and self-consciously English man; while today's residents of Palmerston Boulevard, from what I can tell, are predominantly multiculturists and socialists, with a sprinkling of Sikh converts. Symbolic of the distance between the old and new liberalisms is the massive stone gateway at the entrance to the boulevard, dating from the 1890s, and the center for multicultural education that lies a stone's throw away. Both betoken liberal eras: one from the middle of the last century and the other designating our own time, one associated with imperial England and a Victorian society and the other with a managed and multicultural democracy.

The problem with locating a single liberal tradition in any case did not start the day before yesterday. In America the semantic waters already ran muddy during the interwar years. This can be gathered from looking at those interwar socialists and social democrats who claimed for themselves a liberal pedigree. These efforts at appropriation succeeded, thanks to an obliging professoriate and eventually sympathetic press, but they also called into question whether liberalism forms an "unbroken tradition." There were good reasons that social democrats in the twenties and thirties elected to call themselves "liberal." Some wished to hide the radical nature of their reformist agenda, and most were looking for a self-description that linked them to the American past. Contrary to Louis Hartz's claim, liberalism is not "America's only political tradition," but it is a strong one nonetheless. And it has seemed more congenial to most Americans than socialism. While American workers, noted the German sociologist Werner Sombart ninety years ago, hoped for better material conditions, they also rejected socialist ideology as a European import. This undoubtedly dawned on American social democrats trying to package their programs for their own countrymen. The Socialist Party, they perceived, attracted only a fringe vote outside of a few municipalities, but the "liberal tradition," at least in its Jeffersonian sense, was something most Americans viewed positively.

The appropriation of the term "liberal," however, did not go uncontested. In Austria the free-market economist Ludwig von Mises complained in his major work, *Die Gemeinwirtschaft* (1932): "No one has understood liberalism less than those who have claimed in recent decades to be liberals. They have imagined themselves fighting the 'excrescences' of capitalism; and they have thereby taken over the characteristic asocial thinking of the socialists. A social order has no 'excrescences' that can be merely excised. If a phenomenon develops necessarily out of the effects of a social system based on private control of the means of production, no ethical nor aesthetic whim should condemn it. The speculation that goes on in economic development cannot be damned in its capitalist form because the moral judge has no understanding of its function." Moreover, according to Mises, it makes no sense to condemn capitalism as inferior to socialism as a moral ideal, while praising it as better in practice: "One could with the same justification assert that a perpetual motion machine as a theoretical construct is better than a machine built by the laws of mechanics, even if the first cannot be made to work."[16]

Mises's utilitarian objection to socialism was related to his moral unhappiness about the passing of an age of relative freedom. As he had already observed in 1927: "The world today knows nothing more about liberalism. Outside of England the designation 'liberalism' is utterly despised; in England there are indeed 'liberals,' but most of them are such only in name and really moderate socialists."[17] In the same year, 1927, Guido Ruggiero, after chronicling the turns of European liberalism since the French Revolution, asked with unmistakable dread: "Is the [liberal] state now in decay? It certainly appears to have been exhausted by the gigantic efforts that have been required of it, one following another without interruption. Socialism and nationalism, illiberally employing the liberty bestowed on them, first tried to undermine it from within and to create an autocratic and dictatorial anti-state."[18]

Ruggiero and Mises were both writing against the background of liberalism's accommodation with rowdy bedfellows: nationalist movements in the nineteenth century, and socialism and the welfare state in the twentieth. Both believed these accommodations had added to the burden of defending a separation between the private and public spheres; each thought that the assault on property rights and the adoption of social policies threatened both freedom and proper political authority. Ruggiero ascribed this problem to the "democratization of liberalism," which he traced to the English philosopher John Stuart Mill (1806–1873).[19] It was Mill who first undertook a synthesis of one particular freedom, expressive liberty, with a plan for extensive income redistribution. It was Mill, Ruggiero also noted, who brought to England the technocratic schemes of the father of French sociology, Auguste Comte (1798–1857). In *Considerations on Representative Government* (1861), Mill advocated the creation of a house of lords composed of scientifically educated administrators. By this bow to scientific planners, he hoped to moderate the power of a democratically elected parliamentary lower house.

In 1944 a longtime admirer of Mill but critic of Comte, Friedrich Hayek, published a resonant broadside against welfare state liberalism, *The Road to Serfdom*, later serialized in *Reader's Digest*. Hayek depicted the journey toward a socialized economy as leading toward servitude. He made clear that he himself was decrying social democracy not as a European conservative but as an exponent of individual freedom and rational thinking. What the Nazis and Communists had done in one fell swoop, making everyone serve arbitrary power, Hayek maintained, Anglo-American "reformers" were doing by stages. And they carried out this work relentlessly, while misrepresenting themselves as "liberals."[20]

Hayek scorned the argument that democratic procedures would suffice to protect the citizens of a social democratic regime against the loss of freedom: "We have no interest in making a fetish of democracy. Democracy is essentially a means, a utilitarian device for safeguarding internal peace and individual freedom. Democratic control may prevent power from becoming arbitrary but it does not do so by its mere existence."[21] Far more than his fellow exile from the Nazis, Ludwig von Mises, Hayek questioned the strength of democratic restraints in the face of socialism. He also thought less harshly than Mises about the reactionary opponents of liberalism. Unlike Mises, he did not devote his energies to attacks on the Prussian "state socialism" of the nineteenth century or the social policy of Bismarck as a spawning ground for modern collectivism.[22] For Hayek, the enemies of liberalism who seemed most likely to take power, after Hitler, were on the left, and they wore social democratic colors.

A social democratic liberal who responded angrily to Hayek was Herman Finer in *The Road to Reaction* (1945). Finer appeals to an evolving liberalism that he accuses Hayek of ignoring. According to Finer, Hayek does not take the democratic aspect of liberal democracy seriously enough: he favors democratic elections in order to avoid unrest but does not want the majority to have its way. He also assumes "that the mass of the people are more likely to be swayed by the demagogue who intends to be a dictator, while the people of higher education and intelligence will not." Hayek keeps coming back to the dubious point "that mere argument can sway people in the direction of a policy they do not like, whereas it is well known that people are swayed by their interests in large measure."[23] Because Hayek seeks to curb the majority, Finer explains, he talks about federations in which sovereignty is divided. But Finer suggests that this too is a futile attempt to deny the people the social justice which they seek: "In our time the only form of government which will give Hayek what he wants—namely the protection of economic individualism in the extreme form that he wants it—is dictatorship, which coerces whole peoples, and sneers at rule by persuasion."[24] Thus Hayek extols the idea of democracy but has no stomach for what the people really want, and he attributes "more rationality and honor to millions struggling with each other economically than to millions democratically composing their own laws and controlling their responsible administrations."[25] Finer may have exaggerated the accountability of public administrators, but he is right to notice the squeamishness among free-market liberals in speaking about the democratic will.

Finer then goes on to point out that he himself has liberal as well as social democratic credentials. He affirms his belief in constitutional procedures as a precondition for social reforms and presents socialism as an attempt to overcome "the failures of private enterprise." Finer also points back to John Stuart Mill as a precursor for his own liberalism: unlike Hayek, Mill "did observe and finally concluded that the good of England required socialism."[26] Finer's appeal to Mill is not without precedent among social democratic liberals of his generation. Like J. Salwyn Shapiro and English Labourites, Finer cites Mill as representing a natural progression from the old liberalism to the new, a progression that went back to the mid-nineteenth century. Though John Stuart's father, James Mill, had believed in a market economy, the son had moved gradually toward a new kind of liberalism. It was one combining concern about the status of women and the free exchange of ideas with the acceptance of a democratic welfare state. These stands were supposedly of a piece, including Mill's examination of the "social question." A defender of individual autonomy, Mill had come to recognize what "reactionary" liberals still denied, namely, the need to separate the questions of production and distribution. By the late 1840s he had proposed that redistributionist measures be enacted for the sake of English workers (later social democrats praised Mill for treating property as a function of social evolution). While he understood that legally fixed property claims were necessary for peace in primitive societies, he nonetheless questioned the value of such arrangements in his own day. In the industrial age, Mill explained, property, by remaining an unequally distributed good, led to civil strife and not to general tranquility.

Mill's journey toward social democracy is chronicled in his autobiography, a work long mined for comments on the kind of reconstruction of liberalism favored by American reformers. But there were other English precedents for what later social planners would advocate. The English Liberal Party had begun to embrace the welfare state between 1910 and the First World War, abandoning free trade, introducing social welfare measures, and stripping the House of Lords, with the King's connivance, of any effective veto power. In *The Strange Death of Liberal England, 1910–1914*, George Dangerfield bade a not entirely affectionate farewell to "the true prewar [English] Liberalism supported, as it still was in 1910, by free trade, a majority in Parliament, the ten commandments, and the illusion of Progress."[27]

The changing views on socioeconomic questions among English Liberal politicians reflected their understandable desire to gain working-class votes. This trend also underscored, however, the effect of certain social philosophers of the late-nineteenth century, who struggled to reconcile liberal individualism with communal responsibility. Such thinkers as Bernard Bosanquet (1848–1912) and T. H. Green (1836–1882) distilled for the English public the works of continental philosophers, particularly Hegel's *Philosophy of Right*, in making a case for an ethically engaged state. In books and in lectures these authors took to task the "Manchesterian liberalism" of the mid-nineteenth century, which they equated with commercial values and a night-watchman state. English liberal critics of liberalism insisted that the individual's liberation from coercive and status-bound relations would not bring social improvement, unless it also led to a renewed corporate identity. Thus they demanded that the growing disjunction of the modern age between the individual and established authority must be overcome by the creation of a new synthesis between liberty and order. In *Liberalism* (1911), L. T. Hobhouse, editorialist for the *Manchester Guardian* and admiring critic of Green and the English Hegelians, went one step further than most other Liberal Party members of his time. He called for a revamping of the British economy on the basis of shared power with trade unions. Only in this manner, Hobhouse maintained, could workers become fully integrated into the English nation.[28]

Such Hegelian and organicist concepts were floating in the United States as well and in the late nineteenth century made a powerful impression on the young John Dewey (1859–1952). Dewey picked up these concepts from his professor and later colleague at the University of Michigan George Sylvester Morris (1840–1889). Much of Morris's short life was devoted to lecturing on Hegel's social philosophy and to his magnum opus, *Hegel's Philosophy of the State and History: An Exposition*. Morris also helped Dewey to establish close ties to the philosophy faculty at Johns Hopkins University, where Hegel and T. H. Green were both in favor. But such weighty philosophical speculation did not lead into social planning on this side of the Atlantic. Rather, it provided the window dressing for the new liberalism being formulated in the United States during the interwar years.[29] Arthur A. Ekirch documents the attempts at labeling the "public philosophy" that were implicit in American centralized planning.[30] When Dewey decided to characterize his proposed social reforms as "liberal," he had already tried out "progressive," "corporate," and "organic." The rise of fascism may have rendered rhetorically problematic the last two alternatives to "liberal." And since there were competitors for "progressive" associated with the reform wings of the two major national parties, Dewey and his confreres may have become "liberals" faute de mieux. In any case the social planners grouped around the *New Republic, Common Sense,* and the *Nation* chose "liberal" to describe themselves and their projects. What they wanted, explained Alfred Bingham, a social democratic activist and nephew of the conservative Connecticut senator Hiram Bingham, was a "New Society based on planning."[31]

In "The Future of Liberalism," written for the *Journal of Philosophy* in 1935, Dewey defined the new liberal creed as "commitment to the experimental method and a continuous reconstruction of the ideas of individuality and liberty in intimate connection with changes in social reforms." Contrary to what he thought was the view of classical liberals, Dewey mocked "the monstrosity of the doctrine that assumes that under all conditions governmental actions and individual liberty are found in separate and independent spheres." Yes, nineteenth-century liberals were innovative in their own time, but their descendants seemed to Dewey either economic imperialists or the captives of a frozen past. He called attention to their lack of an historical sense, a failing that results in "absolutism, this ignoring and denial of temporal relativity."[32]

Almost all the appeals to the new liberalism in interwar America invoked Progress, a concept which had also resonated in the older liberal tradition. In John Dewey's *A Common Faith* (1934), this meliorism draws upon Auguste Comte's scheme of human development, which had originated one hundred years earlier. Comte had sketched a course of human improvement extending from a primitive religious through a metaphysical to a social scientific, or positivist, consciousness. Dewey took this Comtean scheme and recast it, having it culminate in "the intense realization and values that inhere in actual connections of human beings with one another." Those who pursue experimental methods and take an active part in social affairs he placed at the point of a fully evolved human consciousness. Dewey's process of movement goes from an oppressive sense of the supernatural through a reflective theological period and onward to the "values of natural human intercourse and mutual dependence."[33] In Lewis Mumford's graphically presented end point, we encounter human consciousness bringing about the global transmission of a distinctively American model of living: "The United States, with its Federal system of government and its strongly centralized executive, is an image of the greater world we must help create for all men."[34] In the face of "fascist barbarism," it seemed necessary to Mumford to move quickly into the inevitable future. The United States, he insisted in 1940, should open its borders to all who wished to come in and then take steps to

14

ensure a "worldwide authority for the allocation and distribution of power and raw materials."[35] In a less generous mood, Charles and Mary Beard linked the course of American Progress to economic growth and technology in *The Rise of American Civilization* (1930). Though the Beards accepted most of the new liberal premises, including the need for social planning, they remained explicitly nationalist in their thinking.[36] This economic nationalism made them increasingly skeptical of the liberal idealism among interventionists before and during the two World Wars. And it may account for the Beards's break with mainstream liberals by the early forties and for their recent popularity among the American Old Right.[37]

The linkage between Progress and social planning allowed interwar liberals to assign changing contents and applications to what they presented as a unified liberal heritage. And once "progressive" liberalism caught on rhetorically and conceptually, this development helped to make liberalism synonymous with both a politically controlled economy and material redistribution. In 1949 Arthur Schlesinger Jr. located American liberalism within the "vital center," between anti-New Deal Republicanism and out-and–out socialism, and few in the United States rose to protest.[38] Though there were liberal parties on the European continent that still treated economic freedom and property rights as sacred principles, in both England and North America that fight was winding down by the late forties. When the avowed social democrat John Kenneth Galbraith celebrated "the liberal hour" in a book by that title in 1960, no one of significance complained that social planning by public administrators went against the real liberal tradition.[39] By then "liberal" had come to mean "progressive," and "progressive" meant being in sync with an evolving and bureaucratically administered society.

Liberalism also changed over time to incorporate two other features, both related to its association with social planning. Both were also implicit in the view of progress as something that affects human consciousness as well as material circumstances. As in other ways, Mill was paradigmatic here. Like other English progressives, including John Bright, Richard Cobden, and James Mill, John Stuart Mill had supported what became the British policy of international free trade. Like his father he believed this policy would benefit English workers while promoting goodwill among peoples. But Mill was also a militant interventionist who believed in the need to propagate what he took to be universal progress. He grew indignant in 1862 when the British government of Lord Palmerston failed to side actively with the American Union. The struggle against slavery became a consuming passion of his throughout the American Civil War. Moreover, like his father, who had written the *History of British India*, Mill went to work for the East India Company and hoped to reform the gender and other social relations which existed among India's inhabitants. In Parliament between 1865 and 1867, Mill returned to the question of "female bondage," calling for the political equality of women and demanding an end to the legal disabilities against them. He also backed what became the Reform Act of 1867, extending the franchise to all English men, and he expressed the wish that the vote be given to women as well.[40]

A frequently heard adage is that history tells less about what really happened than what each generation imagines about the past.[41] This certainly applies to contemporary conceptions of liberalism, in which free trade, political internationalism, and the welfare state are all seen as parts of a composite whole. But these associations have been neither natural nor inevitable. In the nineteenth century most continental liberals were also nationalists and only opportunistically free traders. In England free trade ideas arose mostly among democrats, not mainstream liberals, and among the Philosophical Radicals to whom the French historian Elie Halévy devoted a famous monograph in the 1920s.[42] In twentieth-century America free traders have included both nationalists-isolationists and vigorous internationalists. In 1940 opponents of American intervention in the Second World War, led by William Borah and Hamilton Fish, thought that the removal of tariff barriers would bring peoples together without military force. Those on the other side of the intervention issue, such as Cordell Hull and Henry Stimson, called for American action against imperial Japan to create an international order favorable to free trade.[43] In recent debates over the North American Free Trade Agreement and the General Agreement on Tariffs and Trade, the same difficulty arose about determining the true representatives of the liberal tradition. Those who invoked free trade were mostly very qualified supporters of a market economy, while much of the opposition on the "Old Right" came from free market critics of the welfare state. In the case of presidential hopeful Patrick Buchanan, opposition to unprotected industries went together with attacks on the welfare state, except when it was protecting American jobs.[44]

The impetus toward liberal internationalism may be determined less by an economic outlook than by a commitment to a particular vision. Once liberalism came to signify the march of Progress and the advance of social policy, it could also be made to mandate a civilizing mission.

That explicitly progressive mission explains why European imperialism attracted many on the left, including Karl Marx, the militantly secularist French Radicals of the 1880s, and English Fabian socialists twenty years later. Western imperialists were seen to be the midwives of modernity, who would bring the non-Western world into the new age of science, materialism, and equal rights.[45]

The history of twentieth-century liberalism in any case refutes a critical judgment first put forth by the German legal theorist Carl Schmitt in the 1920s. According to Schmitt, liberals have no real sense of political life or of the intensity of political struggles. They dream instead of "depoliticized" world markets based on economic exchange and legal norms. Liberals view all rights as universal or universally extendable, because they ignore cultural and national differences—or hope they will go away. The same Schmittian refrain has come from the Left, in Theodore Lowi's *The End of Liberalism* (1969). According to Lowi, a distinguished academician who favors well-coordinated social policy, "Liberal government cannot plan. Planning requires the authoritative use of authority," but liberals, who apply "pluralist principles," cannot "overcome the separatist tendencies and self-defeating proclivities of independent functions in government. In short, they are economic negotiators instead of political leaders."[46] In the twentieth century this view of liberalism as "the opposite of the political" has become less and less true. By now successive crusades have taken place, from the presidency of Woodrow Wilson on, to make the world safe for liberalism and democracy. Liberal democracy has become an "armed doctrine" (to use the colorful phrase of Edmund Burke) as well as a human right, and both sides of the American party spectrum have called for the use of force and public money to bring its blessing to other peoples. As Laurence Whitehead explains with regard to this ideological imperative: "One feature distinguishing the United States from all previously dominant or hegemonic powers is a persistent and self-proclaimed commitment to the promotion of democracy as an integral element of its foreign policy and its long-standing confidence that all 'good things,' U.S. influence and security, economic freedom, political liberty, and representative government, go together."[47]

Equally significant, American liberals have insisted at least since the thirties that social and moral improvement requires educational efforts at home and abroad. Letting people go their own way will not suffice to make them open-minded or civic-spirited. The foundations for a planned society go back in Europe to the eighteenth century, and the idea of managed progress provided inspiration for Comte and other social scientists in the mid-nineteenth century. In the United States, Lester Frank Ward (1841–1913), a father of academic sociology and a devotee of Comte, advocated the creation of a "telic and dynamic society" that would pursue rational collective ends. Sociological reformers hoped to implant these ends in all citizens.[48] Ward's concept of "realistic education" influenced heavily Thorstein Veblen, Dewey, and other early-twentieth-century American reformers. Such figures found in public education a training ground for an enlightened democratic citizenry—one that might be cleansed of unseemly religious beliefs, among other flaws. That the projects devised by European social scientists reached America was not surprising, given the cultural ties between the two continents. More interesting was the fact that these lucubrations should come to be seen as liberal. For Hayek, who wrote a diatribe entitled *The Counter Revolution of Science* (1955), this self-description of sociological reformers as "liberals" was patently false. "Totalitarians" such as Comte and his disciples, he said, pretended to believe in freedom and scientific method while respecting neither.[49]

But Mill, whom Hayek did admire for his utilitarian thinking, praised Comte and tried to apply the latter's sociology in the 1840s. A hundred years later it would be widely believed that liberal societies could only survive if they intensively trained their young in liberal values. More accurately put, American social reformers presented a view, which came to prevail, that public officials should preach "liberal democracy." In the mid-thirties Dewey hoped that churches could be encouraged to do the same. To build a new society based on experimental method and communal values, it was not enough to depend on public educators. Dewey hoped to enlist religious leaders in winning acceptance for "human values that are prized and need to be cherished, values that are satisfied and rectified by all human concerns and arrangements." Churches could do this by supplementing the work of public servants. They could "show a more active interest in social affairs, take a definite stand upon social questions as war, economic injustice, political corruption," and, above all, "stimulate action for a divine kingdom on earth."[50]

Other liberals of the period emphasized the fascist threat in making a case for democratic values. The most instructive case in point was Karl Loewenstein in his earnest essay of 1937, "Militant Democracy and Fundamental Rights." Though Loewenstein stops short of proposing national indoctrination in his preferred political values, he ends his warnings about the fascist danger to democracies with these pregnant observations: "In order to overcome the danger of Europe's going fascist,

18

it would be necessary to remove the causes, that is, to change the mental state of this age of the masses and of rationalized emotion. New 'psycho-technical methods' must be found to 'regularize' the fluctuations between rationalism and mysticism."[51]

Loewenstein's hope that therapeutic methods could be devised to make liberal democracy fascism-resistant would become apparent among postwar militant democrats. In this respect the authors and disseminators of *The Authoritarian Personality* and more recent advocates of sensitivity education have not initiated anything that was not already dormant in interwar liberalism. Nor do the recent fears expressed by liberals in regard to the populist masses represent a departure from the interwar liberal devotion to the people. Finer's attempt to appear more democratic than Hayek was simply a ploy. His defense of the people was made in the course of praising their acceptance of public administration and social planning. It is hard to imagine that he would praise their wisdom if they rejected what he calls, euphemistically, "guidance." Loewenstein is entirely candid on this point. "Democracy," he insists, "has to be refined. It should be—at least for the transitional stage until a better social adjustment to the conditions of the technological age has been accomplished—the application of disciplined authority by liberal-minded men, for the ultimate end of liberal government: human dignity and freedom."[52]

Liberal Continuities and Discontinuities

The developmental picture of liberalism here being offered is not intended to be a rogues' gallery. Much of the movement from the old liberalism to the steadily newer occurred because of circumstances common to the industrialized West since the nineteenth century. Urbanization, struggles for universalizing the franchise and for broader distribution of material wealth, and the growing identification of popular government with public administration have all contributed to the reconstitution of political identities. Political taxonomies, like parties, have had to change to keep abreast of social and institutional developments. Less obvious but equally significant, however, has been the shaping of political discourse, a process that has influenced structural changes in the way it has presented and prescribed them. For example, it is not irrelevant to the pace or even the nature of major political changes in the United States that social reforms have been presented as liberal, thereby bestowing upon them the appearance of continuing something hallowed over time. In *Liberalism and its Challenges*, Truman biographer Alonzo L. Hamby equates liberalism with all social welfare programs introduced by the federal government since the presidency of Woodrow Wilson. Though Hamby dissents from post-sixties liberal ventures into affirmative action and minority set-asides, he treats all governmental social planning since the teens as liberal manifestations.[53] What he leaves unexplained is how this accumulation of social programs, all bearing the same label, is related to what used to pass for liberalism in the nineteenth century.

Those who have undertaken to address this question have typically cobbled together presentations of an unchanging and temporally unbounded liberal essence. Though there are multiple variations on this theme, at least three have recurred with some regularity. One is the ascription to Americans of an invariable liberal identity that inevitably permeates all of their political and other activities. Viewed as embodiments of something resembling the Calvinist notion of irresistible grace, Americans are seen to have a liberal status no matter what they do. The political philosopher Leo Strauss and his numerous epigones insist that America was founded as a Lockean nation; thereafter it has stood unchangingly for individual rights to life and property. Strauss's student Thomas Pangle further maintains that the American character was permanently shaped by the country's founding ideas, which were materialistic, utilitarian, and individualistic.[54] The European Catholic traditionalist and exuberant critic of American life Thomas Molnar also speaks of an immutable American character. Molnar argues that the United States was founded as a Protestant commercial republic, and all of its subsequent political and moral problems are traceable to that circumstance.[55] In a kinder spirit Louis Hartz and Lionel Trilling have written on America's permanent liberal culture as reflected in arts and letters.[56] Trilling went so far as to locate the evidence of that culture within a particular imagination and within a temperament that he claimed to find in the national literature.

A second attempt to find liberal continuity is to equate it with characteristically modern assumptions about society and the nature of reality. These assumptions are thought to be particularly persuasive in our time, as alternative ones have lost their hold on the popular imagination. The liberal worldview is alleged to be contractual, individualistic, and secularist. It was supposedly implicit in the attitudes of an earlier age. It found expression among eighteenth-century rationalists, but its full unfolding is taking place only now. A German intellectual historian, Hans Blumenberg, pushes the unfolding liberal heritage even further back in time. In *Die Legitimität der Neuzeit* and in numerous essays, Blumenberg has looked for an operative secular humanist outlook from the age of Copernicus onward.[57] The search for a scientific view of causation during the Renaissance, he explains, reflects attitudes about knowledge and its uses which were typical of rationalist modernity. The detachment of this modernity from older authorities, Blumenberg maintains, began earlier than is often imagined. Looking at the the American side of this modernity, political theorist William Galston makes the point that "liberalism contains within itself the resources it seeks to declare and defend a conception of the good and virtuous life that is in no way truncated."[58] Galston does not deny that liberals may draw some conceptual support from both classical and religious authors, but he is also adamant that liberals do not require these sources for the "content and depth" of their beliefs. He attributes to the spread of liberal openness and rationality a number of characteristics that he believes are embodied in contemporary America: social peace, the rule of law, receptiveness to diversity, a tendency toward inclusiveness, minimum decency, affluence, scope for development, and approximate justice (without achieving full distributive justice), openness to truth, and regard for privacy. According to Galston, we have become the showcase for all these desirable things, and to the extent that they exist, they prove the power of our liberal beliefs, which are not "neutral" but supportive of liberal institutions.[59]

A third approach to presenting a consistent and vital liberal tradition is through reenactment. At the popular level this involves periodic celebrations of past liberal achievements. In the last twenty years Americans have experienced many such rites, from commemorating the Declaration of Independence to expressing gratitude for "two hundred years of a living Bill of Rights" (as a billboard that I passed daily on the way to work used to read). Reenactment also takes a second, more reflective form: engaging in a liberal founding act to justify the transformation of liberalism into social planning. The appeal to a continuous, cognitive refounding of civil society in John Rawls's *A Theory of Justice* (1971) illustrates this kind of reenactment. Rawls, who is both a socialist and a Lockean, provides a contractual theory of society in which property rights are subordinated to "fairness." Rawls tries to conceptualize a society that would be acceptable to all on the basis of justice. Justice, he tells us, is reducible to two principles, to which all of us would give our assent if placed in an "original position" behind a "veil of ignorance." Rawls notes that "the idea of an original position is to set up a fair procedure so that only principles agreed to will be just." None of us in this state would be allowed to have a concrete identity: "If a knowledge of particulars is allowed then the outcome is biased by arbitrary contingencies." This "notion of the original position" would force the participants to "choose principles the consequences of which they are prepared to live with whatever generation they turn out to belong to."[60] In a situation in which all are forced to draw their fortunes from the same bag, we would likely arrive, according to Rawls, at the same two principles of justice: "Each person is to have an equal right to the most extensive basic liberty compatible with similar liberty for others," and "Social and economic inequalities are to be arranged so that they are both a) reasonably expected to be to everyone's advantage, and b) attached to positions and offices open to all."[61]

Despite Rawls's insistence that his own priorities do not violate the first principle of justice, his concern for the second principle, that is, for the "distribution of income and wealth and to the design of organization that makes use of differences in authority and responsibility," overshadows his discussion of justice. He sets down conditions intended to shape its application: Inequalities are permissible only if everyone's position is improved. Moreover, "Unless there is a distribution that makes both persons better off, an equal distribution is to be preferred." Finally, "Inequality is permissible only if by lowering it we make the working class even worse off."[62] Presumably those who think about justice without the burden of particular identities would create and apply such maxims. Behind the veil of ignorance they would be forced to imagine themselves as havenots and would therefore demand a socialist public policy.

Though various approaches to demonstrating liberal continuity have been undertaken, none is believable in the end. For none tells us much about the political life it sets out to describe. All of them lack the "temporal relativity" or historicity that Dewey thought that classical liberals left out of their social views. It is hard to imagine that the present American managerial state is the instantiation of a liberal character descended from the country's founders. Other cultural circumstances must be taken into account to explain our political development. It is equally questionable whether some "disposition" discernible among learned mid-nineteenth-century New Englanders provides the key to understanding our political life in the 1990s. By now America's inhabitants have changed in so many ways that Victorians would have trouble recognizing in them their own successors. Authorial journeys into the past may be instructive, but their value is limited. They do not reveal secrets about today's far more heterogeneous—that is, less traditionally Protestant and less classically liberal—American society. Invocations of an immutable American liberal identity deny what centuries of change have wrought.

It is, furthermore, hard to grasp the value of enumerating the putative achievements of particular societies as proof of their liberal "resources." First, one may question whether these achievements are being accurately described—that is, whether there is social peace and not urban violence and racial hate in the United States, or whether inclusiveness is not really an attempt by public administrators to force groups together, often against their will and in violation of older liberal principles. But, even more to the point, it is not altogether clear what Galston means by liberalism. In the early chapters of his book he associates it with Lockean and classical liberal thinking, but by the end of the same work he is talking about "judicial liberals" and the "liberal" opponents of moral traditionalists.[63] Do all those "liberals" belong to an unbroken chain? That may be the case, but Galston does not provide the evidence to prove it. He also never shows us that today's liberals are truer heirs of Locke, Hume, Kant, or Montesquieu than their pro–free market, "morally traditionalist" opponents. Even less useful is the claim that "autonomous" liberal resources and arguments have changed society. In what way, might we ask, is this true? Does Galston believe that those who have produced desired change over the course of centuries are simply personifications of his own values? In any case he never demonstrates that one can find liberal principles that are entirely unrelated to older sources. As socially and culturally situated beings, most of us do not act exclusively on the basis of any one set of principles. Even in Galston's case, no consistent set emerges from his demonstration.

In Rawls's speculative exercise it is equally doubtful that we are dealing with actual people. It is one thing to devise a "concept of a veil of ignorance" or a "notion of the original position," but quite another to describe what culturally situated groups are likely to think and do. In a review of Rawls's latest book, John Gray offers an appraisal that might apply equally well to *A Theory of Justice*: "The upshot of his theorizing is not a political conception of general human interest but an apology for American institutions as they are perceived from the politically marginal standpoint of American academic liberalism."[64] To justify redistributionist social policy as an extension of liberal principles, Rawls must provide an imaginary founding of society taking place on his own moral terms. This exercise can work only in the absence of "arbitrary contingencies." Otherwise we might have to deal with particular societies that contradict Rawls's premises.

The veil of ignorance not only saves us from noticing distinctive cultural attitudes about economic risk and the welfare state but also permits Rawls to rework an economic theory without telling us. Rawls seizes upon the optimality principle, developed by Léon Walras and Vilfredo Pareto in the late-nineteenth century and then restated by Mises, and gives it a socialist twist. Rawls assumes that a redistribution of goods and honors must follow if we accept the principle that inequalities must benefit all. But here he wants to rework, without calling by name, the theory of optimality by which classical liberal economists reached conclusions totally different from his, namely, that those who are least advantaged fare best under a market economy.[65] Rawls is free to express other conclusions, but he should provide empirical or mathematical evidence for them.

Like other contemporary social democrats who call themselves liberal, Rawls fails to discuss power. The reasons are not the ones Lowi gives, that liberals, being hopeless pluralists, are looking for bargains to be struck by competing economic interests. The real reason, I would argue, is that liberals do not want to be seen as imposing their will upon others. They are philosophically and temperamentally uncomfortable with the power they both exercise and expand. Thus when Rawls approaches the delicate questions of whose advantages the state should take away and in favor of whom, his language becomes suddenly evasive: "In the matter of fair equality of opportunity, I shall not attempt to measure, in any exact way, the degree of justice."[66] But who will make this desired measurement? Obviously public administrators who will be empowered to carry out redistributionist directives bearing on jobs, income, and educational opportunities.

In Finer's polemic against Hayek the denial of the staggering powers being used in the postwar period by English socialists, who were nationalizing key industries and massively redistributing income, amounts to mere hypocrisy. According to Finer, England's march toward socialism was a happy consequence of democracy, "the product of at least three hundred years of severe mental labor, careful reflection, and piece by piece development." Postwar social and economic reconstruction took place on the basis of "party programs . . . thoroughly elaborated in the greatest detail by intra-party discussion and amendment and reconciliation among the many interests that are domesticated in each political party, before they are put forward to the electorate in considerable particularity."[67] Hayek might have responded to this particular civics lesson by pointing out that such intra-party discussion preceding general elections would provide little comfort to those who were being expropriated. One might also recall the pungent observation by the Italian jurist Gianfranco Miglio that "governing takes place not by everyone compromising but by one will yielding to another." In this case it was the opponents of socialism who had to yield to a slightly larger electorate, in allowing costly and irreversible changes to be enacted against them. These changes did not stop with economic redistribution and the nationalization of industries. They eventually led to the resocialization of the British population as administrators reconstructed public education in the postwar years.

Such social planning may be good or bad, depending on one's judgment, but those liberals who devise and carry it out are not innocent souls. They are not the heirs to those legalistic Germans of the 1930s who allowed Hitler to seize power because his party had obtained a parliamentary plurality. They reinterpret constitutions to suit their ends. Nor are they Lowi's tolerant pluralists waiting for cultural and economic interests to flow together under recognized legal norms. Even less do they struggle to uphold academic freedom and the right of (non-minority) groups to private association. Many of the liberals to whom Galston refers have been eager to impose speech codes on educational institutions. They have forced clubs and organizations to open themselves to designated minorities and have introduced laws in Canada, England, and France against ethnically insensitive publications. All of these "defensive" acts have involved the extension of governmental power that liberals fought to expand in the past, particularly in the United States, by increasing the reach of public administration and judges.[68] Such actions are always presented as "defensive," as when agents of the Equal Employment Opportunities Commission sue business people for not hiring arbitrarily set minority quotas or move against banks that have not made enough loans to high-risk members of the underclass. Dealing with the effects of inequality has become a euphemism for current liberalism's assault on what the old liberals called civil society. And the public acceptance of these assaults confirms the old liberal platitude, repeated by Hayek, that all freedoms are inextricably bound together.

Yet it is also clear that the response of free-market and constitutional liberals to democratic changes has not been entirely aboveboard. Finer is right to notice that Hayek accepts democracy only if he can "restrict its meaning arbitrarily," make it subject to "rules which it could not amend." Thus Hayek undertakes in *The Road to Serfdom* to control "the fashionable concentration on democracy," lest it come to undermine liberty. Having created his own legalistic conception of a democracy that stays in its place, in *The Constitution of Liberty* (1960) Hayek confidently identifies all good government with "liberal democracy."[69] In this he follows another liberal, Ludwig von Mises, who in *Liberalism* maintains that democracy, with his meaning always understood, is the best of regimes. But it must be *his* definition that is operative; otherwise there cannot be true democracy, that is, one in which general elections are used to legitimate the application of liberal legal norms. Neither Mises nor Hayek accepts what another classical liberal, Gottfried Dietze, designates as "democracy proper," as opposed to "proper democracy." Neither wishes to live under twentieth-century democracy as it is practiced, as opposed to how it might operate under the guidance of free-market liberals. Mises assures us that "political democracy and economic democracy condition one another. A democratic constitution is the political corollary either of a primitive community of owners or of a market economy."[70]

These statements by Mises and Hayek about a natural harmony between democracy and a market economy might have been understandable in the 1840s. Then James Mill and John Bright dreamt of a fusion between economic and political principles that were still largely untested. These reformers hoped that an extension of the vote to the lower-middle and working classes would be the first step toward creating an unfettered market economy. Such an extended franchise, they believed, would end both Tory privilege and ecclesiastical paternalism and thereby promote commercial liberty throughout society. The second of these predictions was false, as democratic practice amply demonstrates. Within decades of the time that a universal male franchise was introduced in England, France, Germany, and other industrial nations, voters behaved as some nineteenth-century liberals said they would. They supported socialist parties organized with a democratic franchise and drove older, established parties in the direction of redistributionist policies. In the first decade of the twentieth century Max Weber was already associating democracy with both public administration and the welfare state. Although Mises and Hayek do the same, they also pretend that a welfare economy is extraneous to modern democracy. And they wish to have civil servants, rather than political parties, administer decisions arrived at democratically. By doing this, they believe, one might guard against parties growing too strong and threatening legal norms and property arrangements.[71] They ignore a pervasive fact of modern political life: that public administration has affected civil society far more deeply than rule by party patronage. This has come about because of the reputation of civil service as an impartial and scientific tool of governing: whence its rise into the dominant political organization form in modern Western democracies.[72]

Free-market liberalism continues to provide a critical method for studying socialist economies. The same method demonstrates the rationality of the market in gauging relative human needs through pricing. What free-market liberals cannot do is offer an acceptable alternative to modern democracy as it really operates. The most prominent exponents of that liberalism have therefore embraced it selectively, as evidenced by the example of Margaret Thatcher. After years of preaching the virtues of the free market, Thatcher left the British prime ministership with the English welfare state intact. She could not have done otherwise. In the mid-eighties more than 40 million people (or about two-thirds of the total population) in Great Britain received most of their income or welfare benefits (paid to pensioners and to the unemployed) from the government.[73] In a country in which the welfare state is by far the largest employer, Hayek's political-economic model ceases to be relevant.

In the eighties neoconservative political theorists, led by the theologian Michael Novak, hastened to present their own improved version of classical liberalism. "Democratic capitalism," subsequently renamed "welfare state capitalism," was presented as the mature, humanized product of what John Locke, Adam Smith, and other early liberals had in mind for society. Although he has since proved willing to criticize American culture, in *The Spirit of Democratic Capitalism* (1982), Novak exalts the United States and Western Europe as embodiments of a happy fusion between democratic politics and capitalist economics.[74] Out of this coalescence, Novak says, has come a blessing for the human race, which Americans have tried to share with others. While a limited democratic welfare state, together with market incentives, is the political-economic paradigm being recommended, nonetheless it is sometimes hard to distinguish this blessing from social democracy. Novak not only presents public administration as democratic capitalist, but also insists that "social democracy is an acceptable variant on democratic capitalism."[75]

By the end of the twentieth century liberalism has become a pillar of whatever liberal democracy the United States and its imitators are thought to embody. What the United States or those who follow its example do institutionally, politically, or economically signifies liberal democracy in practice. This yardstick seems to be the one most suitable for policy analysts and political theorists alike. And there is a precedent for this form of measurement. After the Second World War, the American government spent treasure and energy to "repoliticize" occupied Germany and Japan on the basis of its liberal democratic ideals. Thus the American system became as linked to a spiritual mission as was the Catholic empire of seventeenth-century Spain. Despite these conversionary efforts, one may be justified to continue to ask whether liberal democracy is not perpetuating an older liberal tradition or whether "liberal democracy," to speak like Thomas Hobbes, is not merely the name we choose to use. This question is by no means idle. If the claimed continuity in tradition does not exist, as I believe is the case, what we are left with is the arbitrary ascription of a label to a fluid political culture. This labeling hides the extent to which the democratic revolution in this century altered older institutions and values. It also conceals the reformulations of liberalism that came to make it coextensive with both social planning and educational socialization. In a penetrating essay for *Harper's* (August 1990), John Lukacs analyzes the course of liberal democracy more accurately than either Frederich Hayek or Margaret Thatcher: "Traditional capitalism is gone in the West, even from the United States. The universal attribute of every country in the world is the welfare state, administered by large bureaucracies. We are all socialists now whether we call ourselves that or not."[76]

Lukacs looks at another factor contributing to this change, beside the advent of democratic electorates and urban working classes. He views the First World War, with its mobilization of entire nations, as the most monumental event of the modern era.[77] Among the changes wrought by that cataclysm was the centralized control of human and material resources among the belligerents, or what the Germans called *Totalwirtschaft*. That command economy, put in the service of a heroic national effort, inspired social planners throughout the Western world. Some became fascists, others communists, and still others Catholic corporatists.

But in America, as Arthur Ekirch observes, the situation was different. The New Deal brain truster Rexford Tugwell viewed his stint in helping to administer America's war industries as an exhilarating experience in "wartime socialism." In 1927 Tugwell regretted that the armistice in 1918 "had brought to a halt a great experiment in the control of production, control of prices, and control of consumption."[78] Like other Americans of his generation, Tugwell decided to call his social planning "liberal," a term that might accentuate its quintessentially American character. Once he and others had done this and their appropriation went, for the most part, unchallenged, the new liberalism came to replace the old. But this did not keep even newer liberalisms from coming along and claiming to be both more democratic and more thoroughly liberal. By now the interwar new liberalism once prevalent in the United States has split into rival sects, one side capturing the postwar conservative movement and renaming itself "neoconservative" and the other, more egalitarian side becoming the left wing of the Democratic Party. Though the revenge of a semantic theft, this development underscores the difficulty of assigning essentialist definitions to a changing ideology. The liberal essence, it can be said, continues to elude.

CHAPTER TWO

Liberalism vs. Democracy

LIBERAL AND DEMOCRATIC MENTALITIES

A PROCESS that drew attention at the turn of the century, and even earlier, was the movement from a bourgeois liberal into a mass democratic society. Not all of those who observed this process made the same judgments about it. Some, including the European socialists and the founding generation of American social planners, welcomed democratization; others, such as Max Weber, considered it to be an inevitable outcome of capitalism, technology, and the spread of the electoral franchise. Still others, typified by Sir James Fitzjames Stephen (1829–1894), prominent jurist and a decidedly anti-egalitarian liberal, protested the unseemly haste with which J. S. Mill and his friends greeted the new democratic age: "The waters are out and no human force can turn them back, but I do not see why as we go with the stream we need sing Hallelujah to the river god."[1]

The tension between liberalism and its successor ideology and between the social classes embodying those ideas provides a recurrent theme in nineteenth-century political debates. François Guizot (1787–1874) the Huguenot prime minister under France's liberal July monarchy and a distinguished historian of England, considered democracy to be as much of a curse as monarchical absolutism. As French prime minister in the 1840s, Guizot fought doggedly against the extension of the limited franchise, the *cens*, from propertied taxpayers to other French citizens. He distinguished sharply in his speeches and political tracts between those civil rights suitable for all citizens, such as freedom of worship, and the vote. By means of the second, Guizot maintained, the lower class could destabilize society, radically redistributing property and bringing resourceful demagogues to power.[2] He believed the bourgeoisie formed a "*classe capacitaire*," those who would be guided by Reason and their stake in society in directing the actions of government. Indeed Guizot recommended the idea of "creating a state through representation which would fully reflect the values of bourgeois electoral law aristocracy."[3] Although in 1831 he fought to give representation to government functionaries and other professionals who paid lower taxes than required for franchise eligibility, he nonetheless argued for the special suitability of the upper middle class for political participation. Only that class combined wealth with formed intelligence.

The English jurist William Lecky (1838–1903), who admired Guizot, devoted his long polemical work *Democracy and Liberty* (1896) to the polarity between liberal order and democratic equality. Surveying England's parliamentary history in the second half of the nineteenth century, Lecky worried that a universal franchise was irreversibly changing both English society and the English state.[4] Not surprisingly, his book appeared at a time when English socialism was becoming a political power, and Lecky devotes more than 140 pages to analyzing this new radicalism. In 1893 the Independent Labour Party officially came into existence in the Yorkshire town of Bradford. Since the elections of 1874, however, avowed socialists had sat in the British Parliament, and socialist labor unions had been around since the 1850s. To the consternation of German liberals, German socialists, meeting in the Saxon town of Gotha, had drafted a program in 1876 calling for public ownership of the means of production. The Gotha socialists also demanded an entire battery of social programs to be introduced by a properly democratized German state.[5] In France the revolutionary socialist Jules Guesde (1845–1922) sat in the Chamber of Deputies from 1893 on, and, as Lecky reminds us, Guesde, in the *Catéchisme Socialiste*, presents the family as an "odious form of property," one destined to give way to a multiplicity of sexual relations for men and women alike.[6]

One way to look at such social quarrels is to observe how dated they are. These battles were supposedly waged between reactionary and democratic liberals. Those liberals who were just and humanitarian, it has been argued, went with changing times, while others who were not, such as the Franco-Italian economist and sociologist Vilfredo Pareto, fell into bad company, and even sometimes into fascism. Implicit in such a view is the distinction that more and more modern liberals have drawn throughout the twentieth century between themselves and those they have replaced. It is a purely strategic stance that minimizes the reality of past conflicts. Like the "mainstream" New Deal liberal historiography in postwar America, this liberal historical view stresses the natural progression of things by which the new liberals took over from the old.

It is possible to perceive continuity in the movement from a bourgeois liberal society into a more democratic one. But that continuity is not the same as direct continuation, as was noted by Max Weber, Joseph Schumpeter, and other early-twentieth-century social commentators. Rather, we are dealing here with a series of points leading from a bourgeois into a postbourgeois age, that is, with a process of displacement that went on for several generations. Thus Weber focused on "rationalization" in analyzing the movement from a bourgeois capitalist toward a bureaucratized socialist society. A liberal bourgeois world created the secularist foundations and economic organization necessary for socialist rule. Another pessimistic social commentator with liberal leanings, Joseph Schumpeter, believed that the middle-class concept of freedom encouraged the expression of critical opposition. This tolerance undermined the belief system of an older liberal society and prepared the way for social democracy. But neither of these attempts by old style European liberals to find links between two distinctive social and political formations denies the differences between them. Both Weber and Schumpeter were looking at the conditions in which social changes took place, and they note the overlaps as well as distinctions between the epochs in question.

Panajotis Kondylis, a Germanophone Greek scholar whose work is not yet widely known, breaks new ground in this respect. Kondylis examines the distinctions between liberal bourgeois and mass democratic societies by looking at their literary and cultural artifacts. Modern democracies differ from premodern ones, according to Kondylis, in that they dissociate citizenship from cultural and ethnic identities and in the way in which mass production affects society. The modern, as opposed to premodern, democrat is not communally situated and has a fluid cultural identity being shaped by a consumer economy.[7] He also inhabits a culture that remains hostile to the older liberal universe. Postmodernism in literature and literary criticism, Kondylis argues, is the latest in a series of cultural strategies aimed at subverting the nineteenth-century liberal order. The refusal to recognize a fixed or authoritative meaning for inherited texts, which is characteristic of postmodernism, represents an assault upon "liberal" education. Contrary to the world of moral and semantic order presided over by an ethical deity, which bourgeois liberals preached, the postmodernists exalt indeterminacy. They decry the acceptance of tradition in discourse, as well as in political matters, as a "fascist" act of domination—or as the inadmissible allowance of the past to intrude upon the present.

Nowhere does Kondylis call for the eradication of postmodernism or make the facile assumption that by opposing it the present generation can resurrect the bourgeois world. He contends that liberal and mass democratic societies are not only distinct but mutually antagonistic and that this antagonism has expressed itself culturally as well as socioeconomically. For over a hundred years bourgeois liberalism has been under attack from authors and artists presenting views about human nature and the nature of existence antithetical to bourgeois convictions. Materialism, atheism, and pluralism have been three such worldviews, which the bourgeoisie long viewed with justifiable suspicion. Deconstructionism is a more recent form of cultural criticism aimed at inherited assumptions about meaning. By now, Kondylis maintains, the old liberals have been reduced to a "rearguard struggle [*Nachhutgefecht*]," while watching their opponents take over culture and education.[8]

But the reason for this reduced liberal presence, Kondylis explains, is not an insidious contamination by a cultural industry separated from the rest of society. Cultural radicals have done well in mass democracies because they continue to target the liberal order that the democrats deposed. The cultural opposition continues to mobilize even after the political war has ended. Victorian rigidity, social status, and elitist attitudes about education have all remained the butts of academic and literary criticism, and this opposition points back to the conditions of strife in which mass democracy arose. This cultural insurgency, Kondylis observes, draws strength from a subversive source that once served liberalism in *its* war against the past. The Enlightenment tradition of critical rationalism was crucial for the war of ideas waged by the bourgeoisie and its defenders against the remnants of an older world. Despite the attempt to integrate this outlook into a bourgeois vision of life, Enlightenment rationalism has played a new destructive role, as the instrument of a war against the bourgeoisie on behalf of openness, skepticism, and material equality.[9]

These pointed observations about the culture of mass democracy do not deny the fact that cultural differences exist among democrats. Deconstructionists and liberal democratic absolutists still fight over the values to be taught in history and literature courses. And some advocates of post–World War Two abstract expressionism, such as Hilton Kramer, have now come to oppose later schools of art as relative cultural traditionalists.[10] Nonetheless, radically antibourgeois movements have remained powerful in our cultures, as mass democracy continues to struggle against the remains of an older heritage. In the United States traditional liberal and agrarian democratic forces stayed alive into the twentieth century and resisted the inroads of the democratic administrative state. Mass democracy needed a cultural as well as political strategy to triumph, and the values and concepts juggled by our literary and now media elites are keys to the emergence of a postliberal society and politics.

Kondylis also makes clear that mass democracy could not have developed without the demographic and economic revolutions that transformed Western Europe in the eighteenth and nineteenth centuries. Industrialization, agricultural modernization, an urban working class, the disappearance of a family-based craft economy, and the operation of assembly-line production were the factors, Kondylis observes, contributing to mass democracy. Although imperial Rome experienced the concentration of uprooted *proletarii* in its swelling, strife-ridden cities, it could not have produced a modern political movement, because it lacked both mass production and mass consumption. Earlier societies had to deal with perpetual scarcity and with the need to share limited resources in a communal setting. The modern West, by contrast, provides more and more material gratification to socially isolated individuals.[11] Its politics are therefore predicated on hedonism and individual self-actualization, values that give an ethical dimension to a consumer economy. Mass democratic politics also advocates material equality, as opposed to the exclusively formal or legal equality preached by nineteenth-century liberals.

By stressing the ties between modern democracy and material pleasure, Kondylis also explains why modern democracy cannot appeal effectively in the long run to an ethic of austerity. At the end of the eighteenth century, both American and French revolutionaries invoked classical ideals of republican simplicity, a practice found preeminently in the political writings of Rousseau. Self-indulgence and luxury were viewed as aristocratic flaws and, among nineteenth-century French republicans, as upper-middle-class vices. Democratic and later socialist revolutionaries even tried to exemplify the moral conduct which they hoped to enforce in a society of equals. The Jacobin socialist Louis Auguste Blanqui (1805–1881) lived and dressed like a priest; and the self-proclaimed republican Sénécal in Gustave Flaubert's novel *L'Education sentimentale* (1869) is made to appear eccentric in his extreme pursuit of virtue. Sénécal is shown embracing dietary and sexual restraints and scorning sumptuous living.[12] In a similar vein, black Marxist president of Zimbabwe Robert Mugabe has denounced the homosexuals in his homeland. Mugabe is outraged that "sodomists and sexual perverts" continue to be found there and scoffs at the idea of "rights for those given to bestiality."[13] All of these revolutionary democratic or socialist appeals to public virtue hark back to republican models that Kondylis views as incompatible with

34

mass democracy. What distinguishes the latter from the former, in his opinion, is the prevalence of hedonism associated with mass production and mass consumption. This ethos express itself as a ceaseless desire for consumption combined with resentment against those who have more access to pleasure.[14]

It was the failure of liberalism, from the standpoint of mass democracy, to move decisively enough toward material equality and individual self-expressiveness that led to its undoing. The defenders of bourgeois liberalism temporized when faced by the sociological evidence of inequality in their own society. They claimed to be more interested in freedom than in the further pursuit of equality but were also more committed to family cohesion and gender distinctions than to individual freedom. The reason for this is clear, according to Kondylis. Bourgeois liberals were both economic innovators and perpetuators of an urban civilization going back to the Middle Ages. In their heyday they spoke about sweeping change, but they were never as dedicated to the social and cultural implications of a consumer economy as were those who replaced them.[15]

Basic to this thesis is the recognition that liberalism is a "bourgeois ideology," a set of ideas and principles indissolubly tied to the Western middle class. This does not mean that liberal principles are reducible to material interests nor that they should be dismissed as a pretext for economic exploitation. In the early 1950s John Plamenatz tried to separate "ideology" from the pejorative associations many Marxists had loaded onto that term. According to Plamenatz, "The word 'ideology' is not used to refer only to explicit beliefs and theories. Those who speak of 'bourgeois ideology' . . . often mean by it beliefs and attitudes implicit in the bourgeois way of speaking and behaving, and sometimes they speak of bourgeois theories and doctrines as if they did little more than make explicit these beliefs and attitudes."[16]

Understood in the cultural sense and not simply as a theoretical instrument of self-justification, liberalism exemplifies "bourgeois ideology." It designates not just liberal ideas but also their social setting, that is, the context without which liberalism becomes merely disembodied concepts or slogans. When Benjamin Constant and François Guizot argued for a political *juste milieu* in the 1820s, in the form of constitutional monarchy, they were not simply advocating moderation or an Aristotelian golden mean. They were looking at the educated *haute bourgeoisie* as a natural leadership class that could maneuver between the equally disastrous shoals of absolute monarchy and democracy. Guizot identified that class with the modern nation-state. He believed that this political order and

35

the bourgeoise would benefit from their historically necessary association.[17] This cultural context does not mean that the French doctrinaires, as the constitutional liberals in post-Napoleonic France called themselves, have nothing to teach our own generation. It is, rather, to insist on the need to avoid tendentious parallels, which arrange past figures and past movements in accordance with current appetites for a usable past.

What I am emphasizing here is the need for contextualization, the avoidance of which typifies contemporary zealotry. Appeals to human rights, as historically unbounded absolutes, now resound in political debates in which opposing sides accuse each other of "relativizing" values. Wars and social policies are justified by invoking "self-evident truths," even though what is true in these truths may be different now from what seemed self-evident about them two hundred years ago. Pointing this out is not the same as relativizing all truth. It is only to question the opportunistic and decontextualized uses to which the past has been bent.

This decontextualization of liberalism can happen in two ways: either when we place liberalism into an eternal present going back and forth in time, or else when we make its real history into a stepping-stone to the present. A particularly striking case of the first comes up in F. G. Bratton's *The Legacy of the Liberal Spirit* (1943), a once widely esteemed defense of the "liberal heritage." In his preface Bratton explains that "liberalism is not to be viewed as a nineteenth-century phenomenon ending with the Second World War. As an attitude toward life it has a history of twenty-five hundred years. It goes back to the Age of Reason and the Reformation and to earlier, distant attempts to establish intellectual freedom and the life of reasons."[18] In the journey that follows, from Plato through Jesus to John Dewey, Bratton celebrates thinkers who he believes have pointed in his own direction. Thus he favorably contrasts one North African Christian Platonist, Origen, with another, Augustine, presenting the first as a protoliberal and the second as an obscurantist.

In *Liberalism*, John Gray also assigns liberal ratings to thinkers who lived long before the liberal era. Gray praises Pericles' "Funeral Oration" (or its reconstruction by the historian Thucydides) for its "statement of liberal egalitarian and individualist principles."[19] He thereby ignores the pervasive stress in that speech on living for the public good, which was paradigmatic for ancient Greek democracy. Modern liberal individualism existed only incipiently, if at all, in Greek antiquity, a point documented in works from N.D. Fustel de Coulanges's *The Ancient City* to Paul Rahe's *Republics Ancient and Modern*.[20]

Among the readings of liberalism which try to shove its past into a triumphalist present are the academic apologetics discussed in the first chapter. In all fairness, it should be said that even probing critics of contemporary liberalism ascribe to it an excessively long genealogy. Christopher Lasch, John P. Diggins, and the ethical philosopher Alasdair MacIntyre have all written critically on the "liberal heritage," which they believe has descended more or less intact from earlier centuries. Faith in material progress as a means of solving moral problems, a buoyant skepticism about religious questions, and, especially in Diggins's analysis, individual autonomy as the end of social policy, are all, in their opinion, permanent aspects of the liberal worldview. This worldview is thought to define liberalism, whether it preaches a free-market economy or the need for social democracy. Diggins and other perceptive commentators contend that people would not go on for generations speaking about a liberal heritage unless one truly existed. Those who admire John Dewey and John Rawls could, for the same reason, find something in Adam Smith and John Locke to admire. Otherwise they would not fix the same label upon all of these *maîtres à penser*.

This view of a liberal heritage is, furthermore, based on a reliable axiom in historical research, that a long-term and widely held belief in the persistence and integrity of a movement cannot be entirely illusory. Note that while classical liberal John Gray sees his own liberalism transformed by modern social democrats, he nonetheless searches for shared ground between himself and them.[21] But this approach raises its own methodological difficulties. It overlooks several generations of agitated debates between liberals and democrats. These debates include Guizot's warnings about the "sovereignty of numbers" and Stephen's assaults on J. S. Mill's faith "that all people should live in society as equals."[22] Indeed much of the political debate in Western Europe from the second half of the nineteenth century into the early decades of the twentieth testifies to the deep divisions between old-fashioned liberals and democratic reformers.

The French anthropologist Louis Dumont, in *Homo Aequalis*, treats as the unifying theme of the modern West the rise of "individualism within the world." Unlike the ascetic ideals of medieval Christianity and Eastern contemplative religions, Western modernity has been characterized by the belief that individual fulfillment should take place within society. This individual consciousness, Dumont explains, does not require that

37

people withdraw from a hierarchical world based on status relations. To the contrary, it has encouraged individuals seeking success and self-expression to find it in a changing and increasingly atomized society.[23] Dumont's analysis treats the intellectual history of the Western world as a steady movement toward expressive individualism, from the Protestant Reformation to the rise of a contractual view of civil society in John Locke and in other early liberal theorists. Implicit in this interpretative perspective is the stress by the German sociologist Ferdinand Tönnies on the movement from traditional communities to functionally oriented and highly mobile societies. Dumont focuses on the cultural and intellectual bases underlying Tönnies's transition from *Gemeinschaft* to *Gesellschaft*, and he places that transition into a continuum of thought going back to the early modern period.[24]

Dumont's thematic stess on "individualism within the world" underscores a problem found in explorations appealing to root causes: they account for both too much and too little. By citing a single force that is made to account for modern culture, Dumont ignores the distinctiveness that marks specific phases of Western history from the Reformation onward.[25] Though clearly he knows that the Protestant idea of the individual experience of divine grace has little to do with contemporary views of individual self-gratification, Dumont's interest in cultural continuity leads him to play down such a difference. His study of individuality in the West causes him to overlook short-term cultural changes, even those with powerful cumulative effects. To the extent that our own study deals with two successive epochs, what Dumont disregards is, for us, significant. Moreover, liberal democracy has accelerated some aspects of that long-range process outlined by Dumont, while making others less important. Material redistribution, as a means of individual fulfillment, has become basic to our own liberal democratic age, while the cohesion of the nuclear family has grown weaker as liberalism has lost out to liberal democracy. Differences in values can be perceived in short-term political transformations, even if the general trend of modernity is what Dumont describes.

Critics of the old bourgeois liberalism are, finally, too hasty in linking liberal concern about the social question to economic interest. As Gertrude Himmelfarb has demonstrated with regard to Victorian attitudes about work and philanthropy, questions of character formation and family responsibility were tied together in the Victorian middle-class mind. Himmelfarb argues that such an association was not a threadbare defense of low factory wages or of the lack of public works programs.

Rather, it came from widely shared assumptions about the social good. The broad middle class, extending from bankers and mill owners to shopkeepers and church canons, rejected a welfare-state conception of government because of what they assumed were its socially destructive effects.[26]

Even if modern liberals disagree with these judgments, their disagreement does not justify substituting their own adaptation for the "liberal tradition." Whether welfare-state democrats and public administrators have refined or degraded the original article is beside the point. What they have done is change that article in ways that would make it unrecognizable to earlier generations. Nor will it do to speak of the *failure* of earlier liberals to see the world like modern liberals. If they had seen the world differently, they would not have been liberals but social democratic advocates of public administration. American historian James Kloppenberg accounts for Weber's liberal skepticism about "such concepts as the 'will of the people' " by pointing to the "longer context of German history." Weber, as interpreted by Kloppenberg, could not imagine the meaningful practice of egalitarian politics because "Germany had no tradition of popular sovereignty and liberals repeatedly put their faiths in elites rather than democracies to accomplish their goals."[27] True, nineteenth-century German bourgeois thought did not produce as much radical ferment as its English and French counterparts. But Weber's liberal doubts about the people's capacity to rule were not restricted at the turn of the century to Germanophone observers. Kloppenberg, as a social democrat who thinks of himself as "liberal," looks for "larger contexts" (i.e., the peculiarities of German history) for his own ideological use: to detach the "liberal tradition" from traditional liberal views that he finds distasteful.[28]

Unlike today's liberals, traditional ones entertained deep reservations about popular rule. A belief that democracy leads inevitably to socialism was common to French liberals of the 1830s and 1840s, and it is equally apparent in Lecky, Pareto, Weber, and other liberal observers at the end of the century. Pareto and Lecky feared that democracy would bring forth a trade union approach to economic policy. Unless put under some kind of control, democratically-elected trade unionists would add to unemployment by driving up wages, which would then harm the most expendable workers. Democratic spokesmen would also agitate to impose tariffs on foreign goods, and this would hurt domestic consumers while unleashing reprisals from those countries whose goods were being excluded. The effects from such economic measures would then be blamed on the owners and captains of industry, and social democratic governments would cite this accusation to justify their confiscation of the means of production.[29]

This fin-de-siècle prediction about trade union democracy revealed the persistent liberal fear about a seizure of property that would take place at the urging of socialists. Despite the French Revolution of 1848, in which bourgeois and social democrats went from being allies to violent enemies, a liberal view did persist that democratized governments would become radical ones. Socialism or rampant social disorder would accompany the advent of a universal franchise. Thus Fitzjames Stephen declared with finality in 1874: "The substance of what I have to say to the disadvantage of the theory and practice of universal suffrage is that it tends to invert what I should have regarded as the true and natural relation between wisdom and folly. I think that wise and good men ought to rule those who are foolish and bad. To say that the sole function of the wise and good is to preach to their neighbors, and that everyone indiscriminately should be left to do what he likes, should be provided with a ratable share of the sovereign power in the shape of the vote, and that the result of this will be the direction of power by wisdom, seems to me the wildest romance that ever got possession of any considerable number of minds."[30] Like Stephen, Lecky feared that democracy, by overwhelming and sweeping away any national leadership, would lead to capricious and unstable government. He predicted almost twenty years before it happened that the House of Lords would be disempowered, and in the 1890s he also warned that "the dissociation of the upper classes from . . . public duty is likely to prove a danger to the community."[31]

Liberal critics of mass democracy offered differing but equally grim predictions about the disposition of power in a democratic age. In the 1870s Stephen could find no cohesive group of political leaders that might create stable rule in the world as imagined by J. S. Mill. His opponents were mere dreamers who, like the "Radicals" (the term by which he designated Mill and his circle), "look forward to an age in which an all-embracing love of Humanity will regenerate the human race."[32] Though the Radicals complain of the "petty social arrangements" in Victorian England, they lack the hardness of mind, Stephen observes, to change things for the better. In time they would be swept aside by better organized fanatics. Another liberal critique of democracy, widespread among the doctrinaires of the 1820s, was its *primitive* character, which made it unsuited for the nineteenth century. Charles Rémusat and Guizot both stressed the idea that democratic republics were a product of classical antiquity. Given their need for cultural homogeneity, severe public morals, and highly restricted citizenship, popular polities did not seem destined to flourish in the nineteenth century. Unlike Guizot's democratic critic, and traveller in the New World, Alexis de Tocqueville, the doctrinaires did not believe that the European future belonged to democracy. They viewed the American experience as sui generis. According to Guizot, Americans had established popular sovereignty because they had been able to build a regime without an inherited class system.[33] Tocqueville's depiction of localism as the essence of American democracy seemed to confirm Guizot's judgment. It offered a political picture that Guizot and other doctrinaires thought had no bearing for France or for Europe in general. A Europe of highly centralized nation states required a stable social pillar drawn from the educated bourgeoisie, in order to maintain political stability. Democratic primitivism, as revealed in the chaos of the French Revolution, was the political alternative, Guizot complained, into which his democratic critics would plunge France and the rest of Europe.

The doctrinaires pointed portentously to the Jacobin rule in 1793 as a precedent for democratizing experiments. As Guizot explained in the essay "De la démocratie dans les sociétés modernes": "Democracy is a cry of war; it is the flag of the party of numbers placed below raised against those above. A flag sometimes raised in the name of the rights of men, but sometimes in the name of crude passions; sometimes raised against the most iniquitous usurpations but also sometimes against legitimate superiority."[34]

While Tocqueville and Guizot underlined the link between American democracy and America's decentralized republic, a new and fateful view of the American regime surfaced in the theorizing of George Bancroft (1800–1891). Jacksonian Democrat, career diplomat, and author of the ten-volume *History of the United States*, Bancroft admired German idealist philosophy, which he popularized in the United States. As a young man he had studied in Göttingen, Berlin, and Heidelberg and, while in Germany, had become intimately familiar with the historical speculation of G. W. F. Hegel.[35] His own work incorporated several unmistakable Hegelian themes: that history showed the progressive unfolding of the divine personality; that this process was reflected in the advance of human liberty; and that liberty had developed most fully in the Protestant Germanic world. For Bancroft, unlike Hegel, however, this progress toward

41

liberty reached its culmination on American soil. Bancroft presents the American people as the ultimate bearers of divinely ordained liberty and makes this point explicit at the end of his *History of the Formation of the Constitution of the United States* (1882): "A new people had arisen without kings or princes or nobles. They were more sincerely religious, better educated, and of nobler minds and of purer morals than the men of any former republic. By calm meditation and friendly councils they had prepared a consitution which, in the union of freedom with strength and order, excelled every one known before."[36]

The spirit of the people thus described was held to be democratic, and Bancroft ascribed to Americans a collective wisdom which found expression in their political architecture. The American federal union, as he saw it, was no mere covenient state but "the only hope for renovating the life of the civilized world."[37] The political institutions fashioned and inspired by America's democratic people assumed in Bancroft's writing a mystical quality, and his insistence that the voice of the people is the voice of God led Tocqueville to remark that "pantheism is the religion most characteristic of democracies."[38]

The American capacity for self-government that Bancroft exalted was not in the end the American propensity for local self-rule. Bancroft glorified a *national* democratic will, and his *History of the United States* ends appropriately with the topic "consolidating the union." According to Bancroft, an American people and an American national government were both inchoately present even before the colonies formed a nation-state: "For all the want of government, their solemn pledge to one another and mutual citizenship and perpetual union made them one people; and that people was superior to its institutions, possessing the vital form which goes before organization and gives it strength."[39]

One does not have to strain to find here a Jacobin imagination hidden behind Hegelian language. A consolidated American national government, a powerful executive representing the popular will, and a global civilizing mission are the visionary expectations that one can read into Bancroft's patriotic scholarship. Although his *History of the United States* deals predominantly with the colonial period, it points more toward the American future than back to the eighteenth century. Bancroft is celebrating the *progress* of the democratic spirit as embodied in the American nation. In the process, he replaces an older American liberal constitutional identity with one that Guizot and Tocqueville might have associated with their own eighteenth-century French revolution.[40]

LIBERAL PESSIMISTS

While Bancroft celebrated the triumphant course of democracy in America, others, among them European liberals, grew increasingly agitated about the inevitability of popular rule. This anxiety, in some cases, became more pronounced as the twentieth century began to unfold and social problems in Europe appeared to be worsening. The most detailed critical treatment of democratic rule produced by a European liberal was *Trasformazioni della Democrazia* (1921) by the sociologist-economist Pareto. Pareto's example, as John Gray remarks, makes dramatically clear how the pre-1914 liberal mind was placed irreversibly "at a crossroads."[41] In the face of a democratic franchise, riotous trade union strikes, and the intrusive presence of public administration, some liberals embraced authoritarian solutions. Of these Pareto was perhaps the best known and the most deliberate, as can be judged from his social writings. In *Trasformazioni* he outlines the characteristics of the democratic epoch and its relationship to the period that had preceded it. In the nineteenth century a parliamentary regime had come to Italy as the result of a fateful alliance between a "demagogic plutocracy" and the popular classes. Both had opposed the rule of landed wealth and the ecclesiastical establishment but drew apart after a liberal, constitutional, and unified Italy had come into existence. Thereafter the laboring class had worked to seize the wealth of the liberal middle class, and by the twentieth century it had also turned against the parliamentary institutions on which the plutocracy had built its political legitimacy.

In the aftermath of the First World War, from which Italy had emerged on the side of the victors but financially crushed, unions took over the railroads, ironworks, and factories in Milan and throughout the industrialized North. Red Guard units were formed to police the worker-occupied areas, and though these units carried out the summary executions of the enemies of the working class, the national government, then under revolving premierships, avoided military force. There was political calculation behind this hesitancy. The largest bloc in the postwar Italian parliament was the Socialists, who in 1919 had voted to nationalize key industries. They and the Catholic social democratic Popolari held enough votes to bring down any government, and both were afraid of estranging their constituents by releasing armed forces against the *sindicalisti*. Meanwhile, landless peasants, *braccianti*, were grabbing land from large estates, as a paralyzed national government conferred on these expropriations ex post facto approval.[42]

Pareto vented particular contempt on Giovanni Giolitti (1842–1928), the aged prime minister who formed his fifth and most disastrous government amid these trials. Pareto mocked Giolitti's "cowardice [*viltà*]" when he responded to Red Guard violence with the statement that intervention would be "tantamount to capital punishment, which would be inappropriate at the present time." Pareto contrasted Giolitti to those fascist squadrons who in the fall of 1919 moved against the "Red baronies" in Bologna and the Po Valley. For Pareto, the plutocracy had become "timorous [*imbelle*] and moronic," and the only groups which now seemed capable of exercising power were nationalists and union leaders: "Among the propertied class the sentiments of self-defense and property are largely spent and have begun to transform themselves into a nebulous, uncertain social responsibility, what others call 'social duty,' used interchangeably with work now defined as a 'right.' In some parts of Italy workers invade the land and perform useless tasks, thereafter claiming the right to receive wages, which the owner has a duty to pay them. The response of many bourgeois is approval."[43] Elsewhere Pareto notes that the hatred and combativeness manifested by the unionists toward the propertied class no longer elicited resistance: "On one side of the class divide one sounds the trumpet and moves on to the assault; on the other, one bows one's head, capitulates, or better yet, joins the enemy and sell one's property for thirty pieces of silver."[44]

In two political commentaries published in 1923, following the fascist advent to power of October 1922, Pareto expressed the hope that Mussolini's regime would restore economic and political order. In January 1923 he perceived "as the major difference between past and present governments that one ignored economic issues, paying attention to demagogic sentiments and particular interests, while the new government is seeking to reestablish an equilibrium between social forces."[45] At the same time, Pareto warned against the danger of taxing heavily those who were salaried or small landowners; and he recommended that moderate unionists be consulted in setting economic policy.

In September 1923 he also suggested how the fascist regime might best reform the structure of government. Pareto urged Mussolini to maintain a free press: "Let the crows caw, but be indefatigable in repressing [rebellious] deeds! Experience demonstrates that leaders who embark upon this path of censorship find headaches, rather than benefits. It may help to imitate ancient Rome: not to occupy oneself with theology but attend only to actions."[46] Pareto also advocated the putting into place of a new parliament, which would express popular sentiments without crippling the executive. Though he readily admitted the failure of Italy's earlier parliamentary experience, he nonetheless thought that the new regime should not operate without elected institutions. He believed such institutions necessary to stabilize and legitimate the fascist order.

In assessing these comments written shortly before Pareto's death, it is important to keep in mind two critical factors. First, there was no reason for Pareto (and others) to believe in 1922 that the Italian fascist regime would later go berserk and ally itself, ideologically and politically, with Nazi Germany. In the early twenties, the Italian fascists expressed neither racist nor anti-Semitic ideas, and they were willing to offer leadership in a country that had broken down economically and was on the verge of political collapse. Second, Pareto saw his own class, the bourgeoisie, as spent and demoralized. And though he hoped to preserve some of its creations, particularly a free market, a free press, and religious liberty, he did not believe that his own social class would be able to do so. He therefore thought it was necessary to turn to what he, like Machiavelli, designated as the "lions," bold warrior forces, to save what had been devised by those who had become "foxes," parliamentary schemers and finessing plutocrats.[47]

What Pareto saw happening in Italy seemed to belong to a broader civilizational context. Throughout his writing, he used the concept of "uniformities," which he applied to both economic and social affairs and which he claimed to have derived from an "experimental research method." The long-term invariability of the income curve and the equivalent advantages to producers of a "perfectly organized" monopoly and of an unimpeded free market are two such laws that are worked out in Pareto's major economic works. In *Trattato di Sociologia generale* (1916), he developed a theory of psychological predispositions to explain social behavior. In this analysis we find six such predispositions, which Pareto called "residues" and associated with changing movements and ideologies, also known as "derivations." The six residues underlying group behavior are the instinct for combination, the persistence of aggregates, the desire to manifest one's beliefs, sociality, the integrity of the individual, and the sexual drive.[48]

It is the instinct for combination and related residues three and four that actuate groups on the rise, while the persistence of aggregates and the concern about individual interest are most characteristic of established elites. Pareto discussed those residues operating within Italian society in the context of his social observations. He believed that the waning of liberalism, conspicuous in his own country, was taking place

45

throughout the industrialized West. The liberal bourgeoisie had lost its assertiveness in the face of an insurgent working class and of other "democratic" forces expressing instincts for combination and group solidarity.

In the First World War, according to Pareto, the parliamentary plutocrats had triumphed over the German military aristocracy but had succumbed to the democratic classes without which they could not have hoped to win the war. The only force now able to resist the revolutionary socialists, Pareto maintained, were the nationalists, who drew upon the same residues prevalent among the socialists. Socialism and nationalism seemed to be related derivations, both resulting from residues leading to collective action.

Among his last published remarks were those on Italian constitutional reform addressed to the new fascist government on 25 September 1923: "Under democratic ideology runs the current of fascism which overflows at the surface. But beneath that runs a countercurrent. Beware lest that countercurrent overflow! Beware lest you bestow upon it power by trying to close it off completely!"[49] Pareto believed that the fascists and their socialist enemies were harnessing the same democratic enthusiasm that a now declining liberal society had given up trying to oppose. He felt that the fascists would have to coexist with social democracy but hoped they would do so on their own terms.

Pareto's appeal to some aspects of the liberal heritage occurred in the face of what he took to be an irrevocable political change. The march toward democracy would continue no matter what, and the "decadence of the Roman plutocracy was only a portent of the destiny towering above our own plutocrats."[50] An activist and redistributionist democratic government was about to arrive, and unlike Lecky a generation earlier, Pareto had no doubt that a corresponding elite was arising to take charge of modern democracy. Political upheavals did not transpire randomly but were the work of purposeful elites, who took advantage of their consequences. Faced by the Italian nationalists and the priesthood of "the social proletariat," Pareto opted for what he considered to be the more moderate democratic leadership. In fact he chose what turned out to be the less farsighted of the two aspiring democratic elites. In the twentieth century, it was the exponents of working-class democracy, not of democratic nationalism, who made the more compelling claim to represent liberal democracy.

Significantly, social democratic planners took over a form of discourse more closely akin to Pareto's than to that of the Italian fascists. In Scandinavia, England, and the United States they appealed to "experimental-scientific" methods in education and public policy, and they presented their takeover of civil society as an act of liberating individuals and upholding their rights. But they also appealed effectively for several generations to democratic legitimacy, unlike the Italian fascists who were forced to manufacture popular endorsements for their plans. It is not surprising that by the end of the century social democratic planning has given rise to what Charles Krauthammer calls "reactionary liberalism: holding fast to the structures and constituencies of the welfare state, come what may."[51] More interesting is the fact that this liberal democracy held up for more than half a century in the most prosperous and literate areas of the world, with popular approval.

This result indicates that some European liberals read the political future with clearer eyes than others. Despite his demonstrated polemical skill, Fitzjames Stephen underestimated J. S. Mill's capacity to plan a popular regime. Mill did not intend to leave the uninstructed masses to do as they please. Maurice Cowling notes that Mill staked his democratic hopes on a Religion of Humanity, "a better religion than any of those which are ordinarily called by that title," and on a "new clerisy" which would work to instill a universal faith in rationality. Unlike the Anglican clergy and most of the English professoriate, Mill's clerisy would propagate scientific method and political sociology, seen as the true science of society.[52] This elite would arise in response to social need and to the spread of secular rationalism. It would train citizens to emulate its own rationality and bring them into fellowship with the advocates of social progress everywhere.

Cowling further argues that Mill's devotion to intellectual freedom was conditioned by his concern about "great minds" being crushed by mediocrity. Mill was less of a libertarian than someone looking out for the "highest natures," "noblest minds," and the advancement of scientific "truth." Note that Mill favored extensive state intervention in the economy and the ongoing redistribution of incomes. He also hoped that his own elite would take charge of the "general culture." It would thereby become possible to teach and apply his own utilitarian ethic, which Mill assumed would bring forth a new social morality. All enlightened citizens would eventually accept the utilitarian notion that the Good is that which maximizes general happiness. But, as Cowling perceives, the "highest end" that men here were imagined to pursue in quest of pleasure was whatever Mill and his confreres desired for themselves. They never doubted that their own social preferences would come to prevail in a democratic age.[53]

Clearly, Fitzjames Stephen and (his younger brother) Leslie Stephen, though both sagacious critics of Mill, did not see fully his authoritarian side. They did not grasp the "inquisitorial certainty" which Cowling exposes at the core of his method of inquiry. Nor did they appreciate the dogmatic way in which Mill generalized about subjects he never studied: "Mill knew little in detail about the history of British society in the two hundred and fifty years before he was born. His denigration of its polity and religion was based neither on close observation nor on exact historical knowledge."[54]

Finally, Mill's liberal critics underestimated the power of his vision of a new clerisy crafting and directing a democratic order. However weak may have been his grasp of the past, Mill evoked a society of democratic planners, which would arise after his death. His twisting of historical data and fudging of laws of human progress were of less significance than Mill's ability to foresee mass democracy at work. No other mid-nineteenth-century figure, including Tocqueville, exhibited such understanding of the dawning democratic age, even if that understanding, in Mill's case, was ideologically colored. And only one European liberal, Max Weber, revealed comparable insight in plotting the likely course of modern democracy. Unlike those liberals who trembled over the fate of property and parliamentary civility, Weber associated democratic life with the "iron cage of bureaucracy." Like Pareto, he was willing to entrust democratic government to plebiscitary leaders, not because of the fear of anarchy but because of his dread of bureaucratic despotism.[55]

In an oft-quoted letter from Weber to the sociologist of elites Robert Michels at the end of the First World War, Weber questions the intelligence or honesty of those who exalt the "will of the people." He goes on to admit that "genuine wills of the people have ceased to exist for me; they are fictitious. All ideas aiming at abolishing the dominance of man over man are 'Utopian.' "[56] In 1918 Weber observed even more incisively: "In large states everywhere, modern democracy is becoming a bureaucratized democracy. And it must be so; for it is replacing the aristocratic or other titular officials by a paid civil service. It is the same everywhere, it is the same within parties too. It is inevitable."[57] Despite the attempt by Weber's critics to attribute such remarks to the "anemia of German liberalism," what they indicate is Weber's deep perception of a secular trend: the intertwining of mass democracy and public administration as the shape of things to come.

✻ CHAPTER THREE ✻

Public Administration and Liberal Democracy

BUILDING THE WELFARE STATE

THE ASSOCIATION of public administration with liberal democracy is by now taken for granted. At the end of the twentieth century, this relation seems both natural and unavoidable. According to journalists and the authors of college textbooks, justice and freedom can only operate harmoniously in a liberal democratic welfare state. Almost all Western governments now embrace that idea, and these governments' shared features have come to outweigh their cultural and institutional distinctions. In each of them professional administrators oversee the details of popular government, look after social services, regulate commerce, and provide for suitable transfers of income. In such welfare states, democracy has become synonymous with economic policy, usually signifying the distribution of entitlements or allowances, and services, and at least some public management of national resources, key industries, and corporate wealth.

There are, of course, degrees in the way different countries have pursued these activities. But these relate to differences of degree and not of kind. Whether a particular democratic welfare state adds utilities to its public sector or controls them indirectly by determining wage levels, hiring practices, and permitted profits, is a practical decision. But the government's position of control remains awesomely powerful in either case. This became so in a mass democratic age, when entire populations began to demand an "equitable" distribution of wealth and of access to consumer goods. The creation of this state mechanism (what the French call aptly *le dispositif social*) took place in response to popular demand; that is, enlarged electorates produced mandates for a changed regime. It also drew legitimacy from a "liberal" creed: government exists to promote individual gratification. Absent that responsibility, the state is no longer living up to an implicit social contract.

Until recently, however, there was no necessary tie between a publicly administered unitary state and liberal democratic ideology. Before the

French Revolution, public administration was a tool of monarchical sovereignty. Kings raised commoners (*novi homines*) to look after the public realm, to devise means for augmenting their revenues, and to mete out uniform justice throughout their territories. It was monarchs in Austria, Spain, Prussia, and France who set up schools of cameral science and public law, where future government lawyers and administrators studied.[1] As Tocqueville noted in the mid-nineteenth century, a highly centralized national administration did not first originate in France with the Revolution. It was the gift bequeathed to Jacobin France by the monarchy that the revolutionaries overthrew.[2] In the nineteenth century, public administration continued to develop in all major European states, no matter what their political complexion. From Tsarist Russia to liberal monarchical England and to republican France, public servants grew in importance and visibility.

The German philosopher G. W. F. Hegel (1770–1831) assigned to public administration an exalted role in the *Philosophy of Right* (1821–22). It "represented the generality" and carried out the daily work of a modern nation state without the taint of "social or material particularity."[3] In April, 1831, the government of the newly established July Monarchy recommended the integration of members of the public class into an expanded franchise. In addition to professors, military officers, physicians, and lawyers resident in their electoral districts for at least five years, the electorate was to be opened up to judges and their staffs. Guizot and others who formulated the original recommendation also hoped to extend the vote to local administrators managing populations of at least thirty thousand and to the chief officials in federal and municipal districts (*départements* and *arrondissements*). Significantly it was the republican Left in the French Assembly that defeated this specific proposal for extending the franchise. Looking at state officials as the instrument of political reaction, intransigent democrats voted for limiting the vote to upper-middle-class property holders and to members of the liberal professions.[4]

The growing demand for social services and income redistribution in the present century did not bring about entirely by itself a new political order. That order faced competitors for several generations before becoming the only respectable political model. In the interwar period it had to deal with two rival models of public management, and material redistribution, both of which had considerable followings. In *The Managerial Revolution* (1941), James Burnham underlined this rivalry and pointed to the common features of Soviet Communism, National Socialism, and welfare-state democracy. In all of them, Burnham believed, a new class of state administrators had succeeded to political power by deftly manipulating popular rhetoric and redistributionist slogans. What further united these managerial experiments was their distinctiveness from capitalism and socialism (as either would have been understood in the early-twentieth century). The new managerial state was built on neither a market economy nor true social equality. Rather, it elevated a managerial class which already had positioned itself in a corporate economy and would now provide state-authorized social services.[5]

For many, the fascists and communists seemed able to furnish those services while holding out the promise of regeneration for their societies. A vast literature exists for the rise and spread of the Communist movement in the West as well as outside of it, and it may be useful to recall that at the end of the Second World War the Communist Parties of Italy and France were the largest political organizations in those countries and commanded millions of votes. A less well-known fact, which John Diggins and John Lukacs have highlighted, was the widespread popularity enjoyed by fascism throughout the twenties and thirties.[6] Despite the assassination of the socialist leader Giacomo Matteoti by fascist *squadristi* in June 1924, Mussolini remained popular among social reformers into the 1930s. A generally favorable view of his economic policies and style of leadership could be found in the *New Republic* and in other publications supportive of social planning. And within Italy itself, as the historian of fascism Renzo De Felice makes clear, Mussolini was generally perceived as a modernizer as well as a Latin nationalist. His fascist national revolution was hailed as an Italian path to restored political greatness and economic growth.

The appeal of this path, which was felt by, among other groups, revisionist Zionists and the back-to-Africa followers of Marcus Garvey, became less pronounced in the mid-1930s. By then Mussolini overreached in trying to create an empire, and Latin fascism became overshadowed by its more disagreeable German variant. Even more significantly, European fascists, under the disastrous leadership of Adolf Hitler, incited and lost the Second World War. In that struggle the Communists, after switching sides, came out, together with the "democracies," as the perceived champions of the Good. In time, the Communists also lost credibility because of their inept planning and persistent brutality. The collapse of the Soviet Union and its Eastern European satellite states in 1989 discredited conclusively that model of socialist government, though by then its appeal in the Western world had shrunk considerably, outside of rarefied circles of Marxist Leninist intellectuals.

The liberal democratic welfare state defeated fascism and communism partly by default. It survived after contributing to their downfall, and it picked up support from those who either defected or were converted from the two failed models. It also exhibited certain strengths its rivals never possessed. Liberal democracies have generally desisted from physical brutality in dealing with internal opposition. They have also tolerated opposition even while seeking to manage civil society. Liberal democracies have been, for the most part, economically prosperous, encouraging the coexistence of markets and private initiative with a public sector and a regulated economy.

From the Second World War through the 1970s, most Western countries saw the steady expansion of both GNP and the social welfare net. In 1945 France introduced social security (having had only one national social program before, accident insurance for workers, established in 1898). By the 1960s the French national administration collected and dispensed funds for a multitude of allowances (*prestations*) and social insurance programs, without having to lower the national standard of living. Despite increased government taxing, the French per capita Gross Domestic Product doubled between 1960 and 1982. By the early eighties the average Frenchman received almost $10,000 yearly after taxes, putting him well ahead of his English and Italian and only slightly behind his German counterparts. This growth took place in a country, moreover, in which subsidies to the agricultural sector remained almost as large as the revenues collected from the income tax.[7] In Germany even greater prosperity occurred in the wake of ruinous defeat in the Second World War. According to documented studies by Karl Hardach and Eric Owen Smith, the postwar *Wunderwirtschaft* not only reindustrialized Germany but left it with the highest GDP of any major industrial power after the United States. This took place together with the establishment of enlarged welfare states at the provincial and federal levels. Today German wage earners pay at least half their income back to the government.[8] In the United States the GNP and standard of living both rose in the postwar years. From the sixties into the nineties, the American GNP continued to rise despite the steadily greater share of earnings taken by the government. Between 1991 and 1995, U.S. tax collection soared by one-third.

In England the postwar democratic welfare state may be harder to justify. It has not taken shape amid prosperity, but it has survived, notwithstanding the economic crises that have dogged it since the late forties. Between 1913 and 1938 the English GNP doubled, and at the end of the Second World War England remained the most prosperous (or economically the least damaged) of the European industrial powers. Under these circumstances it seemed possible, according to the "Beveridge Report on Social Life," submitted to the cabinet in 1944, to move decisively toward English social democracy.[9] The postwar Labor government of Clement Atlee did exactly that, creating a national health service, pouring increased monies into public education, and nationalizing mines, utilities, transportation, steel, and other major industries. Though the distribution of consumer goods rose in the late forties, by the early fifties English voters, bothered by the very modest rise in living standards, brought the Conservatives back into power. But the returned opposition left most of Labour's work untouched. In the sixties Conservative prime minister Harold Macmillan competed with Labour in promising expanded social services. Both major parties were then committed to a large national welfare state. In the seventies Labour Prime Minister Harold Wilson responded to militant demands and the threats of strikes by union leaders by announcing a new "social contract." Thereafter, it was said, the government would negotiate with those working in nationalized industries instead of trying to intimidate them. This conciliatory approach did nothing to improve obsolescent national enterprises or to stem the loss of jobs. By 1979, when the Thatcher government came to power, English unemployment stood at 1.5 million, the highest since the Great Depression. Real wages in England had been falling for almost a decade, and the economy had contracted in two of the previous four years.[10]

Despite these disasters, an observation made by Harry Schwartz about English health services can apply equally well to other aspects of the English welfare state: to most of those living under this form of government it has been hugely successful.[11] It is seen to protect them against utter dearth, and despite the reprivatization of major industries undertaken in the eighties, the public sector remains the largest English employer. A working- and middle-class concern is that the influx of Third World population from the Commonwealth will erode the financial base of the English welfare state. This concern is becoming widespread and, according to polls taken from the late seventies, has grown into a burning issue for a majority of the English.

The trend toward public control, with only intermittent setbacks, has continued throughout the Western world for more than half a century. It has blurred any sharp and permanent distinction between public and private enterprise. The proportion of the work force made up of public employees is already approaching 50 percent in France, Germany, Holland, Norway, and Denmark, and is, significantly, well over 60 percent in Sweden (where over 85 percent of earned income is taxable).[12]

At first blush it would seem that the United States has a smaller public sector than European industrial democracies. According to the *Annual Report* figures published by the U.S. Council of Economic Advisors, government employment accounts for about 15 percent of the national labor force, excluding military personnel. Even with that Factored in, however, government-authorized jobs remain less than 30 percent of full-time employment in the United States.[13] But other circumstances should be considered to obtain an accurate picture of the American public sector. Government budgets grew from 26 percent to over 40 percent of the American GNP from the mid-fifties into the early nineties. As the economic historian Robert Higgs notes, moreover, the American government in the present century has expanded six times as much as economic growth.[14] While a smaller and smaller percentage of earnings has been left to jobholders in the form of disposable income, the public sector has continued to grow, most strikingly since the sixties.

Equally important, its control is far greater than the number of jobs it directly creates. The distribution of public funds and the awarding of licenses and contracts have allowed the American government to supervise what it has not authorized explicitly. A study by the economist Thomas DiLorenzo traces the extent of this "hidden" growth of the public sector. DiLorenzo demonstrates that this growth has been sufficiently dramatic to invalidate the often made contrast between American free enterprise and European statism. Controlled economic activity need not take the form of public sector employment. Nor does government spending in the United States have to conform to the budgetary guidelines found in the *Annual Report*. Though the Congressional Budget and Impoundment Control Act of 1974 and the resulting Congressional Budget Office were designed to set overall targets for revenues and expenditures, the United States Congress has evaded the intended restraints.[15] Congressmen have resorted to off-budget outlays, as in the funding of synthetic fuel research and the 1995 bailout of the Mexican currency. Neither major party has resisted this circumvention of budgetary limits.

In view of this analysis it may be premature for American movement conservatives to celebrate "the death of socialism," or to join the *American Enterprise* symposiast who in July 1995 proclaimed that "the Gingrich revolution is a rollback of both the 1960s and 1930s."[16] With all due respect to American postwar debates, no American or European political party seems likely to roll back the welfare state. A party may dispute anticipated tax increases to cover entitlements or allowances, and it may even muddy discussion by equating the "American welfare state" with Aid to Dependent Children. Finally, it may even be made to appear that socialism is vanishing because direct government ownership of the means of production has lost its mantra-like appeal among self-declared socialists. That is to say, the criterion of socialism given by Emile Durkheim, Karl Marx, and others at the end of the last century, nationalization of industry, is no longer a popular idea, even among social reformers.[17]

But what has taken its place in liberal democracies is a more enduring form of collectivism, the perceived growth of public administration as an instrument of equity. This has gone forward as liberal democratic states intrude on economic and social activities without, at least in the United States, nationalizing anything outright. The terms "socialism" and "capitalism" no longer describe the process at work, which is one of administrative engulfment. In a probing response to conservative movement predictions about the end of socialism, *New Republic* senior editor John B. Judis notes the obvious fact that government control of the economy has not gone away. Judis looks forward to an international regulation of capital, under an enlightened global administration that protects "international labor rights." But this development will occur, Judis explains, without the linguistic and genealogical burdens of past socialist models: "It is unlikely anyone will describe this new international as 'socialist.' And I certainly don't think that future intellectuals will describe themselves as 'Marxists' in the same worshipful way as past generations."[18]

THE POLITICS OF SOCIALIZATION

An indisputable strength of liberal democracy is its power to incorporate both liberal and democratic elements in defining its character. This absorption of political forms nonetheless has been selective and determined by what is compatible in each element with modern public administration. From democracy, liberal democrats have taken their insistence on general elections, carried out with minimal voting restrictions, and they have stressed the characteristically democratic values of political and social equality. Like nineteenth-century liberals, they have turned to party organizations to stage elections and to arrange for a "rotation of governments" behind which administration can do its daily work. Liberal democrats also appeal to an expanded notion of freedom, what L. T. Hobhouse called "the self-directing power of personality." Basic to this thinking is the belief in a progression from a selfish, antisocial view of freedom to a fuller, more compassionate one. This progression is thought possible because of the formation of a science of society, and because of public administrators trained in the "experimental-scientific method" in preparation for managing their fellow citizens.[19]

In the early twentieth century, Anglo-American social planners fleshed out this vision of a liberal democratic future. In *Liberalism and Social Action*, drawn from his Page-Barbour Lectures at the University of Virginia in 1935, Dewey discusses the new "scientific" liberalism. Unlike the nineteenth-century liberals, who "lacked historic sense and interest" and were "frozen" in free-market doctrine, the new liberals view society as being "in continuous growth." This growth poses no mystery for these new liberals who, unlike earlier ones, are not "blinded by their own special interpretations of liberty, individuality and intelligence."[20] Dewey's liberals, who are not "historically conditioned," can grasp and control the constant features of a world otherwise in flux. The reason for this is their acquisition of a scientific method which, together with technology, has been the "active force in producing the revolutionary changes society is undergoing." Through the understanding of social data, "the engineering mind in the invention and projection of far-reaching social plans" can furnish liberal democracy with a "concrete program of action." This, Dewey argues, is particularly urgent at the present time. Faced by authoritarian ideologies that feature their own forms of social control, liberal democrats must learn to profit fully from "scientific method and experimental intelligence." They must respond to any "narrowing of choice" between fascists and communists with their own call for "discipline, order, and organization." Indeed "regimentation of material and mechanical forces is the only way by which the mass of individuals can be released from the regimentation and consequent suppression of their cultural possibilities."[21]

Aside from the defense of a "scientifically" regimented economy, Dewey's lectures make a sustained plea for government as a vehicle of public education. Unlike the old liberals who held "a conception of individuality as something ready-made, already possessed, and needing only the removal of certain legal restrictions," the new liberalism demands extensive socialization. It seeks to prepare individuals for the "conflict between institutions and habits originating in the pre-scientific and pre-technological age and the new forces generated by science and technology."

Such training, in a properly administered society, will open up "cultural possibilities" based on "cooperative and experimental science."[22]

Education was the keystone of social planning for Dewey and Deweyite social reformers, and for several generations their ideas ruled American schools of education, starting with the one where Dewey taught, Columbia University. Moreover, the call to restructure public education around scientific and democratic values goes back to the dawn of liberal collectivist thinking. Like the "renascent liberalism" in Dewey's Page-Barbour Lectures, the "constructive liberalism" expounded by L. T. Hobhouse in 1911 prescribes that the state be an "overparent": "It is on the basis of the rights of the child, of his protection against parental neglect, of the equality of opportunity which he may claim as a future citizen and of his training to fill his place as a grown-up person in the social system" that the state should assume this function, which includes the right to education.[23] By the twenties and thirties, this role of "overparent" would entail far more in the minds of democratic social planners. As Allan Carlson and Nikolaj-Klaus von Kreitor demonstrate in studies of Gunnar and Alva Myrdal as architects of Swedish social democracy, Scandinavian reformers in the interwar years treated public education as a means of national socialization. The Myrdals argued that the Swedish state, by monopolizing educational activities, could mold entire families in accordance with scientific collectivist methods. Until after World War Two, that ethos was not always identifiably leftist. In the thirties it included glorification of the *Folknemmet* (national home), a Sterilization Act for racially and genetically defective individuals, and the acceptance of other forms of eugenic engineering. A longtime justification for Swedish social planning was the need to increase the natality of the Nordic peoples in a changing economic environment. What provided the common link in all phases of Swedish social democracy, however, was the combination of public administration with a vision of social reconstruction. Educational reform as well as economic control were foundational for whatever social changes were envisaged by Swedish social democrats.[24]

Liberal democratic education has become increasingly different from its older liberal predecessor. It acquired two functions: shaping social personality and helping to fill the social space. When Prussian reformers introduced the *Volksschule* during the Napoleonic Wars and when in the 1830s liberal ministers reformed and expanded French primary and secondary education, the justifications were both practical and nonegalitarian. The members of a modern nation, it was said, had to be literate in order to be employable, and besides, it was believed, national unity required some type of shared learning. The French minister of education at the time, Guizot, took pains to distinguish between his national plan and a democratic one whereby public schools would be used to level down society.[25] Liberal democratic education, by contrast, has aimed explicitly at changing social structure and social attitudes. A conspicuous case in point is postwar West Germany where since 1945 "remolding the civic culture" has been a duty of both public educators and public administrators. In *The German Polity*, David Conradt outlines the extent of this program, with obvious approval. Resocialization in Germany has aimed at inculcating democracy and encouraging Germans to "overcome their past [*Vergangenheitsbewältigung*]." The horrors of the Nazi era are regularly invoked to explain this national effort at creating a democratic culture.[26]

At the end of the Second World War in Europe, *Time* featured expert testimony by prominent social scientists on what measures should be taken to transform the "German character." Basic to these suggestions was the need to reconstruct the German family. German males were seen as "passive-aggressive" bearers of the "authoritarian personality," who were prone to follow undemocratic leaders.[27] They presumably developed these personalities because of defective relations to their wives and children, and the German household was presented as a spawning ground for social pathology contributing to dictatorship and strife.

This therapeutic zeal common to journalists, academics, and politicians may be traced to the passions of war, especially one fought against the representatives of a murderous ideology. But this analytic discussion was not limited to plans for an occupied Germany. What it proposed was no different from what American liberal democratic theorists would be doing at home. These reformers advocated the diffusion of "critical thinking" about traditional belief systems, and by the seventies they introduced measures to produce gender equality in the home and workplace. These proposals were equated with progress and science, and the failure of others to accept them became proof positive that public experts were needed to make liberal democracy work.

In *Liberalism in Contemporary America*, Dwight D. Murphey shows how liberals in the first half of the century presented their cultural and educational agendas as practical responses to socioeconomic pressures.[28] For example, Dewey calls for the social use of intelligence to forestall an impending "crisis in democracy." He then attributes that crisis to the failure to apply to American political life "scientific procedure." Though Dewey advocates the resocialization of his fellow Americans, he claims to be guided only by science in his pursuit of the common good. He contrasts "the state of intelligence in politics to the physical control of nature" and looks forward in the area of social questions to the "outstanding demonstration of the meaning of organized intelligence" already achieved by technology.[29] Note that the crisis to which Dewey refers is moral and social, and his responses, as his biographer Robert B. Westbrook remarks, expressed his own moral judgments. By the 1950s some of Dewey's values, particularly his commitment to self-government, had lost out to his own scientific and technical procedures. His disciples S. M. Lipset, Robert Dahl, and Arthur Bestor abandoned the plan for genuine popular government and, according to Westbrook, came to identify democracy with electoral laws and an expertly run welfare state. Calling themselves "realists," they also "conflated description and prescription. . . . All too often a description of the way politics works in the United States provided realists with their normative conception of what democracy should be."[30]

The work of Dewey's friend Herbert Croly also illustrates the practice of hiding personal preferences behind "historical necessities" and appeals to science. In the end he too reduced democracy to a set of procedural and administrative problems. In *The Promise of American Life* (1909), Croly maintains that the Jeffersonian model of local democracy is no longer appropriate for the new industrial age. One could not depend on outdated social habits in preparing Americans to compete in a "world economy." In *Progressive Democracy* (1918), Croly comes back to the same theme in constructing a brief for long-range national economic planning.[31]

This future Wilsonian, soon to be editor of the *New Republic*, was as much concerned about social education as he was about America's economic place in the world. He complained about American provincialism and spoke of the need to adapt German social planning to a unified American people. Though Wilsonian liberals supported the Allied side in 1914, Croly continued to be well-disposed toward German state socialists. He professed admiration for Hegel's attempt to integrate the sphere of individual liberty into the ethical will of a unified state. Croly fretted little that the "march of constructive national democracy" would be over the body of democratic localism. Indeed, he wished to accelerate that march by having the federal government socialize the American people. He insisted their political problems could be traced to an "erroneous democratic theory," one that sacrificed collective education to individual interest. In the new democracy "the nation must offer to the individual a formative and inspiring opportunity for public service." All learning must be made into a "national educational experience," and those who shape the new state must realize that "democracy cannot be disentangled from an aspiration toward human perfectibility and the adoption of measures looking in the direction of realizing such an aspiration."[32]

Walter Weyl, Croly's collaborator at the *New Republic,* was more explicit about the "progressively diffused education" that would nurture a modern industrial society. In *The New Democracy* (1912), Weyl makes the point that economic changes and social grievances require centralized planning, but such planning can only succeed if accompanied by a "socialization of education." A sober democracy demands that citizens be willing to control their appetites and national consumption.[33] Instead of "capitalist anarchy of production and anarchy of consumption," the new democratic leadership must prepare citizens to think entirely of the collective good: "The future education of the masses cannot be the traditional Procrustean, unrelated, and undifferentiated education of yesterday. It must be an education which will aid society, the conservation of the life and health of the citizens in their progressive development."[34]

This socialization of education proposed by Dewey, Weyl, and Croly was both attitudinal and vocational. It called for training citizens to be economically useful but also to look upon resources and consumer goods as a public benefit. Though Croly, Weyl, and the *New Republic* placed some emphasis on experimental science in the schools, this analytic tool seemed to them more important for public administrators than for the masses of citizens. The "individual" for whom these thinkers planned was expected to accept their judgments, after receiving the proper social education. Croly believed that "a democratic nation must not accept human nature as it is but must move in the direction of improvement." Without a regime that sought this improvement, the unenlightened individual would harm himself and others. This was the temptation faced by those who embraced the "false tradition" of an unplanned economy: "The popular enjoyment of practically unrestricted economic opportunities is a condition which makes for individual bondage."[35]

By the thirties and forties the program of socialization which American reformers of the Progressive era had outlined became more heavily cultural. The writings of Horace Kallen (1882–1974), one of Dewey's close associates and a founder of the New School for Social Research, indicate this turning toward social control presented as positive freedom. Though Kallen popularized the term "cultural pluralism," his "approach to liberty" left rather limited room for social or cultural diversity. Such diversity had to fit Kallen's definition of democratic humanism: that which "cannot favor any race or cult of man over any other; nor any human doctrine and discipline over any other." In the "orchestrations of humanism with democracy" offered by Kallen, there is no place for orthodox Christianity, particularly in its ridiculed Catholic form. Democratic humanism, which is the appropriate outlook for a democratic society, can only tolerate a tolerant deity, one who "brings forth impartially all the infinite diversities of experience and who allows men to survive or to perish by their own dispositions and abilities."[36]

The democratic pluralism and democratic humanism that Kallen advocates are intended to benefit all of mankind, and so he moves in his pluralist vision beyond national planning toward a global perspective. He invokes a future "international mind" that would be informed by scientific attitudes and envisages a United Nations consisting entirely of democratic nations. This internationalism would lead to social reforms that Kallen would be pursuing at home.[37] These would entail public ownership of some of the means of production and substantial redistribution of wealth, both aimed at furthering individual human betterment and the "liberal spirit." Kallen perceived no contradiction between his economic measures and free enterprise, which "satisfies the natural preference of natural men."[38] His economic policies were intended to humanize "great economic and financial undertakings" that "deal with men and women as if they were merely animate tools, merely beasts of burden." Among those forms taken by "arbitrary and authoritative" rule of the kind that Kallen wished to abolish are "religious establishments and political orders, which are as totalitarian as cartels and monopolies as hierarchical as armies."[39] Liberal democracy should lead to the overthrow of such "tyrannical" structures, which Kallen associates specifically with General Franco's regime in Spain. It would not be an unjustified speculative leap to think that these structures, for Kallen, included Catholic theocracy and corporate capitalism, both of which he detested. What is left unanswered is what or who would control that "government for the people" that Kallen trusted would bring down anachronistic powers.

It was not strange that liberal social planners in the United States and elsewhere stressed public education and values-formation in the context of defining "industrial democracy." Their project of rebuilding society presupposed the filling of the social space with appropriate ideas and concerns. What had to be decided was not whether a socialization of education should occur but what public ideology squared best with social progress. On this point there were differences which became perceptible over time. These reflected the changing views of historical progress and of the power the state might properly claim in remolding individual lives and communal habits.

From the founding of the *New Republic* and the Progressive era down to the 1960s, liberal collectivists in America appealed to a science of-public administration and to the ideals of a *national* welfare state. Both scientific method and the national interest were ready counterweights to be used by social planners against local opposition. Nationalization of decision-making has remained a useful process down to the present for American reformers intent upon removing perceived patterns of social and gender discrimination. Multiculturalism, the movement toward open borders, and the extension of Fourteenth Amendment protections to illegal aliens have signaled the journey of American liberalism from a national to a global educational purpose. This trend in the United States has grown particularly pronounced in "civil rights policy making." As two sympathetic analysts, Anthony Champagne and Stuart Nagel, observe in surveys of such policy initiatives: "Equality is not a concept withoutcontroversy. Changes interfere with human prejudice, tradition, and economic demands. Compliance with laws is a function of the benefits of noncompliance being outweighed by the benefits of compliance. It is important to note that courts have become havens for oppressed groups in our society. The other branches are more responsive to established, more powerful groups who can influence elections and provide funds for campaigns."[40] Aside from the questionable reference to "powerful groups," which can certainly be applied to policymaking judges and administrators, Champagne and Nagel are correct to view compliance to social policy as an essential object of a nationalized American administration. Contemporary policymakers have set out to bring to their society equality of esteem and pursue this end by trying to modify social behavior.

The Liberal Democratic Model

Several objections can be registered to this study of an evolving liberal democratic ideology. This ideology, it can be argued, is barely worth discussing. It describes a mere by-product of socioeconomic changes that would have occurred without individual visionaries or collective visions. Industrialization, urbanization, and other processes engendered industrial democracies, which then developed into welfare states out of popular demand. These welfare states required managers to deal with their complex problems, much as corporate capitalism called forth a similar managerial elite.

A related form of this corporate argument can be found in the Marxist analysis of C. Wright Mills and James Weinstein. These sociologists do not deny the cultural and social impact of political bureaucratization, but they attribute it to the extension of corporate capitalism into government. Once business titans organize a late-capitalist global economy, the resulting economy imposes its own corporate structure upon the state. Thus there emerges a capitalist welfare regime that mirrors an already bureaucratized economy.[41] In a variation of this theme, the counterrevolutionary populist exponent of Mills, Samuel T. Francis, has stressed the "isomorphic" nature of polity, the economy, and society present in a managerial order. All of these elements of human association have become assimilated to the same bureaucratic model that dominates the present age. For Francis, like Mills and James Burnham, ideology takes a backseat to social forces in explaining modern political organization. For all of these thinkers, moral visions are the mere accompaniments of the process by which classes make themselves economically dominant and try to control other groups. In the language of Antonio Gramsci, values are the means by which the ruling class establishes its "cultural hegemony." They therefore wield no power outside of their instrumental use.[42]

Although sympathetic to these attempts to unmask managerial ideology, it seems to me that all of them fail to take ideas and values seriously. One could organize a welfare state that provides social services without instilling a liberal democratic ideology. Similarly, one could have built the German autobahnen and increased the social benefits of German workers in the 1930s without carrying out a Nazi revolution. Likewise it would be possible for the American government to provide entitlement programs for its middle class without enforcing what are now unpopular quotas for designated minorities.[43] In all of these cases welfare states in industrialized societies have done more than address the majority's material demands. They have also tried to shape or reshape social relations to fit particular worldviews.

Equally important, it is hard to demonstrate that managerial elites have consistently benefited by pushing their own bodies of belief. Nazi administrators, to the extent they embraced Hitler's global vision, were rushing headlong into cosmic violence and arbitrary personal rule. Another telling example can be cited to demonstrate our point. No major American newspaper nor presidential candidate, save for Pat Buchanan, has called for restricting immigration, and neither the liberal Democratic *New York Times* nor the pro-business Republican *Wall Street Journal* will even publish an immigration-restrictionist argument except to ridicule it.[44] Yet faced by what is now predominantly Third World immigration (between 1981 and 1990, 35 percent of *legal* American immigrants came from Central and South America), the majority of respondents to both *New York Times/* CBS and *Newsweek* polls in 1993 favored significant reductions in the number of immigrants being admitted into the United States. By a 50 percent to 30 percent margin *New York Times* respondents also believed that immigrants "cause problems rather than contribute to the country."[45] On the immigration question, including social services to illegal immigrants, American political and journalistic elites are almost without exception pitted against a growing popular consensus. The reason is not undemocratic arrogance, as claimed by their populist opponents. The elites' understanding of democracy is based on globalist and managerial premises that most people do not accept wholeheartedly. Its adherents in government embrace that ideology out of genuine conviction. They insist on agreement even with aspects of their worldview that are least likely to resonate among the American people. When conservative Republican Congressman Dick Armey lectures his Texas constituents on the need for even higher levels of immigration from Mexico, it is not opportunism but ideological fervor that explains his behavior.[46]

It is also factually incorrect to believe that those who built the modern welfare state were impervious to its theoretical architects. Croly's *The Promise of American Life* had a profound effect on both Theodore Roosevelt and Woodrow Wilson, a fact well-documented by Arthur S. Link. According to Link, it is impossible to overestimate the impact of *The Promise of American Life* on Roosevelt, who in 1909 was searching to define his own political nationalism: "Roosevelt read the book with enthusiastic approval, and it helped him systematize his own ideas. In any event, he at once began to translate Croly's abstruse and heavy language into living political principles that the rank and file could comprehend."[47] Croly chastised and supported Woodrow Wilson, who responded to both actions with respect. In an oft-quoted editorial in the *New Republic*, published on 21 November 1914, Croly scolded Wilson for believing that his "economic reorganization" of the American nation should end with the creation of two agencies, the Federal Reserve Board and the Federal Trade Commission. Wilson's satisfaction with such meager change, thundered Croly, "shows he is a dangerous and unsound thinker upon contemporary political and social problems."[48] Wilson took this scolding to heart and worked to prove by example and by consulting Progressive intellectuals that he was worthy of their esteem. In 1916 he cultivated them for reelection as president, and Link marvels at "the way in which independent progressives—the social workers, sociologists, and articulate intellectuals—moved into the Wilson camp."[49]

A similar development occurred during the New Deal, as former brain truster Raymond Moley notes, when Franklin D. Roosevelt's administration moved decisively toward controlling business in the fall of 1935. Having seen himself stymied by the Supreme Court, which struck down the National Recovery Act and other forms of federal interference in intrastate commerce, FDR stressed the need for structural changes in American government. His relations with industrialists and corporate executives, as shown by Moley, Basil Rauch, and Allan Brinkley, became increasingly adversarial.[50] Moreover, his attempted packing of the Supreme Court to create a favorable majority dramatized his willingness to override opposing branches of the federal government. By 1936 FDR had forged an open alliance with organized labor, by which the newly formed mass industrial union, the CIO, became joined to the Democratic Party. FDR's spirited support for the National Labor Relations Act in 1935, sponsored by New York Senator Robert Wagner, betokened this burgeoning alliance with the working class. After the passage of the act, the federal government created a National Labor Relations Board, which oversaw labor-management disputes. It also guaranteed to unions the rights to organize and collectively bargain, regardless of the wishes of managers or owners.[51]

It is possible to see FDR's actions as driven by nonideological concerns; for example, his own political position in a country beset by depression and in which wealthy industrialists were electorally outnumbered, or his exasperation with a hostile Supreme Court. There is also no reason to assume that all New Deal politicians read Rexford Tugwell or agreed with the industrial policies of those brain trusters FDR periodically consulted. Besides, Democratic politicians, like Republican ones, then as much as now, were interested in holding offices and enjoying the benefits of their incumbency. Even so, FDR, like Woodrow Wilson, a president whom he had served and admired, and like his cousin, Theodore Roosevelt, had considered himself a Progressive. His trusted advisors, such as Tugwell, Harold Ickes, Adolf Berle, and Raymond Moley (before Moley's defection from the New Deal), read the *New Republic*, respected Croly, and identified their own liberalism with social planning. Like Wilson, the Swedish social democrats and the English Labourites, FDR did not live and act in an ideological void. His moves to nationalize economic problems, to put the federal government on the side of mass unions, and to provide for scientific management of social issues reflected the liberal collectivism becoming dominant in his time. In the United States these stands had the explicit endorsement of those whom Link sees as moving into the Wilson camp in 1916, "the social workers, sociologists, and articulate intellectuals."

Too much has been made of the fact that the liberal, social democratic welfare state was conceived or planned as something different from what it became. For example, like John Dewey, the Wilsonian founders of the *New Republic*, Walter Weyl and Walter Lippmann, were self-declared socialists; and their mentor and cofounder, Croly, did not deny the use of that term in describing his own politics. In 1932, brain truster Rexford Tugwell expressed unabashed admiration for Soviet industrial policies. In one memorable statement, Tugwell explained that "the interest of the liberals among us in the institutions of the new Russia of the Soviets has created wide popular interest in 'planning.' "[52]

Such remarks can be misleading for those plotting a genealogy for the democratic welfare state. Some American Progressives and New Dealers were deeply impressed by the Soviet experiment, and others, like the young Horace Kallen, endorsed with equal enthusiasm the model of social planning then associated with Mussolini.[53] There were also discernible ethnic nationalist and eugenic concerns in the platforms of interwar Scandinavian socialism, and certainly there is evidence of radical rightist impulses operative in Swedish social democracy into the early forties.

But this appeal to interwar historical data misses an obvious point. Managerial ideologies have borrowed from each other and invoked the same "historical crisis" without becoming identical. The attempt to find a common denominator for all modern managerial regimes has produced useful speculation, as attested by the works of Burnham, Adolph Berle, and Bruno Rizzi. But one should not rely exclusively on this denominator, lest it divert us from the crucial differences among managerial states. The distinctions between Nazi Germany and Western welfare states overshadowed the shared forms of public administration, which Burnham outlined in 1940. Focusing on structural similarities can be instructive but should not come at the cost of ignoring institutional and ideological differences. Only one political managerial model has triumphed in the industrial West by the end of the twentieth century, and that model is by now recognizably American and intertwined with liberal democratic ideology.

In *Crisis and Leviathan* a principled libertarian, Robert Higgs, critically surveys the evolution of the American liberal democratic welfare state. The picture drawn in detail is one of a steadily expanding federal administration interfering increasingly in the private sphere. Wars and other calls for national mobilization have had a "ratcheting effect" on administrative expansion, and executive power since the New Deal is said to have personalized bureaucratic sovereignty.[54] Looking at the cumulative results of this managerial dominance, Higgs notes a "substantial expansion of government authority in our economic decision-making. . . . "Given capitalist colors by the form of private property rights, the system has denied the substance of any right whenever governmental authorities have found it expedient to do so."[55] In this system of economic control and diminishing property rights, Higgs insists, the federal government (and its derivative state administrations furnished with federal funds and directives) can redefine or infringe on any group's liberty. This encroachment on property in the name of industrial planning and social equity became the icebreaker for the state's continuing invasion of society.

Another critical libertarian view of the American administrative state is offered by Northwestern professor of law Gary Lawson. In a study of federal agencies and their powers since the New Deal, Lawson observes that "the post–New Deal administrative state is unconstitutional, and its validation by the legal system amounts to nothing less than a bloodless revolution.[56] This modern regime is predicated upon a constitutionally dubious power, asserted by Congress and the president but found nowhere in the Constitution: the delegation to nonelected agencies of continuing oversight and judicial authority. Lawson notes that the Constitution does not allow any branch of the federal government to create new and permanent instruments of public control; nor should Congress be able to confer upon these agencies judicial powers, which were intended in Article Three for a system of courts. It is furthermore questionable, according to Lawson, whether the Commerce Clause in Article One can be honestly applied to justify the twentieth-century administrative state. That clause provides for congressional oversight of interstate commerce but is not a standing invitation to establish agencies. It does not, for example, give Congress the power to regulate *all* economic activities, as opposed to mere commerce, and it does not authorize Congress or its created instruments to interfere in commercial enterprises entirely within states.

Lawson points to an interpretative problem that even jurists who do not share his politics acknowledge to be real: the American administrative state rests on its own political, or political-scientific, logic and not on constitutional legitimacy. As one social democratic legal scholar, Bruce Ackerman, admits, it may be necessary to ignore this "deficient ratification" of the post–New Deal administrative state and to treat that authority as a constitutional given.[57] Reluctantly, Lawson concurs with this point. If given a choice between constitutional propriety and public administration dispensing material favors, most voters would gladly take the second, he maintains. And he concludes his observations with this provocative passage: "Modern champions of the administrative state seem loathe to abandon the sheltering language of constitutionalism. But tactical considerations aside, it is not at all clear why this is so. . . . After all, the moral relevance of the Constitution is hardly self-evident."[58]

What Higgs overlooks but Lawson does not is the resounding popular success of what they condemn. The liberal democratic welfare state gained vast power because it gave to most people what they wanted. The "substantial expansion" of its authority into "economic decision-making" fortified its base; and one reason this secular process has continued until now is that the welfare state has built a consensus around economic management. The redistribution of earnings and the furnishing of social services have both middle- and lower-class backing, and as Kevin Phillips proves in a study of American voter reaction, any perceived threat to middle-class entitlement programs can destroy a conservative candidate running for elected office in almost any voting district.[59] It is this democratic consensus for government economic policy that has allowed the American government to go beyond welfare-state measures into social engineering. The management of economic democracy has provided public administrators with what Carl Schmitt calls "social legitimation for the exercise of political power"—popular acceptance of a claim to moral authority made by those expanding their political control. More and more administrators have used that authority to implement a liberal democratic ideology to which they have assigned global implications.

This socializing mission has also assumed messianic tones, and both John Dewey and U.S. Commissioner of Education John Ward Studebaker affirmed the importance of bringing to Americans their own "democratic faith."[60] In this view, liberal democracy is not about a set of procedures or constitutional arrangements. It is a "living faith" which the American government is to impress first, on its own citizens and eventually, on the rest of humanity. In a massive biographical study, *In the Time of the Americans: F.D.R., Truman, Eisenhower, Marshall, and MacArthur,* David Fromkin, professor of international relations at Boston University, makes an observation telling as much about his own faith as the one attributed to his subjects: "In the First World War, Wilson had inspired people Franklin Roosevelt's and Harry Truman's and Dwight Eisenhower's age to go out and change the politics of the rest of the planet. It took nearly a century; it was by no means entirely of their own doing, and for the most part they did not realize where the forces would lead that they were putting into motion . . . but, in the end, they did it."[61]

This passage underscores the belief in the imperative to export liberal democratic ideology. America is not to be a state or society of the kind that exists elsewhere, but the instantiation of a political model informed by the "democratic faith." Today that faith is filtered through a managerial state, which expresses faith through abstract ideals assumed to have universal validity. That faith must be made to apply to others if its truths are the permanent and transcendent ones that its proponents claim they are. But the content of those truths has changed over the last eighty years, and today's democratic ideology of pluralism has weakened the legitimacy of the state that proclaims it. For the pluralist version of the democratic faith has come to incorporate doctrines that are breeding popular discontent. As Gary Lawson reminds us, the modern administrative state stands or falls not on constitutional legality but on the demand for its services. When those services carry disagreeable social and cultural costs, the "liberal democratic" regime faces an erosion of its popular legitimacy as well as constitutional foundation. The appeal to a partly resurrected nineteenth-century liberal vocabulary of rights will not cause these problems to go away. As the astute critics of modern liberalism Paul Piccone and Gary Ulmen note, the same trick has been tried too often to hide the fact that the administrative state is now widely viewed as undemocratic.[62]

This problem does not cease to exist because the regime in question claims to be "liberal." By now that decontextualized term means what the user wishes it to signify, providing that he can browbeat others into accepting his definition. Basic to this liberalism is that freedom be presented as what judges, public administrators, and journalists see fit to impose on other people. Presumably no one would be free, because inequality and discrimination would be rampant, unless our lives were supervised by experts. This freedom, which the administrative state guarantees, is what today's democratic faith is about; and for more than half a century it has worn the tag "pluralist."

The supposed essence of liberal democratic life, pluralism, has made its own semantic journey through the decades in various guises. Its advocates have claimed to be pursuing strategies of national unity, enhanced freedom, and cultural diversity but have contributed steadily to a different result, the growth of state managerial power. In recent years pluralists inside and outside of government have pushed social designs such as cultural inclusiveness, "secular-scientific" thinking, and global education upon increasingly resistant citizens. Whence the perception of Christopher Lasch in "The Revolt of the Elites" that a gulf is widening in America between the political-professional class and everyone else: "The masses today have lost interest in revolution. Indeed their political instincts are demonstrably more conservative than those of their self-appointed spokesmen and would-be liberators." Furthermore, Lasch continues, "Upper-middle-class liberals have mounted a crusade to sanitize American society . . . to censor everything from pornography to 'hate speech' and at the same time, incongruously to extend the range of personal choice in matters where most people feel the need for solid moral guidelines."[63]

The invective directed by Lasch against America's transnational elite is noteworthy in view of its source. By no means an apologist for the political economy of pre–New Deal America, Lasch is an avowed egalitarian. A morally conservative socialist, he celebrates blue-collar habits of mind against those of yuppie administrators and cultural revolutionaries. Another man of the Left now turned against administrative rule, Pierre Rosanvallon, points out the inescapable tie between pluralism and the ascendancy of experts. In an interview with *L'Express* (25 March 1993), Rosanvallon asserts that "pluralism results in misunderstandings as in the lack of rationality: on one side stand competent experts and on the other the incompetent many. For the latter to be rational and informed, it suffices that one accepts the opinions of the former."[64] Like Lasch, Rosanvallon stresses the structural presuppositions of pluralist ideology. Without the rule of administrators and social experts, that is to say, pluralism would not have remained for so long the American "democratic faith."

A question that remains to be considered in terms of this rule is whether successive attempts, presented as pluraslism, to formulate and update the "democratic faith" have internal consistency. That question should be approached by shifting the focus from any further consideration of a "liberal tradition" to the role of social planning within liberal democratic regimes. From that developmental perspective, it is possible to understand how pluralism became the justification for interventionist social policies. Contemporary pluralists, it will be argued, have not strayed far from the purposes or methods of their social engineering predecessors. Rather, they have widened the scope and definition of socialization to include behavior modification and the creation of a "sensitive" civic culture.

✳ CHAPTER FOUR ✳

Pluralism and Liberal Democracy

A WORLD DEMOCRATIC EMPIRE

ALREADY for some time now a debate has been going on about the "New Class" and its values. Typical of this discussion is *The Revolt of the Elites*, in which Christoper Lasch relates America's business and political leadership to a degenerate liberal culture. A collection of driven and deracinated achievers fixated on financial rewards and mental and physical well-being, Lasch's New Class is seen to embody the materialist mentality of a late capitalist society. It resists community or any fixed identity, be it ethnic, religious, or gender, that does not offer material or sensual reward. It also scorns any appeal to the collective good that does not benefit individual interest.[1]

Such comments on New Class hedonism and hyperindividualism typify a communitarian critique that concentrates predominantly on cultural and moral issues. While those who offer this kind of critique are mostly self-described socialists or social democrats—e.g., Charles Taylor, Jean Bethke-Elshtain, and Elizabeth Fox-Genovese—they speak passionately about the loss of an ethic of personal responsibility. They also envisage a combination of certain aspects of late modernity, such as women's rights and a planned economy, with a return to a putatively traditional social morality.[2] Because of these concerns communitarians sometimes land up on the same side as American neoconservatives, who also deplore the attack on the family and the impact of postmodernism on American education. In this neoconservative view, shared by some communitarians and expressed most conspicuously by Irving Kristol and William Bennett, it is not political and economic powers but the antisocial postmodernist values of New Class verbalists that are sowing moral confusion. Indeed, neoconservatives conveniently dissociate *their* New Class from government administration and multinational corporations.[3] Having headed federal agencies that fund cultural activities in the 1980s and having received hundreds of millions of dollars from large corporations, neoconservatives may have a practical interest in ignoring the New Class identity of their benefactors.

But, as the German social theorist Jürgen Habermas observes, the neo-conservatives have constructed social criticism which is suspended in mid-air. Their comments on New Class culture make no attempt to correlate patterns of belief with political and economic structures. Such critics want us to believe, however implausible it may be, that culture operates without reference to structural contexts. *Their* New Class manages to influence and at times even to control society, without at the same time representing the dominant forms of political and social organization.[4] It commands exclusively by verbal and artistic weapons, or so we are led to think.

In opposition to this view, it will be argued that any meaningful discussion of politically dominant values must take into account those who exercise force and enjoy a significant degree of economic power, in this case by cajoling and intimidating the wealthy and by redistributing income. Without such support, values do not become dominant; nor is it proper to speak about elites unless one means a group disposing of material and political resources. The preceding chapter set out to describe the developing democratic welfare state in order to highlight the formation of a dominant political class. It is one with considerable material power but does not directly own productive forces. And while this class's influence is massive and persuasive, individual members do not stand out. It is of course possible for others to share the benefits of this elite through association (for example, neoconservative journalists who defend the federal welfare state and multinational corporations). Nonetheless, journalists cannot become associated with those above them except to the extent that they uphold compatible views or convert others to their ideas. Those who express sharply opposing views to those in positions of political leadership are cast out as extremists and cannot expect to become part of the respectable opposition.

What are called New Class attitudes refer to the configuration of ideas linked to the modern administrative state. Two presuppositions for that regime are the mass democratic identification of government with both social planning and material benefits and the prevalence of a pluralist worldview. It may be said that pluralism is the ideology of the administrative state, providing two considerations are kept in mind. The first is that pluralist ideology is not reducible to class interest consciously pursued. Pluralists believe in their ideology and are not likely to exchange it for another body of ideas on the basis of anticipated gains. The second consideration is that the pluralist ideologues who praise and serve the administrative state are held together by a worldview which seems, to them,

73

entirely true. A particular view of reality informs their planning and, as Karl Mannheim said with regard to utopias, spurs them on "to transcend the present social reality by shattering it."[5] In the case of the administrative state, that transformational task requires the carrying out of perpetual revolution. Both the regime and those who define and defend its beliefs have pushed and continue to push society toward a continuing self-transformation.

It will also be contended that pluralist ideology is necessarily globalist. This has become the case for at least three reasons. The first and most obvious is the transnational character of modern bureaucratic society. Administration ascribes to itself a rationality that transcends cultural specificity. It is the rules of bureaucratic organization that seek, or are alleged, to provide the moral substance of a society thus governed, and those rules, as Weber notes, are seen to be coextensive with a universal science of management. The second reason for the globalism inherent in pluralist ideology is the quest for validation of its own premise. What are called "human rights" and "human dignity" can only be made to appear such if all or most of humanity accepts the same ideology. Otherwise pluralism loses its status as a universal verity and becomes, to all appearances, a subjective judgment and special interest.

Finally, pluralism has attained international currency through its identification with America as a superpower. Already by mid-century, American advocates of liberal democracy were proclaiming what they took to be a global mandate. What they defended was not the outlook of a particular people nor the artifact of any one culture. They regarded their beliefs as universally applicable; and the "right to democracy," which is what a legal advisor to the Clinton administration explained in 1994 that American troops were enforcing in Haiti, came out of the established view of liberal democracy as a universal creed. In the 1980s President Ronald Reagan defined America's mission as the spread of its democratic faith, and throughout his administration and that of Margaret Thatcher in England, "global democracy" remained the cosmic counterpoint in the struggle against world Communism.[6] This faith finds eloquent expression in the final section of S. M. Lipset's *Political Man*. A work written in the fifties by a democratic socialist and celebrated for its detailed and dispassionate treatment of political typology, Lipset's study ends with this striking credal statement: "A basic premise of this book is that democracy is not only or even primarily a means by which different groups can attain their ends or seek the good society; it is the good society itself in operation."[7]

It is clear what Lipset means by democracy: a welfare state subject to periodic elections and protecting freedom of expression. Lipset points to the pluralist character of American democracy, by which he means the tolerance of religious and political diversity. But he also enunciates a dogmatic pluralist faith, insisting that *only* his political preferences can lead to the "good society." That society is already "in operation," presumably in the United States and in other countries of the world whose institutions are similar. It is only a short step from that view to the more explicitly interventionist call for global democracy. Would it not be humanitarian, one might infer, for those constructing the only good society in history to induce others to embrace it?

Contrary to one widely shared fallacy, such beliefs are not at all peculiar to American enthusiasts for the Cold War. They have been around since the early-twentieth century and have characterized forward-thinking intellectuals both before and after the Cold War. John Dewey's hopes for social planning based on experimental science, Horace Kallen's call for a scientifically managed and expandable "cultural pluralism," and Auguste Comte's and J. S. Mill's formulation in the last century of a universal positivist method for social reorganization have all contributed to the optimism of modern liberal democracy. American nationalists can claim as their heritage this vision of a planned society, inasmuch as their own country has become its most prominent laboratory. As *National Review* editor John O'Sullivan notes, "For much of the world's left the U.S. is today a utopia."[8]

Through much of the second half of this century, however, the United States did not enjoy the widespread approval of intellectuals, nor was it seen as the most promising representative of social planning. Its recent success as a model comes from surviving the downfall of managerial rivals and from using its political and cultural presence to advance its version of popular government. What Reagan-Thatcher conservatives and their counterparts on the European continent call "liberal democracy" presupposes the operation of public administration as essential for democratic governance. The praise of the "democratic welfare state" that crops up regularly in the *Wall Street Journal* brings to mind both John Dewey and Woodrow Wilson, though admittedly its Republican converts give a wider berth to corporate capitalism than was the case with New Deal or Progressive social planners.[9] The expression of admiration for Wilson, FDR, and John F. Kennedy among today's American conservatives is not merely dissembling. It testifies to their acceptance of a managerial welfare state as a point of departure for public policy.[10]

A related question about political presuppositions is the one debated in postwar Germany about whether a workable parliamentary democracy can be grounded on "minimal consensus." German political sociologists Ralf Dahrendorff, Richard Lowenthal, and Stephan Eisel have asked whether Germany's constitutional democracy can withstand a critical challenge simply on the basis of procedural rules and the state's monopoly of force. Is there also no need, German intellectuals ask, for other beliefs as a prerequisite for a stable democracy, particularly in view of the Nazi experience? One traditional German liberal, Wolfgang Mommsen, answers "no." Mommsen maintains that it may be counterproductive to allow administrators and educators to interfere in German society because of an unsubstantiated fear that present-day Germany will go the way of the Weimar Republic.[11]

Others have insisted on the need for a more extensive education of the German people in order to safeguard their democracy. Dahrendorff stresses the importance of gender equality in the family, Eisel the "teaching of human rights" as a political doctrine, and they and others have opposed any attempt to limit the right of asylum to refugees (proclaimed in the German Grundgesetz of 1947, the founding document of the West German government). Jürgen Habermas would go even further to "protect" German democracy. In "Recht und Gewalt-ein deutsches Trauma" and in commentaries for the *Frankfurter Allgemeine Zeitung*, Habermas belittles any attempt to define German liberal democracy strictly in terms of "*Minimalkonsens.*" In a nation such as Germany, Habermas explains, whose entire political culture has been authoritarian, it is foolish to try to defend democracy merely by setting up rules.[12] Basic to this task is the radical refounding of the German people as a democratic-constitutional citizenry. One can achieve this end, according to Habermas, only by viewing the entire predemocratic history of Germany as a prelude to Nazism. Habermas favors increased immigration into the federal republic to overcome its association with a discredited German past. Since he believes that German identity should rest entirely on a postwar civic patriotism, there is no reason that it must be specifically German, except linguistic convenience. The only other reason Habermas can find for even minimal German cultural identity is negative: the need for German atonement for the Nazi past, which should take the form of democratic socialization.

Habermas wishes to expiate German sins by obliterating a distinctive German identity, but self-proclaimed American nationalists advocate for their own country what Habermas intends to be a German atonement. They too wish to live in a "universal nation" with open borders and a changing cultural character. *Wall Street Journal* columnist Ben Wattenberg and Congressman Richard Armey hold these patriotic positions, which most Europeans would reject for their own lands as an invitation to national suicide.[13] In the United States, however, these universalist tenets belong to a liberal democratic consensus within the political and journalistic elite.[14]

The recent media campaign against Republican presidential hopeful Patrick J. Buchanan highlights the problem of challenging the evolving pluralist character of the American regime. The terms "political extremist" and "Nazi," which journalists hurled daily at Buchanan, conveyed indignation about the rejection of pluralism by a political celebrity. Buchanan had expressed moral reservations about homosexuals and feminists and had called for a five-year moratorium on legal immigration into the United States. Such views outraged his former colleagues in journalism and the media, and most Americans polled shared the belief that Buchanan was an "extremist," if not an outright Nazi. But the offensive positions, journalists also observed, were characteristic of the 1950s.[15] In the intervening decades a pluralist doctrine, which has become the hallmark of non-Nazi humanity, had established itself in the Western world.

Though public administrators and judges have assumed the duty of enforcing this doctrine, it is intellectuals who have defined it throughout the century. In this labor they have built steadily on the engineering achievements of earlier generations, going back to the Progressive era. It is therefore imperative for a survey of pluralist thinking to look at its interwar forms and then at its further development from mid-century on. The discussions among concerned Germans about democratic reeducation for their people corresponded to other deliberations that took place among equally engaged American intellectuals about socializing "democratic" citizens in their country. These socializing plans became increasingly ambitious after the Second World War, in response to what was perceived as the danger of nondemocratic thinking.

In any investigation of liberal democracy from the Progressive era onward, it is important to distinguish between long-term beliefs and short-term variables. At least some early Progressives, including Woodrow Wilson, espoused racial segregation, American nationalism, and other ideas that later ceased to be politically acceptable. But these teachings were subject to change and did not represent the Progressives' most enduring contributions to modern ideology. These contributions were linking liberal democracy to "scientific" administration and planning a "modern community" that is indeterminately extendible. Three modifications occurred as the Progressive agenda was put into practice. One, globalist thinking overtook the older Progressive concern with national conscious-ness. The Progressive appeal to nationalist sentiment was always, to some extent, strategic. It was part of an effort to raise public administration as a reforming force against local institutions alleged to be corrupt. Two, hereditarian explanations for social behavior, once popular among the Progressives, yielded by the interwar period to environmental determin-ism. Margaret Mead, Franz Boas, and J. B. Watson were three prominent social scientists who contributed to this change of position. All of them cited the methodological faults of hereditarians but also claimed for their research a scientific precision that was dubious.[16] Watson exagger-ated the possibility of totally conditioning the human organism, and Boas's attempt to explain skull formations among groups as creative ad-aptations to environment flew in the face of evolutionary evidence. The environmentalists, however, prevailed in the court of public opinion be-cause of their appearance of holding the moral high ground. They ar-gued that people could be improved by altering their environment. And this alteration could be planned by social experts, who would guide the liberal democracies already under reconstruction.[17]

The third modification was that social planners went from advocating a scientifically retrained society to making a critical distinction between scientific administrators and properly conditioned subjects. In several groundbreaking studies, John C. Burnham traces the rise of social psy-chology in America during the Progressive era.[18] Social reformers turned quickly to a discipline and method whose exponents claimed for them-selves the ability to alter undesirable behavior. They took what had once been considered unvarnished vice and turned it into dysfunctional be-havior, a condition that required "expert" knowledge to be treated. At first this knowledge was applied to dealing with gambling, drinking, and family violence, but by the thirties social psychologists went from family counseling into industries and large corporations. Assembly line produc-tion and corporate integration were taking their toll on the individual worker, and management solicited experts who might be able to deal with the troubled spirits in their work force. The struggle against fascism and the "social deviance" associated with that particular ideology aided the ascent of social psychologists into public administration. In the thir-ties and forties, Eleanor Roosevelt spoke out in favor of that develop-ment, and the U.S. Commissioner of Education recommended the pub-lic use of social psychology, which was held to be vital in creating a "mentally healthy" democracy.

Even before the First World War such popularizers of psychology as H. Addington Bruce were at work in the United States advertising a socially relevant approach to their discipline. Bruce noted that functional mental disorders were on the rise but insisted that this was not attributable to "defective inheritance as the primary cause."[19] This "decline results primarily from environmental conditions caused by man himself" and could therefore be remedied by creating a different environment. Bruce also cited the work being done in Europe on the subconscious and argued that the power of suggestion could be made to work on dysfunctional minds. His writings on psychology over several decades, observes commentator Paul M. Dennis, typified the attempt to make psychology into a "highly visible and utilitarian science." It also reflected the increasing politicization undergone by theorists and practitioners of psychology. Bruce and other popularizing psychologists of his generation were drawn to Progressive politics and presented research that supported their ideological predilections. According to Dennis, Bruce accepted Progressive tenets, which "included faith in science (including the social sciences), emphasis on environmental manipulation as an instrument of change and an egalitarian view that assumed people to be basically good and more similar than different."[20]

The invasion of government and the courts by behavioral scientists has produced what Thomas Szasz calls "the therapeutic state." Psychiatrists and social psychologists have been given social status, according to Szasz, and their moral and political judgments, though not always founded on hard, empirical science, are taken to be "expert." These experts today can affect decisions about the responsibility of criminals, the right to control property, and the custody of children. "Psychiatric theologians" have been able to impose their private political opinions as "scientific" truth, and Szasz cites the fact that the American Psychiatric Association now defines the involuntary treatment and incarceration of mental patients as "health rights." Szasz also observes, "If people believe that health values justify coercion, but that moral and political do not, those who wish to coerce others will tend to enlarge the category of health values at the expense of moral values."[21] "Health values" have also become socialized through a global managerial culture. Since 1976 the United Nations, through its International Covenant on Economic, Cultural, and Social Rights, has elevated "the enjoyment of the highest standard . . . of mental health" to a sacred entitlement. Henceforth governments must ensure a sound state of mind as a "human right."[22]

Christopher Lasch explains the process by which the therapeutic segment of the managerial elite won moral acceptance. Despite the fact that its claims to be providing "mental health" were always self-serving and highly subjective, the therapeutic class offered ethical leadership in the absence of shared principles. By defining emotional well-being as both a social good and the overcoming of what is individually and collectively dangerous, the behavioral scientists have been able to impose their absolutes upon a culturally fluid society. In *The True and Only Heaven* Lasch explores the implications for postwar politics of the *Authoritarian Personality*. A chief contributor to this anthology, Theodor Adorno, abandoned his earlier work as a cultural critic to become a proponent of governmentally imposed social therapy. According to Lasch, Adorno condemns undesirable political attitudes as "prejudice," and "by defining prejudice as a 'social disease' substituted a medical for a political idiom." In the end, Adorno and his colleagues "relegated a broad range of controversial issues to the clinic—to 'scientific' study as opposed to philosophical and political debate."[23]

Despite the claims by Adorno and his colleagues to be defending the working class as "the major bearer of liberal ideas," Lasch also notes that mixed in with this praise were expressions of contempt for actual workers. *The Authoritarian Personality* speaks about the need to "indoctrinate" the working class "so as to modify those attitudes centering around authoritarianism, which are more pronounced in this group than in most others."[24] Adorno worried that the American blue-collar class expressed racial prejudice and attributed this misfortune to status anxiety. The proposed cure, social reeducation by the state, fitted the mind-set that midwived the series to which *The Authoritarian Personality* belonged. Starting in 1949, the American Jewish Committee sponsored a succession of books by behavioral scientists. The series reflected the fears aroused by the Nazi persecution of Jews: almost all of the contributors, such as Paul Lazarfeld, Theodor Adorno, Max Horkheimer, Leo Loewenthal, and Bruno Bettelheim, were refugees from or victims of Nazism with Jewish ancestry. The appearance of their books also coincided with the postwar reaction to the advances of Soviet Communism: the authors feared that the passionately anti-Communist junior senator from Wisconsin, Joseph McCarthy, had become a point man for right-wing authoritarian prejudice.[25]

A leitmotif throughout this series is that liberal democracy is being endangered by authoritarian prejudice. Two examples of this evil are racism and anti-Semitism, which most of the authors link to traditional belief systems and repeatedly to blue-collar Americans. Somber warnings about misguided workers mark both the *The Authoritarian Personality* and an address (turned into a book) by S. M. Lipset, "Working Class Authoritarianism." Delivered originally before the social democratic anti-communist Congress for Cultural Freedom in 1955, Lipset's remarks about prejudiced union members seem remarkable for someone then associated with the democratic Left.[26] Lipset's close friend, the historian Richard Hofstadter, was also a self-described man of the Left who feared the "paranoid style" of nonurban Americans and of workers who had not been properly socialized. In lectures about those he found culturally and politically alien, Lasch explains, Hofstadter was lavish in his use of therapeutic terms.[27]

It may be instructive to contrast these broadsides against "prejudice" to other attitudes expressed at the same time by Walter Lippmann. In *The Public Philosophy* and *The Price of Freedom*, both written in the fifties, Lippmann calls for a responsible governing class able to show independent judgment and resist popular passions. In *The Public Philosophy* he deplores "the functional derangement of the relationship between the mass of people and the government. . . . Where mass opinion dominates the government, there is a morbid derangement of the true function of power. The derangement brings about the enfeeblement, verging on paralysis, of the capacity to govern. This breakdown in the constitutional order is the cause of the precipitate and catastrophic decline of Western society."[28]

Reading such passages brings to mind what may have been two of their inspirations, José Ortega y Gassett's *Revolt of the Masses* and Irving Babbitt's *Democracy and Leadership*. Both of these interwar classics offer the opinion that, absent a natural leadership class, modern mass democracy is doomed. By the fifties Lippmann, who had assumed the role of being a conservative but sympathetic critic of liberal democracy, set out to provide his own diagnosis of democratic "maladies." Without leaders trained in civility and without a "public philosophy" around which peoples can rally, Lippmann maintains, the "eclipse of democracy" is inevitable. The choice for the Western democracies is either to follow natural leaders within a constitutional regime or to move toward "totalitarian democracy."

Lippmann's call for liberal democratic regeneration begs certain questions. How exactly does one create a civilized citizen with liberal virtues who will make a responsible use of freedom? Is it possible to mass-produce such a type in a modern society in order to protect liberal democracy against itself? And where exactly does one find the leaders whom these citizens will recognize as being fit to "administer governments"? In Lippmann's age people must be trained to administer what he perceives to be a "complex" society. Why remind us then of the death of Socrates and the "inwardness of the ruling man" when the real subject is modern public administration?[29]

Lippmann invokes a humanistic ideal of leadership that may have grown obsolete by the time that he wrote *The Public Philosophy*. His Christian and classical ideas about authority and civility were out of place in a managerial state of the kind he himself had advocated as an editor of the *New Republic*. The placing of administrators beyond popular control would not have brought them into touch with their second and higher nature. More likely, it would have allowed them to do exactly as they pleased. Nor is it clear how Lippmann's proposed "accommodation" between religionists and skeptics would have restored a public philosophy. By the fifties it was not philosophers but social scientists and therapists who were setting the tone of government. As a desperate plea to change political course, there is a certain nobility in Lippmann's work. But it may be too little too late. The elite that managed the American government even then could not have been interested in Socrates' acceptance of death or in a stoic model for political leaders.

Nonetheless, Lippmann was right to direct attention toward the likely connection between settled beliefs and constitutional order. The stability and credibility of the latter, he maintains, depend on public restraint and the "mastery of human nature in the raw by an acquired rational second nature. . . . In the literal sense, the principles of the good society must be unpopular until they have prevailed sufficiently to alter the popular impulses. For the popular impulses are opposed to public principles. These principles cannot be made to prevail if they are discredited—if they are dismissed, as superstition, as obscurantism, as meaningless metaphysics, as reactionary, as self-seeking to rationalizations."[30]

Lippmann's talk about the need for moral and social traditions showed him moving away from those Progressive intellectuals he had once admired. He had come to reject their trashing of metaphysical certitudes and looked back to a time when people "did agree that there was a valid law which, whether it was the commandment of love or the reason of things, was transcendent." The systematic attempt to reduce such belief to a "psychological experience and no more" undermined the possibility of moral consensus within political life. What the new democratic theorists had done in debunking this consensus was to leave the mass of people to their own impulses. This made the popular will unstable and prepared to way for a "Jacobin conception of the emancipated and sovereign people."[31]

Lippmann's observation about the political danger of subverting moral habits was no doubt unconvincing to those he criticized. Liberal democrats had long cultivated a skeptical attitude toward received knowledge other than their own. Indeed they quoted with approval Mill's aphorism (from *On Liberty*) that "the despotism of custom is a standing hindrance to human advancement." Lippmann's friend Dewey had gone after metaphysics as mere debris left from prescientific thinking. What the elder Lippmann styled "public philosophy" would have deeply offended this critic of the past. Nor was it compatible with what some liberals had viewed as modern thinking at the end of the last century. It was not a socialist but a Victorian liberal, Edward Beesley, who in his confessional essay "Why I Am a Liberal" (1885) asserted that "the right course in practical politics cannot be ascertained by mere reference to the will of the people at any given moment but must be sought in conformity with the laws of order and progress revealed in the scientific study of man and his environment."[32] While Beesley was no democratic social planner, his skepticism toward the past points toward the Progressive wedding of social planning with social science.

The attitudes mentioned by Lippmann had become characteristic of forward-thinking intellectuals by the first half of the century. Lippmann grasped this fully as he laid out the culturally adversarial role played by these intellectuals in relation to the moral wisdom of the past: "I do not contend, though I hope, that the decline of Western society will be arrested if the teachers in our schools and universities come back to the great tradition of the public philosophy. But I do contend that the decline, which is already far advanced, cannot be corrected if the prevailing philosophers oppose the restoration and renewal and if they impugn rather than support the validity of an order which is superior to the values that J. P. Sartre tells each man 'to invent.' "[33]

PLURALISM AS PUBLIC PHILOSOPHY

In *The Public Philosophy* Lippmann expresses concerns about the implications of value-relativity that parallel those of other postwar political commentators. For example, Anglo-Catholic John H. Hallowell shared Lippmann's anxiety that value-relativists were coming to define the liberal democratic outlook. Like Lippmann, Hallowell believed that the "impugning" of the inherited moral order would undermine the capacity of Americans for self-government.[34] What neither he nor Lippmann saw fully, any more than did the postwar conservative movement that also attacked behavioral scientists, is that the impugning of inherited beliefs was merely a first step in the pluralist process of change. First it is necessary, that is to say, to evacuate what Kallen ridiculed as "Christianism" and "metaphysical rationalization" before one can erect a scientific and mentally healthy future. Insisting that all values are equal and that all values are reducible to individual preferences are the mere opening shots in a cultural confrontation. They are ways of dealing with older worldviews or ingrained attitudes, which liberal democratic pluralists see as obstacles to their own social projects. In a study of social criticism in eighteenth-century France, Reinhart Koselleck points to similar intentions among the bourgeois supporters of the Enlightenment. According to Koselleck, an assault took place in France before the French Revolution on long-respected political and ecclesiastical institutions, and a rising bourgeoisie financed this attack in its own bid for power. The middle class patronized social critics who cried out against political discrimination and who, finally, prophesied upheavals unless "enlightened" warnings were heeded and aristocratic and clerical privileges ended. Like the modern political class and its journalistic allies, eighteenth-century rationalists and their patrons appealed to "universal rights" that expressed their own particular aspirations.[35]

It tells much about our intellectual climate that those who today examine cultural pluralism and value-relativity ignore the real use of these concepts. They take for granted that value-relativity is somehow connected to liberal democracy. Religious traditionalists try to minimize that connection while nonetheless professing liberal democratic beliefs. Overlooked is the function played by the relativity in question. For example, Horace Kallen did not dispense entirely with moral preferences after asserting that values are nothing more than "irrational" private interests. Rather, he proposed the application of "creative intelligence" to determine which preferences were the most worthwhile. Kallen also made a distinction between "conciliatory" and "expressive" ideas: the first, he maintained, included otherworldly rationalizations for early failures, such as Christian theology, while the second were driven by a hope of human betterment.[36] Despite his apparent reduction of values to relational and subjective interests, Kallen devised ways of privileging his own values by identifying them with a universal good.

84

Kallen's treatment of values must be understood as one of several strategies pursued by pluralist thinkers developing modern behavioral agendas. What has made these strategies effective and these agendas compelling is not the airtight reasoning behind them. Some of the most respected pluralists present hand-to-mouth arguments, but these arguments have prevailed in the court of public opinion because they jibe with what the managerial state is doing. To ask a regime engaged in behavior modification to go on with its work for the sake of "tolerance" or "niceness" is to address the converted. And to use the terms "liberal" and "democratic" in the postliberal and postdemocratic senses in which they are now routinely applied is to avoid being controversial or "insensitive." The argumentative ruses adopted to consolidate the political status quo go from forcing an argument to actual intimidation. They begin by appealing to unproved premises, which the reader is nudged into accepting, move on to therapeutic criteria for right reasoning, and finally, as seen in recent hate speech and anti-Holocaust revisionist laws, end by reverting to the *argumentum baculinum,* which may mean arresting those considered criminally insensitive.

At stake here is not the idle pastime of scribes. It is an attempt undertaken by prominent intellectuals to elevate pluralism into behavioral coercion. The least credible defenders of pluralism, among the intellectual class, have been those in a state of denial about underlying assumptions. In *The End of the Republican Era,* former president of the American Political Science Association Theodore Lowi makes two startling admissions about a liberal democratic regime that he claims to admire: one, bureaucratic interventionism is now shaping liberal democratic politics; and two, the interventionism practiced by the "instrumentalist state" has become therapeutic. The individual is made to bear less and less responsibility for his actions, and members of society are "indemnified regardless of fault." In the therapeutic liberal state, "the patron is more concerned than the client for the welfare of the client," and failure and deviance are taken as measures of victimization that require special indemnification.[37]

Lowi studiously ignores the value-aspect of the arrangements he delineates. He persists in treating liberal democracy, which he associates with pluralism, as a mere way of doing things, one to which he has gravitated as a "Jewish liberal cultural relativist." He credits modern liberal democracy with "the tremendous contribution liberalism has made to the theory of democracy by its attempt to cleanse the political process of morality," and he rails against the religious Right for its unseemly "moralization of national politics."[38] Lowi overlooks the values, particularly sensitivity,

85

that democratic pluralists impose in their role as guardians of mental health. He assumes in an equally axiomatic way that his own concern for equality exists in a moral vacuum or as a function of technique. But bureaucratic structures and patron-client relationships have existed in societies other than our own and have not always been wedded to Lowi's "liberalism." In some societies political authorities have been associated with views about social morality that presumably differed from Lowi's. In Louis Dumont's formulation, some cultures are based on a model of *homo hierarchicus* and others on one of *homo aequalis*.[39] Some societies, and some thinkers, moreover, make no pretense about promoting their principles, while others, by contrast, hide them behind technical jargon and "self-evident" truths about tolerance.

A straightforward approach to value-assertion is the one taken by a professor of philosophy at Harvard University, Hilary Putnam. Like Dewey, Putnam has insisted that all values are provisional and subject to scientific investigation, including statements about the social good. As Dewey explained, insight about "rational goods" must come from the "authority of knowledge," which can only be exercised by "those competent in science."[40] The question is whether Dewey's preferred value of social democratic equality represents for him and his disciples a provisional understanding of the social good, or whether this particular value was and is to be held as an article of democratic faith. While Putnam does not take up that question specifically, he does perceive the tension between pluralistic skepticism and his and Dewey's social democratic vision: "The fundamental idea that I stick to is that there are right and wrong moral judgments and better and worse moral outlooks and that is the way we talk and think and also the way we are going to go on talking and thinking."[41] Putnam stresses the inevitability of moral choice in justifying his own value-preferences and offers a candidly subjectivist position in discussing moral and political issues.

Like Horace Kallen, Oxford professor of jurisprudence Ronald Dworkin has to smuggle in *his* privileged rights in what is intended as a defense of cultural diversity. Although rights, like values, are traced to individual interests, for Dworkin, one particular right trumps others, the demand for social equality on behalf of aggrieved minorities. In a study of the Supreme Court case *DeFunis v. Odegaard* (1994), in which a Jewish applicant sued the University of Washington Law School on grounds of reverse discrimination, Dworkin dismisses DeFunis's complaint as morally unconvincing. Though DeFunis had higher grades and test scores than the minority applicants who were admitted, his right to admission rested, for Dworkin, on disputable grounds, namely, "intellectualism" and the promise of impartial protection for the rights of all American citizens under the Fourteenth Amendment. Dworkin allows his egalitarian preferences to color his reading of the Fourteenth Amendment. The equal protection under the law which that amendment guarantees does not "outlaw whatever policies violate equality," nor does that clause support the view that "racial classifications that make society as a whole more equal" are constitutionally acceptable.[42] Dworkin is not above playing with constitutional phrases to make them fit his own predilections.

The reason for his value-preferences, we learn, is that "in certain circumstances a policy which puts many individuals at a disadvantage is nonetheless justified because it makes the community as a whole better off." That result is achieved if compensatory justice is applied to those who personally or through their ancestors had suffered unequal treatment in the past. Members of these groups deserve not only "equal treatment" but "treatment as an equal," which is the right "to be treated with the same respect and concern as anyone else." But that respect, we then find out, entails unequal treatment, as if one had "two children and one is dying of a disease."[43] According to Dworkin, the afflicted child (and by analogy a member of a disadvantaged group) deserves special consideration, and he believes this can be given without denying just treatment to his sibling (and thus to people like DeFunis).

Dworkin's analogy here is obviously strained; beyond this, however, one is struck by his assumptions about himself as a lawgiver. By what claim does he speak as the moral conscience of American society? What gives *his* highest value such paramount importance that other values— meritocracy, equal protection of citizens under the law, and the principle of colorblind justice—seem less worthy than his own. It is one thing in a free society to claim the right to make private judgments. It is quite another to insist that a majority of the community be put at disadvantage in order that one's own value be imposed. Dworkin's position exemplifies what Max Weber characterized as the "tyranny of values." In nontraditional societies without recognized moral authorities, intellectuals compete, according to Weber, to make their private value-preferences generally accepted. Such "assertions of a highest value [*Höchstwertsetzung*]" become typical of a society which declares itself open to discussion but is searching at the same time for moral bearings.[44]

There is a distinction drawn by Dworkin that allows him to place his value beyond contention. As two of his critics, John Gray and Robert George, note, Dworkin intends to make his rights and his value function "prepolitically," through courts that are inaccessible to majority opinion or the legislative will.[45] In a liberal pluralist society, Dworkin insists, "rights" must come before "policy," and while popular assemblies are entitled to legislate up to a point, they must be subject to judges who can define and uphold human rights. Analyzing such thinking about rights as found in Rawls and Dworkin, Gray makes the pregnant observation that the "end-result . . . is not the simple transposition of political life into legal contexts but rather the corrosion of political life itself. The treatment of all important issues of restraint of liberty as questions of constitutional rights has the consequence that they cease to be issues that are politically negotiable."[46] Although Gray is right that Dworkin is allergic to popular government, he mistakenly describes him as a rights-obsessed "liberal."[47] This overlooks the fact noted by George that what Dworkin is defending is not some quintessential Lockean civil society. He favors social engineering taking place without popular restraints, and courts in the United States and in Europe have become a vehicle for carrying out change under the guise of guaranteeing newly discovered human rights. Dworkin's defense of affirmative action, with its invitations to judicial activism, illustrates what he means by liberal rights in a pluralist society.

An even more revealing statement about the pluralist agenda is the one found in the work of Amy Gutmann, director of the Princeton University Center for Human Values. Gutmann is especially harsh in describing the "essentialist" character of traditional liberal arts education. Such learning, she believes, favors the opinions of particular elites—white, male, heterosexual, Christian ones—at the expense of other groups who until now have not received proper cultural consideration. Against this "intellectual idolatry," which would limit humanistic education to "tried-and-true virtues," Gutmann calls for opening academic discussions to the works of black and feminist authors who address contemporary moral and political concerns. She quotes approvingly Emerson's adage "Each age must write its own books" and then attaches her own gloss: "Why? Because well-educated, open-minded people and liberal democratic citizens must think for themselves."[48]

Gutmann's demand for academic multiculturalism, which would place in the curriculum such authors as Toni Morrison and Simone de Beauvoir alongside Plato and Aristotle, is by no means an invitation to "mutually exclusive and disrespecting cultures." Gutmann in fact criticizes deconstructionists for claiming that cultures are intellectually self-contained and cannot learn from each other. Although most of them speak "in the name of exploited and oppressed," they do not pursue a "realistic vision: neither universities nor politics can effectively pursue their valued ends without mutual respect among the various cultures they contain." In the name of multicultural respect, Gutmann explains, "Some differences—racism and anti-Semitism are obvious examples— ought not to be respected." She lists among the unacceptable types of discourse "ethnic, sexist, homophobic and other forms of offensive speech directed against members of a disadvantaged group."[49] Gutmann is willing to tolerate some forms of speech she does not agree with: "A multicultural society is bound to include a wide range of such respectable moral disagreements [e.g., differences about abortion rights], which offers us the opportunity to defend our views before morally serious people." But these do not include those guilty of "misogyny, racial and ethnic hatred, or rationalization of self-interest and group interest parading as historical or scientific knowledge."[50]

The last qualification on "morally respectable speech" adds a special twist to Gutmann's warnings about "hate speech challenging members of liberal democratic communities." Such incidents are made to include "rationalization[s] of self-interest and group interest parading" as scholarship. It is also explained that offensive speech may be directed against "members of any disadvantaged group." Less evident is whether members of those groups can also be guilty of "hate speech" if they disparage members of any other group. It does not seem coincidental that two groups into which Gutmann herself fits, Jews and women, are held to be "disadvantaged." Why these groups in the United States should merit handicap consideration in discourse is never sufficiently explained. Although anti-Semitism produced ugly repercussions in Europe, it has never been as widespread in the United States and is certainly not harming contemporary American Jews, such as myself or Professor Gutmann. Another problem inherent in Gutmann's prescriptions concerns the appointment of an umpire to oversee liberal democracy: who gets to decide in her society which opinions are "morally respectable" or merely "rationalizations" of interest "parading" as something more serious? One may assume that it will be elite university professors and others in their circle who will make this decision. Canadian philosopher Charles Taylor complains that advocates of multicultural politics and education often labor under two mistaken assumptions: they judge positively other cultures about which they are ignorant, and they prematurely load on to them the "homogenizing assumptions" about all "worthy" cultures that they construct for themselves as Western liberal democrats.[51] This "underestimating of differences" does not seem to be the worst flaw noticeable among liberal democratic pluralists. In their hands multiculturalism has become an instrument of control, one designed to privilege their own concerns and to stigmatize those who think differently.

Instructive in this regard is a defense of affirmative action programs published in *Tikkun*, a leading American liberal magazine, by an associate editor and professor of ethics, Peter Gabel. Gabel complains that privileged access for minorities to jobs, government contracts, and student places is being justified in terms of meritocracy. He mocks the conventional liberal belief that preferential treatment is only a temporary expedient intended to help minorities fit into a competitive way of life and asks, "Why should we support a merit-based theory of affirmative action that legitimizes arrangements that are evil in themselves and that breed injustice and racial hatred?" Gabel contrasts to a meritocracy appealing to "test results based on shallow detached verbal manipulations" his own ideal of a "spiritually transformed civil society."[52]

Given his rejection of unjust meritocracy, on what moral grounds, one wonders, is Gabel building his alternate vision. At one point he declaims against "phony meritocracy," but thereupon he shifts his attack from the practice to the concept of a merit-based society. Like Michael Lerner, his associate at *Tikkun* and Hillary Clinton's self-proclaimed mentor, Gabel believes that any attempt to measure professional or scholastic worth by objective testing "breeds injustice and racial hatred." It is therefore best to have the government set aside things for minorities in order to "heal societal division."[53] Gabel and Lerner both delight in the language of healing and happily fall back upon it whenever they discuss social policy. They assume certain apparently self-evident linkages. Both spirituality and justice signify the inclusion of other groups in a diverse society. This prescribed inclusiveness ought to express itself in therapeutic gestures ("healing" and "caring" being two of the favorite terms of *Tikkun*), and public administrators should be charged with the task of spiritually transforming the rest of us. In all such exhortations to reach out and care, there are hidden assumptions about the operation of democracy. Citizenship is a passive activity, which one allows to be done to oneself for the sake of feeling good or making others feel good about themselves.

The Platonic image found in the *Republic* of healing (*iatrikē*) as the essence of governing runs through this type of discourse, which calls for social control and inclusiveness. One also finds embedded here another image from Plato, about the erotic nature of living in a just community. In the *Tikkun* social vision, however, political eros does not point back to a Platonic realm of eternal ideas. Its foundation is not a shared concept of truth located in a presumably unchanging reality but enforced fellowship that comes through sensitizing administrators. In this therapeutic view, public administration will decide which group receives which benefit or is forced to suffer which liability, for the sake of general self-esteem and maximal healing. Appeals to justice and virtue are the justification for liberal democratic psychology being practiced on citizens turned into patients.

Essential to this tendency are the political and cultural attitudes that American social scientists had begun to push by mid-century. The linking of liberal democratic pluralism to the war against prejudice and discrimination was the critical moment in creating Gutmann's multicultural concepts and Lerner's politics. From this linkage came the possibility of defining pluralism therapeutically. Not all cultures need to be treated with the same respect; some are presumptive sources of bigotry while others are designated victims of prejudice. Moreover, the victimized cultures do not have to be real ones in any anthropological sense. They are only collections of opinions thought appropriate for victims and useful to multicultural pluralists. As their critics point out, multicultural pluralists never choose to represent a diversity that does not express their own values. *Their* blacks and *their* Jews are neither homophobes nor sexists but living proof of the values that multiculturists intend to instill.[54]

For almost half a century the defense of liberal democratic pluralism has been tied to therapeutic politics. Having reduced inherited moral truths to individual value-choices, the pluralists are now in a position to proclaim *their* value-preferences as an alternative to the war of all against all. At first they defended these preferences in terms of experimental science or as inescapable paths toward modernization, but they eventually followed the course revealed by Lasch and Szasz: condemning stubborn dissenters as pathological. This dehumanization of dissent was already present in Adorno's conception of personality disorder. For Adorno and his collaborators on *The Authoritarian Personality*, values and attitudes were functions of personality, by which they understood "a readiness for behavior rather than behavior itself." Adorno maintained that "personality structure may be such as to render the individual susceptible to antidemocratic propaganda" and that "a certain psychological structure of the individual" predisposed him to both fascism and anti-Semitism.[55] His research and that of his collaborators were not intended as mere exercises in statistical correlation. In the foreword to the *Studies in Prejudice* series that Adorno and his group's research inaugurates, the general editors, Max Horkheimer and S. H. Flowerman, announce that "our aim is not merely to describe prejudice but to explain it in order to help in its eradication. Eradication means reeducation scientifically planned on the basis of understanding scientifically arrived at."[56]

The obligatory focus in *The Authoritarian Personality* and throughout the series, anti-Semitism, skews the research in several ways. First, it exaggerates the depth and incidence of anti-Semitic prejudice in American life. It takes what even in 1950 was a residual bias, and probably not as widespread as anti-Catholic prejudice, and treats it as the leading danger to American political institutions. In chapter 3 of *The Authoritarian Personality*, for example, Daniel J. Levinson expresses the view: "As a social movement anti-Semitism presents a major threat to democracy: it is one of the most powerful psychological vehicles for antidemocratic political movements and it provides . . . perhaps the most effective spearhead for an attack on our entire social structure."[57] The references made to "our social structure" suggest that the topic at hand is not Nazi anti-Semitism but the anti-Jewish prejudice in postwar America.

In looking for evidence of an allegedly pervasive prejudice, the researchers make too much of the critical statements about Jews attributed to their respondents. They also link anti-Semitism arbitrarily to any critical attitudes expressed about the American welfare state. An analysis of one interviewee, "Mack," exemplifies both of these methodological flaws. Unlike a second interviewee, "Larry," a Republican who accepts the New Deal and believes in gender equality and tolerance toward homosexuals, Mack is presented as a "pseudodemocrat." Mack believes that Jews are clannish and "won't intermingle," and though a self-identified Democrat, he thinks government planning in the United States may have gone too far.[58] Adorno describes Mack as a "pseudoconservative, . . . who would abolish the very institutions with which he appears to identify himself. It has frequently been remarked that should fascism become a powerful force in America, it would parade under the banner of traditional American democracy. Thus the slogan 'rugged individualism'—which apparently expresses the liberal concept of free competition—actually refers to the uncontrolled and arbitrary politics of the strongest powers in business."[59]

Adorno rates Mack as "high on ethnocentrism," though it is hard to infer this from the data presented. Mack speaks well about Irish, Poles, and most Protestants, and his only reservation about Jews is that they prefer their own kind to others. Considering the fears openly registered by American Jewish leadership about Jewish assimilation and Jewish intermarriage and considering that Mack may have actually experienced Jewish clannishness, his attitudes do not seem unreasonable. Mack mentions that he would be willing to date and even marry a Jewish woman, providing she did not treat him as an outsider. More important than the assumption of unproved prejudice are the interpreters' insistence that Mack's anti-Semitism typifies his attitude toward "outgroups like the Jews, Roosevelt and the Washington bureaucrats."[60] Curiously, Adorno himself in *The Dialectic of the Enlightenment,* written during the War, had offered a far more devastating criticism of the modern bureaucratic state than any later associated with "pseudodemocrats." Adorno attacked administrative collectivism as spurious democracy and identified it with a totalitarian development leading from the Enlightenment to Nazism. Adorno changed his own judgment sufficiently to scold Mack for having second thoughts about the growth of American bureaucratic government. This volte-face is all the more remarkable in view of the persistence of the critique of impersonal bureaucratic structures among the German emigrés in whose circle Adorno moved. Hannah Arendt and Max Horkheimer continued to produce such criticism into the postwar years, though like Adorno they sometimes conveniently associated the prevalence of bureaucratic control with a capitalist dynamic.[61] In *The Authoritarian Personality* Adorno also depicts Mack as perverted because of his quest for power instead of love. Mack expresses his belief in the need for male dominance in the home, which is seen to indicate a cluster of troubling, interrelated personality traits: "conventionalism, repression, and a cult of strength and masculinity."[62]

Mack is also made to exemplify "pseudoconservatism," which for Adorno goes together with anti-Semitism and the authoritarian personality. The pseudoconservative "feels compelled to profess democratic ideals" because of an "increasingly bad conscience," brought on by the awareness of "the rapid development of important conservative layers of American society into the direction of labor baiting and race hatred." Unlike a traditional conservative, the pseudoconservative does not state openly his prejudices, and "this may help to explain why it is so hard to find any striking examples for genuine conservatism on high scores [for ethnocentrism]." According to Adorno, pseudoconservatism manifests itself in the "usurpation complex," a rebellious attitude against elites who supposedly usurped the pseudoconservatives' power. Adorno believes that populist protests against the governing class, masked as war against privilege, express this pseudoconservative rebelliousness: "Government by representation is accused of preventing democracy. Roosevelt and the

New Deal particularly are said to have usurped power and to have entrenched themselves dictatorially." Predictably, Adorno compares the populist pseudoconservatives in America to those who prepared the way for Hitler: "To them progressives in the government are the real usurpers . . . because they assume a power position or several for the 'right people.' Legitimate rulers are those who are actually in command of the machinery of production—not those who owe their ephemeral power to formal political processes." Pseudoconservatives blame progressive national administrations for what "those who control American industry" have really done. They attribute social problems to halfhearted socialists instead of recognizing "the dangerous contradictions between economic inequality and formal political equality."[63]

The plea by Adorno and other contributors to the *Studies in Prejudice* series on behalf of social planning and economic reorganization is both continuing and unmistakable. In examinations of "prejudice," certain traits unacceptable to the authors are forced together and made to appear symptomatic of an authoritarian personality. Those who submit to economically dominant groups wish to oppress outsiders (particularly Jews and blacks), express a fatalistic outlook, and seek to overpower women. Such people, we are told, abounded in the "prehistory of German fascism," and therefore the preservation and expansion of a democratic way of life requires a national commitment to "re-education" for the sake of egalitarian ideals.[64] What makes this task particularly urgent is that pseudoconservatives pretend to believe what they reject. Only deft psychologists would be able to smoke them out by picking up on their political discontent. But special care must be taken to unmask authoritarian, anti-Semitic personalities lurking behind apparently mild criticism of the state. Mack is a "traditional Democrat" and (like Adorno after the War) an opponent of anti-Communism, but his grumblings about the New Deal supposedly betray him as a bigot, particularly given his beliefs about male dominance and Jewish ethnocentricity. These attitudes justify speculation about Mack's psychic abnormality and his possible genetic propensity for crime.[65]

One should not view Adorno's analysis as the work of an isolated refugee socialist, without bearing on American political culture. His collaborators on the *The Authoritarian Personality* and all the contributors to *Studies in Prejudice* held respected academic positions, and even a generally reasonable participant in the project, S. M. Lipset, did not dispute Adorno's conclusions. The American Jewish Committee, which promoted the series and financed the *Studies*, had become by the early fifties the Cold War liberal sponsor of *Commentary* magazine. The Committee and *Commentary* were concerned about defending liberal democratic values against, on the one side, anti-Semites and "traditional" anti–New Deal conservatives and, on the other, the assembled forces of world Communism.[66] And for those thereafter engaged in debates about liberal democracy, it became convenient to treat one's opponents as prejudiced and sick. Political debate, as Lasch notes, would be limited to increasingly narrow parameters of dissent, and whoever crossed those lines would be singled out as enemies of democracy and bearers of social disease. Defenders of welfare state democracy, who, like Arthur Schlesinger, Jr., saw themselves as upholding the "vital center," would thus acquire a new arrow for their quiver. Being a pro-welfare-state liberal internationalist betokened not only virtue but also mental well-being.[67]

In *After Virtue*, ethical philosopher Alasdair MacIntyre notes the value-invention characteristic of modern culture and treats it as symptomatic of the breakdown of traditional social authorities. Even more striking than this value-inventiveness is the accompanying tendency to impose values in the context of battling prejudice. Liberal democratic pluralism has come to denote a process of sensitization. And the behavior modification required by this conditioning is something that demands the intervention of social experts. This behavior modification, moreover, must go on indefinitely. The sensitivity needed to practice "democracy" or to enter the political conversation continues to rise. Unlike his counterpart of 1960, today's public personality must master gender-inclusive language, remain abreast of the changing designations for designated minorities, and say nothing to offend gays. The apparent reasons for these restraints are the growing compassion and openness being practiced by society. But the real reason may be widespread fear. People are afraid to engage in pathologically described dissent or to oppose the favored values of journalists and government administrators.

A PLURALIST GLOBAL SOCIETY

A critical moment in the association of pluralism with a global society was reached in the United States in the 1960s. At that time American politicians and journalists emphatically came to identify their country as a universal nation. They presented the civil rights revolution as a crucible for reforming American identity. A connection emerged between establishing equal political rights for American blacks and breaking down na-

95

tional barriers. The first was thought to mandate the second, as social commentator Chilton Williamson Jr. explains. The Immigration and Nationality Act passed in 1965 was more than an "homage to the late president [John Kennedy]. It was substantially the legacy of the desegregation campaign of the 1950s, an extension of the civil rights movement of the 1960s and of anticolonial sentiment following World War II." Moreover, Willamson adds: "By 1964 Rosa Parks, the Freedom Riders, and Martin Luther King, Jr. were recognized gods in the pantheon created by a mythology more potent and influential even than immigration; it was the genius of the architects of immigration reform that they recognized the possibility for conflating the two and amalgamating them as statute law."[68]

The drive toward extending equal citizenship at home and the opening of America's borders to larger and larger numbers of Third World immigrants became related tendencies in the sixties. As Williamson notes, religious and political publications, like *Christian Century* and the *New Republic,* and such national leaders as Robert and Edward Kennedy exalted these twin missions of outreach.[69] Immigration expansion and pursuing the politics of inclusiveness at home were both testimonies to an American commitment to pluralism that developed during the Great Society era. Note that one enduring legacy of that period was a new consensus about America as a fluid society and culture held together by a shared repugnance for discrimination. The point is not only that some choose to make a connection between civil rights and immigration rights, one that the *New York Times* now makes with regularity. It is, rather, that pluralism as a privileged Amerian creed was brought into play to justify both sets of presumed rights. It has been invoked since then to justify the movement toward a universal society together with the stifling of dissent about the implications of that movement.

In *Alien Nation,* Peter Brimelow, editor of *Forbes,* complains about the way he and other critics of liberal immigration policy have had their views subjected to "psychoanalytic babble."[70] Accusations of prejudice, with ominous references to the Holocaust and Jim Crow laws, have drowned out critical observations about the economics of increased Third World immigration, particularly from Mexico. Brimelow approaches increased immigration in terms of both its economic and cultural costs, and he makes a compelling case that since the revision of American immigration laws in 1965 and congressional legislation to reunite families, the influx of largely Third World immigrants, with few marketable skills and little incentive to assimilate, has continued to grow.

The indifference of American administration has made this influx even larger and has allowed the total immigration into the United States to rise to over one million annually. It would be exaggeration to say that Brimelow, Lawrence Auster, Dan Stein, Wayne Lutton, and other immigration restrictionists offer unfailingly accurate judgments. But they do present documented arguments that enjoy popular support. By contrast, neither is true of the journalists and academicians who dismiss rival views as "projections of personal fears, phobias, and fantasies."[71] Brimelow cites damaging evidence to prove his point. One feature piece in the *New York Times* (13 December 1992), by Deborah Sontag, describes the oppositions in California to *illegal* immigration as "rudeness goes public." Sontag states: "Across the country and particularly in California, Americans have felt freer to voice a rude hospitality that at other times they might have considered racist or xenophobic. Those who call for a freeze on immigration, however saw the mood as a harbinger of a new conservatism ahead."[72] A leading advocate of increased American immigration, Julian Simon, observes in the *Economic Consequences of Immigration* his own "delight in looking at the variety of faces I see on the subway when I visit New York." So great is Simon's delight in the diversity of New York that, in recalling the sight, "I get tears in my eyes."[73] On an equally personal note the director of Brandeis University's Institute for Jewish Advocacy and an early sponsor of the *Studies in Prejudice*, Earl Raab, notes with pleasure that "half of the American population will soon be non-white and non-European." Raab expresses relief that "we have topped the point where a Nazi-Aryan party will be able to prevail in this country." The climate of opposition to ethnic bigotry "has not yet been perfected but the heterogeneous nature of our population tends to make it irreversible."[74] Despite Raab's views about the source of America's improved mental health, it might be asked whether his fears about American Nazis justify the continued imposition of an unpopular social policy. Is the likely alternative in any case the apocalyptic specter conjured up by Raab? A more plausible alternative would be a return to the moderate levels of immigration characteristic of the 1950s.

Finally, does the passion for heterogeneity voiced by Simon and the national press justify the pariah status assigned to those who feel otherwise? Here again the treatment of dissenters, which in this case may describe the majority of American citizens, shows the cost of liberal democratic pluralist argumentation. Not only have the immigration restrictionists supposedly forgotten the presumed lessons of Nazism, but they have also turned their backs on the "American liberal tradition." In the *Detroit Free Press*, a visiting scholar at the Cato Institute, Sikha Dahmia, accuses immigration restrictionists, most notably Peter Brimelow, of a "cognitive failure that blurs the distinction between America and England and the Soviet Union." According to Dahmia, a "commitment to individual rights" kept the Founders from giving to Congress "the constitutional authority to keep out immigrants who might dilute that [broad social] consensus [about democracy]." It also requires that "America's borders remain open to those who threaten neither person nor property."[75]

Contrary to these statements, the U.S. Congress is not forbidden to restrict immigration and passed a law to that effect in 1924. Moreover, most of the American Founders were in favor of limiting citizenship to those who would not be culturally hostile to republican institutions.[76] In *The Federalist Papers*, number 2, John Jay goes beyond that in stating other requirements for a flourishing American republican government. An American federal union is possible, Jay explains, because "providence has been pleased to give this one connected country to one united people—a people descended from the same ancestors, speaking the same language, attached to the same principles of government, very similar in manners and customs." Nowhere in *The Federalist Papers*, a liberal document that defends dual federalism and distributed powers, is there evidence of Dahmia's inalienable right to cross borders while "pursuing private good."[77] Historically speaking, this is not a liberal right, but one confected by twentieth-century publicists and then asserted as a test of human decency and mental health. Once put into effect, it undermines popular consent by taking away from citizens any control over the composition of their political society. Note that this debate is not predominantly about the costs of immigration but about whether one can take the other side without being run down as an antipluralist. Once condemned as such, one loses one's standing as a liberal and a democrat and one's right to participate in public discussion at major universities and within the media.

A Canadian scholar, Stephen Brooks, calls attention to "plastic words that have moral connotations and the effect of precluding open debate."[78] Surveying government-sponsored panels and legislation in Canada dealing with gender-oppression and xenophobia, Brooks perceives the same fuzzy vocabulary surfacing again and again. Such words as "aberration," "empowerment," "human right," "prejudice," "equality," and "family violence" are the terms of choice for both behavioral experts and public administrators, and they serve to "construct the political imagination by conflating morality and scientific authority."[79] Brooks cites the German political scientist Uwe Pörksen on the degeneration of language into psycho-administrative jargon. Like Pörksen, he analyzes the overlapping vocabularies among social scientific textbooks, human rights documents, and UNESCO pronouncements. In all of these publications Brooks sees the same habits in operation: the reduction of political and cultural questions to "things that can be administered, planned and developed," and the presentation of private opinions as "expert" judgment. The most arresting illustration of these tendencies is the shifting meaning of violence in a report issued by the Canadian Panel on Violence against Women in 1993. Though this advisory board was intended to guide public administrators in dealing with violence, it was interested more in reconstructing the family than in halting physical abuse. Thus it employs the word "violence," Brooks observes, "to describe acts as different as murder and maintaining exclusive [male] control over household finances."[80]

None of these practices strays very far from the pluralist idea that has unfolded in this century. From its inception, pluralism was intended to close off discussion with individuals and groups who were held to be insufficiently progressive. Early pluralists hoped to overcome the past by exposing what was nonscientific about it or by relegating it to private life. Maurice Cowling makes this point in regard to Mill's devotion to critical thinking. It was "a means of persuading men to arrange society in a way different from the way in which societies had been arranged hitherto. It is as aggressive in relation to other ways of organizing society as any other doctrine and as erosive of existing institutions. It assumes that conscientious decisions will usually be decisions contrary to existing practice, and that conscientious decisions can only be made by self-conscious reference to 'rational principle.' "[81]

The appeal by twentieth-century pluralists to scientific method was also ideologically—and even messianically—driven. It ignored scientific data that interfered with environmentalist assumptions and misrepresented socialist faith as "scientific planning." By mid-century pluralism had moved from an experimental science of society to incorporate programs of behavior modification. These were imagined as necessary to build a more tolerant world, in which people would be antiseptically free of "fascist" prejudice. The fear of prejudice reinforced the environmentalist dogmas, common to pluralists, that racial and ethnic differences are insignificant and may disappear entirely with the application of expert social policies. The students of Franz Boas were particularly fierce in assailing those who held differing views, and during the Second World War, according to historian Pat Shipman, they accused their critics of harboring Nazi sympathies.[82]

In 1944, when UNESCO appointed a committee to draft a statement on the prospects for world harmony, it turned predictably to Boasians to give this undertaking a high-sounding tone. In the UNESCO statement are words that must have astounded evolutionary scientists and raised questions about the objectivity of its environmentalist authors: "Biological studies lend support to the ethic of universal brotherhood, for man is born with drives toward universal cooperation."[83] In writings later produced on American racial problems by the authors of this passage, Ashley Montagu and Otto Klineberg, one encounters another equally dubious view, that races are almost entirely social constructs. One supposed proof of this cited by Klineberg and Gunnar Myrdal (a Swedish social scientist also influenced by Boasian environmentalism) was the lack of evidence for innate cognitive differences between Negroes and whites.[84] This assumption was no more demonstrable in the fifties than it is now, although it has endured as a pluralist and environmentalist article of faith. Like other Boasians, Montagu and Klineberg alternated between the espousal of social policies derived from questionable empirical premises and appeals to value-relativity. Rendering their relativist pose particularly suspect was their readiness to make explicit and implicit moral judgments about cultures.[85]

Stephen Goldberg observes another obscurantist feature in social scientists trying to combine pluralism with environmentalism. They are so preoccupied with the role of prejudice in creating hostile environments that they perpetually deny the obvious, that stereotypes are rough generalizations about groups derived from long-term observation. Such generalizations are usually correct in describing group tendencies and in predicting certain collective actions, even if they do not adequately account for differences among individuals. Nonetheless, as Goldberg explains, the self-described pluralist and prominent psychologist Gordon Allport went out of his way in *The Nature of Prejudice* (1954) to reject stereotypes as factually inaccurate as well as socially harmful. For Allport and a great many other social scientists, nothing is intuitively correct unless it is politically so.[86]

The contradiction between pluralism's supposed devotion to scientific method and its practice of ideological control is no more glaring than another, even older contradiction within the pluralist idea. It is one that goes back to the early decades of the century and to pluralism's formative stage. Early exponents of pluralism, such as Harold Laski in England and Dewey, Kallen, and Sidney Hook in the United States, could never fully reconcile their hope for a society based on voluntary association and the free exchange of ideas with a collectivized economy and centralized educational planning. Laski, who by the mid-twenties called for nationalized industries in England and eventually came to praise Soviet "economic democracy," began his political and legal writings as a critic of state sovereignty.[87] Two sympathetic commentators, Isaac Kramnick and Barry Sheerman, note Laski's suspicion of government even when he proposes construction of a socialist state in his most widely known work, *A Grammar of Politics* (1925). Here one finds a "layering of pluralist suspicion" and the curious "interplay of statism and pluralism."[88] Laski's response to his own suspicion was that state power was good, as long as it aimed at removing, rather than increasing, social inequality.

R. B. Westbrook finds the same ambivalent attitude toward government in the writings of the early Dewey, though by the 1920s Dewey's respect for the state as an instrument of social change had grown enormously. Dewey still referred to the state as a secondary institution in relation to the "associated living" that went on outside of it, yet he also came to see government as basic to the realization of democratic pluralism: "Even though Dewey's state remained a 'conductor' of sorts, most pluralists would have regarded the regulatory power he assigned to it as fearful, given the tendency to abuse power. Dewey was unwilling to set any inherent limitations on the activities of the state, for such limitations could, under certain circumstances, be harmful to the public interest."[89] There was a tension between Dewey's notion of a pluralist society "giving play to the diversity of human powers" and a government which, in the name of the public interest, could intervene whenever it felt necessary. But Dewey tried to resolve that tension, particularly in lectures delivered in China in 1921, by pointing to the "good state." In such a state "officers genuinely serve the public interest," and their effect on social groups is "very important and, potentially, very beneficial."[90]

Clearly the kind of regime to which Dewey (and Laski in *A Grammar of Politics*) refers is the new administrative state, and what distinguishes it from earlier authoritarian or socially unjust governments is its management by experts committed to equality. During the First World War, both Laski and Dewey stressed the nature of that struggle as one between authoritarianism and an evolving democratic "world order." Dewey was quite explicit in linking the second to Wilson's "crusade for democracy," which he believed required the building of an American national welfare

101

state and a world democratic mission. Scientific democratic administration became the key to Dewey's hope for a new "state mechanism" that would contribute to and even decide on the "modes of behavior" for a pluralistic democratic society.[91]

What made such a plan seem workable was that for the early pluralists and their multicultural descendants society would have fewer and fewer traditional groups. The kind of pluralist society that Dewey and Kallen envisaged would go beyond rooted ethnic communities. It would become the evolving creation of "free" individual participants, setting goals under scientific direction and having their material interests monitored by a "conductor state." The world as conceived by pluralists was there to be managed and to be made culturally safe for its framers: Eastern and Central European Jews fearful of traditional Gentile mores and the uprooted descendants of New England Calvinists looking for the New Jerusalem under scientific management.

But what made this vision more than the wish-projection of individuals in search of new collective identities was its timeliness. Its contradictions mattered less than its historical mission: to bestow content upon liberal democracy as the ideology of the modern managerial state. Although pluralism has continued to play this role, contradictions have come along to shake its foundations. The pathologization of dissent has been the final tactic for staving off its assailants, as pluralist ideology has been reduced to a hollow shell, like its often indistinguishable cousin, liberalism. These internal problems, nonetheless, have not spelled doom for pluralism as a public religion attached to those in power. Like the court Zoroastrianism of the late Persian Empire, pluralism endures as both a syncretistic cult and the symbol of centralized administration.

THE PLURALIST WAR AGAINST DISSENT

In defense of American pluralism, Jürgen Habermas recounts his experience as a young German growing up under American occupation and influence: "The political culture of the Federal Republic would be worse today if it had not absorbed the inspirations of American political culture in the first postwar decades. The Federal Republic exposed itself without reservation to the West for the first time. We thus took over the Enlightenment, grasped the mind-altering power of pluralism and became acquainted with the radical democratic spirit of pragmatism from Peirce and Mead to Dewey."[92] Despite the extent of this forced transformation,

Habermas fears that German constitutionalists are now retreating from a radical democratic pluralism into the indigenous German concept of the *Rechtsstaat*, a mere government under law that does not aim at resocialization. Under the residual impact of the "Lutheran tradition of a state church and its pessimistic anthropology" and of "a young conservatism whose heritage is one of compromise with modernity," Germany's social liberals "are not strong enough to rid themselves of the questionable mortgage of German liberalism."[93] Habermas's criticism is directed at the heritage of nineteenth-century bourgeois liberalism, which he believes is impeding the march toward social democracy.

The question that is never addressed in all such defenses of imposed pluralism is whether it is congruous with self-government. To whatever extent democracy is about that particular activity, it must be asked whether pluralism is democratic. Is self-government compatible with therapeutic crusades against "prejudice," carried out by public administrators? All classical democracy was decidedly antipluralist. As Aristotle notes in the *Constitution of Athens*, the great popular advocate Pericles gained public recognition by striking from the voting lists those who could not trace back their Athenian descent three generations. Cleansing the Athenian franchise of those not descended from authorized citizens (*astoi*) was then considered to be a democratic act.[94] As classicist Paul Veyne explains, moreover, openness to new residents has characterized empires, but not popular government until the present century, and that change, according to Veyne, may have been due to the fusion of democratic legitimacy with an imperial structure.[95] Modern liberal democracy behaves like an empire in its absorption of peoples, while appealing formally to a popular mandate. But that does not mean that, absent a globalist vision or fluid cultural identity, democracy ceases to exist. There is no reason to equate democracy, as popular self-government, with either of these conditions.

In almost all the major issues that now pit self-identified peoples against public administration and judicial experts, this definitional problem is basic. What exactly determines the character of democratic societies, aside from the government's activity in redistributing income and national benefits? Is that regime's "disposition," to borrow Aristotle's term, one of perpetual openness engineered from above; or is its character shaped by mutually recognized citizens living in a distinctive cultural space? The pluralist attempt to define modern democracy underlines the shifting ideological emphasis from a nineteenth- to a twentieth-century form of government. While the characteristic political debates in

Western Europe a hundred years ago dealt with the boundaries between civil society and the state, by now those boundaries have become irrelevant. The state has worked to refashion civil society by selectively defending individual claims and by embracing the interests of favored victims and other groups. It has thereby contributed to the present concern about democratic citizenship in a situation of forced politicization.

Today pluralism operates as a court religion, while having less and less intellectual credibility. Betraying the plastic terminology in which its directives are framed are the additions to the "Human Rights Code" passed in the Canadian province of Ontario in 1994. The Code cites "human dignity" to justify the criminalization of "conduct or communication [that] promotes the superiority or inferiority of a person or class because of race, class, or sexual orientation."[96] The law has already been applied to prosecute scholars making hereditarian arguments about social behavior, and its proponents defend this muzzling as necessary for "human dignity." But never are we told whence that dignity is derived. It is certainly not the one to which the Bible, a text that unequivocally condemns certain "sexual orientations," refers. Nor are we speaking here about the dignity of nonengineered academic discourse, an act that the supporters of the Ontario Human Rights Code consider to be criminal if judged insensitive. Yet the pluralist advocates of human rights codes that now operate in Canada, Australia, England, and on the European continent assume there is a human dignity. Indeed this dignity is so widely and passionately accepted, or so it is asserted, that we must criminalize unkind communication. In the name of that supposedly axiomatic dignity, we are called upon to suppress scholarship and even to imprison its authors.[97]

It is incorrect to believe that such measures are being taken to further instrumentalist ends (i.e., to reduce friction or promote civil peace). If that were all the managerial state and its pluralist priesthood were seeking, they might go about that end differently. They might try to control immigration and allow communities to enforce those behavioral and cultural standards accepted by most of their citizens. Those who wished to live differently would have to go elsewhere. But these are not the solutions favored by pluralist proponents of social harmony, who are not interested primarily in civil peace. They aim at "openness," "inclusiveness," and other ideals that require the monitoring of groups by public administrators and behavioral scientists.

The identification of immigration restrictionists with undemocratic bigotry has taken a punitive turn in France. There opponents of liberal immigration policy have been threatened with imprisonment under a federal law, passed in 1972, forbidding "provocation to discrimination, to violence, or to hatred against a person or group of persons by reason of their origin." The same law, furthermore, prohibits "public defamation of a person or group of persons by reason of their origin or belonging or nonbelonging to an ethnic body, nation, race or determined religion."[98] When a columnist for the *Quotidien de Paris*, Christian Charrière, called for stringent controls of immigration into France, "anti-racist" activists, led by LICRA (*Ligue Internationale Contre le Racisme et l'Antisémitisme*), brought criminal charges against him under the 1972 legislation. A Paris court found Charrière guilty of "provoking hate" by characterizing Third World immigration as a "proliferating invasion" and thereupon imposed a heavy fine.[99] Other "insensitive" writers in France and elsewhere in Europe have been threatened with jail for "inciting discrimination," that is, for expressing attitudes that are contrary to "antiracism."

As a French deputy, Aymar Achille-Fould, who sponsored the 1972 law, observed in a parliamentary discussion: "Racism is born with man. It is in his nature at all times, and it is necessary for civilization and culture to exert considerable effort to avoid that which gives human beings the rules of discrimination."[100] But does democracy or liberalism, properly understood, require that such a therapeutic effort be made? Why should citizens not have a liberal or democratic right to limit the number or composition of the persons or groups or persons entering their country? And why is an uncooperative attitude toward the plan of antiracists ipso facto proof of an unredeemed human nature? Again we are faced by the demand for escalating proof from the pluralists in order to demonstrate that those who oppose any aspect of their multicultural projects are not dangerous bigots. The French law of 1972 not only prohibits provocation for discrimination against persons on the basis of origin but criminalizes discriminatory behavior on the part of public officials directed against persons because of "ways of life [*moeurs*]." No sooner was this passed than litigation began on behalf of pedophiles and transvestites, as well as homosexuals who objected to discriminatory attitudes that they claimed to have encountered from the public sphere.[101] One wonders how far the French state will have to reform itself to fit its own pluralist criteria or what new signs of tolerance passive citizens will still be called upon to give in order to avoid the stigma of discrimination.

Since the early 1970s, moreover, laws have been enacted in France, Austria, and Germany, and by the European Parliament to treat as a criminal offense revisionist views of the Holocaust and critical remarks about the judgments for crimes against humanity rendered by the Nuremberg Tribunal in 1946.[102] One relevant French piece of legislation, passed in July 1990, received the overwhelming backing of the French Communist Party, and of Jewish and immigrant groups organized to resist "racism." The Loi Gayssot (named for the Communist deputy who proposed it) requires, among other things, that publications print any objection to their contents from designated antiracist groups and representatives.[103] The distinguished historian of French Communism Annie Kriegel has denounced the Loi Gaysott as "a form of Communist repression," but there is credit (or blame) to be shared with non-Communists. One lawyer who has represented the criminal defendants in cases dealing with hate speech, Eric Delcroix, has documented the widespread involvement of French Jewish organizations in efforts to criminalize unwelcome speech and historical research. Delcroix and Kriegel raise questions about whether Jewish activists who wish to preserve the memory of the Holocaust have drawn a worthwhile lesson from Nazi tyranny.[104]

Even more significant, however, has been the role of publicists, professors, and university students as *vigies délatrices*, self-appointed vigilance committees that gather information about suspected hate criminals and hand it over to state prosecutors. At Lyons such a committee brought professional ruin and, finally, death threats to an experimental psychologist, Bernard Notin, who had included Holocaust revisionist doubts in a footnote to a scientific article. The journal in which the article appeared was forced by law to delete the offending page; Notin was temporarily dismissed from his job and dragged through criminal proceedings.[105] Both at Lyons and at Nantes academic vigilance committees have been formed to aid in the search for revisionist and racist opinions and to bring pressure on the university administrations to dismiss summarily those guilty of "offenses of opinion [*délits d'opinions*]." Administrations are also pressured to notify state prosecutors in order to punish the accused.[106]

The use of force to compel sensitive behavior is entirely appropriate, according to Martine Valdès-Boulouque, vice president of the European Commission against Racism and Intolerance attached to the Council of Europe and a former assistant prosecutor of the Paris Court of Appeals (*tribunal de grande instance de Paris*). Valdès-Boulouque, who is proud of helping to punish suspected Holocaust revisionists and other sources of criminal opinion, warned in an interview with *Le Monde* (12 January 1994) of a "progressive raising of prohibitions." Unless more drastic actions were taken, particularly police surveillance of book vendors, she cautioned, the fight for tolerance could not be won. Valdès-Boulouque was especially bothered by the "vexing problem of bookstores which live only for the diffusion of that poisonous food, racism, and its variant, revisionism."[107] Ironically, the office in the French Ministry of Interior that now oversees the censorship of such reading matter is the "direction des libertés publiques."

While certain vocational and ethnic groups have been in the forefront of the pluralist war for sensitivity and tolerance, an indispensable force throughout has been the managerial state. As the new monarchies in early modern Europe imposed religious orthodoxy as a means of centralization, likewise have managerial democracies sought to unify their populations by controlling and modifying behavior. A movement from such control to the suppression of speech has been a logical progression, once speech could be categorized as a kind of behavior. Since March 1994, for example, the U.S. Department of Education has been monitoring "harrassing" speech in educational institutions, which means anywhere in the facilities and even by uninvited visitors. The published guidelines for this civil rights initiative mention written and oral communications as forms of conduct that may result in "creating a hostile environment."[108]

Despite the differences among self-defined pluralists, one may draw this conclusion from the vantage point of the 1990s: there has been far more continuity than discontinuity in the development of pluralism as both a political ideal and administrative practice. Though some democratic pluralists criticize the current cultural diversity, this may be a case of the revolution devouring its children.[109] Dewey, Kallen, Laski, and other pluralists laid the conceptual foundations for a public administration that has come to fruition in the second half of the century. It is committed to social reconstruction and to using education to rebuild culture, and it prefers to deal not with traditional communities but with more easily influenced aggregations of individuals. Pluralist groups are now subject to governmentally determined social concern, and Mary Frances Berry, chairman of the United States Commission on Civil Rights, underscores the new view of identity when she reminds us that "civil rights laws were not passed to protect the rights of white men."[110] This statement indicates how pluralists look upon the government's role in validating identity. From their perspective, communities are collections of claimants whose collective character hinges on being certified by administrators and their advisors. Official communities in the United States now consist of "minorities," a designation applied to homosexuals but not, for example, to Calabrian Catholics or Levantine Jews. Needless

107

to say, this pluralist policy is still open to change, depending on the interests of the state and the concerns of intellectuals.

A commonly heard objection to affirmative action programs carried out by the government is that "reverse discrimination" brings injustice to white males. Such programs, we are told, allow courts and administrators to deny equal rights to some in order to compensate for the socioeconomic disadvantages ascribed to others or to their ancestors.[111] Such plans are condemned on the grounds that "two wrongs do not make a right." They also are seen to violate the claim to equal justice that the civil rights movement once supposedly embodied.

Such programs, however, are not a return to older patterns of social discrimination with the shoe on the other foot. In its pluralist phase, the present regime assigns "ethnicity" and other generic categories to rearrangeable groups of citizens as an exercise of power. Preparing the way for this exercise was the work done by generations of social environmentalists. By deprecating such inherited biological categories as race and gender and by reducing identity to social constructs and, finally, victim status, environmentalists did not challenge the state's power to assign collective identities. They opened the door to the practice by which administrators and judges could classify their subjects in ever more arbitrary ways. On official government documents, American citizens now dutifully list their "ethnicity," which can be one or more of the following categories: "male," "female," "Asian," "Native American," "white," "Hispanic," or "African American." Needless to say, these identities are mostly unrelated to ethnicity and are in some cases whimsical combinations of ethnic and racial groupings: for example, Japanese and Indian Dravidian "Asians," or Castilian Spanish and predominantly Negroid Puerto Rican "Hispanics." But insofar as these classifications are creations or residues of social policy, scientific precision is no longer needed to define or hand out group identities.[112]

The managerial state has also given strong encouragement to multicultural activities and curricula that are intended to showcase the genius of designated victims. In the process political pluralists have gained further educational control, as when the U.S. Commission on Civil Rights in January 1995 ordered Wesleyan University and the University of Connecticut to discipline faculty members who were exhibiting insensitivity. Professors at both universities failed to "concentrate on multicultural and diversity issues" or to "give appropriate weight to their consideration."[113] In the face of such orders and their accompanying justification, older pluralists may wince with embarrassment. But they overlook the by now centennial character of a bedrock pluralist belief, that the modern state should socialize its population to be right-thinking liberal democrats. Once initiated, this mission continued beyond the point at which the moderate pluralists wished to have it stop. For if the state is to be empowered, as all pluralists believe it must, to fight "prejudice" through social engineering, why should it limit its energies to "anti-Semites" or "racists"? The pluralist mandate for change can be and has been applied to other ambitious ventures, which like earlier ones have come at the expense of social freedom. With due respect to its former practitioners now suffering second thoughts, all phases of pluralism reveal the same tendencies, the ascendancy of the managerial state and its restructuring of social relations. Whether a humanistic conception or an arrogant court religion, pluralism has consistently justified a socially intrusive public administration. And by its own politicizing momentum, it has contributed to a postliberal democratic age, to which pluralists continue to attach misleading liberal labels.

Mass Democracy and the
Populist Alternative

I T HAS long been customary to relate calls for direct democracy and for expressions of the popular will to a revolt from below. Abundant political commentary exists for this view, and one can cite, among those who expressed it, Walter Lippmann, Irving Babbitt, José Ortega y Gassett, and the framers of the American Constitution. All such thinkers warned against giving "the people" their head, and they affirmed the need for educated minorities that could rein in popular passions and reckless appetites.

As the second chapter makes clear, bureaucratic government was entirely acceptable to nineteenth-century liberals, providing that certain conditions were met. Administrators were expected to uphold properly made laws impartially, respect the sanctity of property and the family, and behave with personal rectitude. It was also hoped that public servants would act as a check on the popular will and the partisan aspects of government. A reading of Hegel's *Philosophy of Right* or François Guizot's addresses to the French Chamber of Deputies should confirm this point. Hegel's references to *Staatsbeamte* as a class with no interest but the public good was by no means an invitation to social engineering.[1] It was an attempt at recognizing the intended role of unobtrusive guardians of public order, who would also, as a last resort, deal with otherwise insoluble social problems. Furthermore, Guizot, in introducing French public education in 1833, went out of his way to disavow any Jacobin intent. As one interpreter explains: for Guizot "instruction was not a means of advancing human equality. Its purpose was to render cohesive a society which rests upon the inequality of faculties. It had for an object avoiding the democratic peril defined as social confusion."[2] By providing every Frenchman with minimal vocational training and some degree of shared culture, the liberal July Monarchy hoped to create national unity and at least a tolerable general living standard. But the pursuit of this aim was not viewed as inherently democratic. It was an attempt by the state to ward off the "democratic peril," seen as an upsurge of social disorder that would give rise to a revolutionary dictatorship.

In many ways populism seems to be the polar opposite of the politics practiced by nineteenth-century liberal states. In Latin America populists have promoted both redistributionist economics and public works programs. Dictators such as Juan Peron in Argentina and Getulio Vargas in Brazil appealed directly to the people when they crushed social and institutional opposition to their personal rule. In the United States the Populist or People's Party, organized in Omaha in 1892, backed positions that were anathema to traditional liberals. The American populists advocated unlimited coinage of silver, a graduated income tax, state control of public utilities, particularly of railroads, and direct election of federal senators.[3] Though inimical to classical liberals, such populist positions have attracted the communitarian socialist Christopher Lasch, particularly since they were wedded to conservative cultural attitudes.[4] The Populist Party represented the agrarian American heartland and mobilized its constituents against the alliance of corporate capital with expanding federal government. Populists hoped to locate effective governing control in the states and expressed open disdain for the commerce and culture of the Eastern cities. Their call for referenda and for other direct consultations of the popular will were aimed at circumventing entrenched powers, and for the populists those powers were typically associated with distant urban elites, especially in New York and Washington.

What is indeed a strange twist in the history of populist movements has come in the way direct democracy and the popular will are currently invoked. For at least twenty years, starting with the French National Front in the 1970s, movements that have labeled themselves populist have incorporated large chunks of the nineteenth-century liberal legacy. This has not always been clear, and the editorializing that has occurred against populist "racists" and "counterrevolutionaries" has made it even harder to notice this fact. In the National Front's program, published in 1985, party leader Jean-Marie Le Pen repeatedly presented himself and his cohorts as French national liberals: "We defend economic liberties because without these there are no political liberties. As nationalists we wish in all domains to preserve the greatest possible national independence, and we know this will happen not from withdrawing into ourselves, but from a vigorous offensive of which only an economic system based on free enterprise and competition is capable."[5]

Critics of the National Front and of its controversial leader have traced its political outlook to "extreme rightist" currents, from pagan fascist to

Catholic clericalist, and from diehard supporters of the Vichy government to French Algerian refugees. (In 1965 these refugees entered
French politics behind their presidential candidate and fellow French
Algerian Jean-Louis Tixier-Vignancour.)[6] The National Front has also
been likened to the following of Pierre Poujade, the politician who ral-
lied rural France in the 1950s in what became a vociferous tax revolt. But,
as the French psephologist Pascal Perrineau demonstrates, the electoral
regions in which National Frontists from the mid-eighties onward and
Le Pen as their presidential candidate have had the most success are not
the electoral strongholds of either the Poujadistes or the Tixier-Vignan-
couristes. Poujadistes made electoral inroads almost entirely in rural regions, especially Maine, the Vendée, and Berry, while the French refugees from Algeria only scored well in areas full of *pieds-noirs* (as the
Algerian refugees were known).[7] By contrast, the National Front has
gathered strength throughout the eastern part of France, and particularly in the southeast around Marseilles. In some elections it has gar-
nered more than 20 percent of the votes in the Paris Basin and in the
industrialized areas along the Rhine, Rhone, and Loire Rivers. In and
around Paris, Frontists have attracted both shopkeepers and industrial
workers, and in the presidential election of April 1988, Le Pen drew
significant numbers of votes from all socioeconomic groups.[8]

This appeal may be partly attributed to the timely issues which Le Pen
has hammered away at, particularly immigration and criminal violence,
which he has linked directly and indirectly to the North African "invasion" of France. Certainly he and his party never miss the opportunity to
point to the cultural and physical threat posed to French national identity by the presence of a large, mostly unassimilated Muslim, North African population. Le Pen has, furthermore, cast himself and the National
Front as the one true alternative to the "gang of four" (the two right-
centrist parties together with the Socialists and Communists). Voting for
the National Front and holding referenda on controversial political issues after the National Assembly votes on them are the ways Frenchmen
are told they can regain power over the state. By these populist means,
lepénistes insist, voters can make the "gang of four" responsive to the
French nation.[9] The National Front has also been inventive in combining
programs and electorates, in appealing to both free-market and pro-envi-
ronmentalist constituencies, and in seeking the support of the Catholic
Right without offering it more than rhetorical gestures. (Despite his culti-
vation of a pious image, Le Pen was embroiled in a divorce battle with a
sultry wife whom he lost to a former lieutenant. He then lost the lieuten-

ant, who bolted his party and denounced him to a hostile newspaper, *Le Monde*, as a capricious brute.)[10]

The character of the National Front has remained predominantly national liberal, however ingeniously or cynically its politicians reach out to Catholic rural or working-class electorates. The party program of 1984 combines appeals to a national identity and national culture with proposals for denationalizing industries, limiting public administration, and providing tax relief to business.[11] It also invokes the example of Margaret Thatcher in emphasizing the need to put unions back in their place. In 1984 Le Pen inveighed against a practice (introduced in 1946) of having union representatives play a key role in the distribution of federal funds for social programs (the *Caisse Sociale*). He has also periodically complained about the power of the Force Ouvrière and the Confédération Générale de Travail, the national union organizations with which France's current president, Jacques Chirac, is locked in battle.[12]

Despite Le Pen's flirtation in the sixties and early seventies with France's traditionalist (Catholic nationalist) Right and its interwar corporatist economics, by the mid-seventies he had come to define himself as a national liberal. This Breton politician with close ties to Algerian French refugees began to frequent the Club de l'Horloge, a group of young conservatives who had broken away from the anticapitalist French New Right. While that Right, under the leadership of flamboyant publicist Alain de Benoist, celebrates Celtic-Graeco-Roman religion coupled with organic economics, the Club de l'Horloge seeks to harmonize European Christian civilization with the free market. Often it seems to be promoting the Christian humanist classical liberalism defended by the economist Wilhelm von Roepke and by postwar American conservatives. But the Club de l'Horloge has a harder edge. It has taken a strong stand against France being flooded by non-Europeans and speaks of the nation state as the necessary political structure for the contemporary West.[13] It has also provided key advisors for the National Front, most notably Jean-Yves Le Gallou.

Critics of the National Front insist that it is intent on restoring the past, though which past is not agreed on by all of its interpreters. Typically its detractors depict it as full of French neo-Nazis trying to bring back Nazi totalitarianism or its Vichy counterpart. Almost all of these assessments are ideologically colored.[14] They emphasize Le Pen's anti-Semitism, which is either exaggerated or else inferred from his stance on immigration and French national identity. There is no doubt that Le Pen has made tasteless jokes about Jews to his colleagues and on September 13,

1987 opined in an interview with *Le Monde* that whether or not the Nazis killed their victims in gas chambers "is a point of detail in the history of the Second World War." Still, it is far from clear that he is the ferocious anti-Semite denounced in *Le Monde*.[15] The tasteless jokes were in some cases reported by personal enemies who defected from his party, and their reports, it may be guessed, were not entirely accurate. Nor is there convincing evidence that Le Pen does not believe in the reality of the Holocaust. Rather, he has disparaged its relative historical significance at least on one occasion. He has also emphatically stated that those who lament Nazi crimes most loudly often fail to notice the even greater enormities committed by the Communists.[16]

It must be kept in mind that French Jewish organizations, almost without exception, support the social Left. As in Canada and the United States, most Jews in France are enthusiastically behind liberal immigration policies, gay rights, and pro-feminist legislation. It is only natural that they and the National Front be at loggerheads; and while Le Pen has picked away imprudently at Jewish sensitivities, particularly when the Holocaust is brought up to support socially liberal measures, Jewish organizations would not likely have held back in any case in condemning his social views.[17]

Le Pen has also been unrelenting in criticizing the double standard among Jewish and Arab nationalists who favor multiculturalism for France. Why, he asks, is particularity to be the privilege of a Jewish or Arab state, while Frenchmen must consent to the eradication of *their* collective identity? All the same, the National Front has not called for denying Jews their full rights as French citizens. It has not attacked them as racially alien, though it has engaged in ridicule of its Jewish political opponents. It is therefore questionable whether the National Front should be compared to Nazi or Vichy leadership, which stripped Jews of civil rights and brought about their physical destruction. Sparring with French Jewish spokesmen is not the same as persecuting Jews or even advocating that practice.

As Pierre-André Taguieff and American commentator Franklin Adler point out, moreover, the casting of Le Pen as an interwar Nazi type has already begun to backfire. Imitating their critics on the Left, Le Pen and his followers now depict themselves as an aggrieved group being denied the right to ethnic difference that others are enjoying in their country. They have put together their own "antiracist" organization, L'Alliance Générale contre le Racisme et pour le Respect de l'Identité Francaise et Chrétienne, and insist that the same respect accorded to non-French and non-Christian minorities is due to traditional French Christians.[18] When this courtesy is not extended, the members of the Alliance intend to sue their defamers under the same antihate laws invoked by their opponents on the Left. Such a strategy may help the Front play the same game as its enemies, but it does so at a price, increasing the power of the managerial state as an arbiter of victimological claims. It is the government, after all, that must decide whether the Front's "right to difference" is one to be respected.

Le Pen and his followers have also incurred attacks in the French press for identifying modern France with the kingdom of Charles Martel and Charlemagne.[19] In his apostrophes to the "historic France of forty kings and fifteen hundred years," Le Pen is accused of ignoring the changing character of his country. But in their fixation on fluidity, Le Pen's critics end up denying to France any claim to national continuity.[20] Nations can endure even while changing. The claim by Eastern and Central European Jews to be the descendants of ancient Semitic tribes represents a less believable assertion of national continuity than the one made for Frenchmen by the National Front. But the Jewish claim to continued peoplehood, which provides moral justification for the modern Israeli state, is one that many of Le Pen's Jewish and Christian critics accept. Such an acceptance seems appropriate, particularly after the destruction of European Jewry, as a collective reparation for injuries inflicted by anti-Semites. But Le Pen's question remains valid nonetheless. Why should Frenchmen who have inhabited the same land, spoken (more or less) the same language for centuries, and who share an extended gene pool not have the same right to believe in their nationhood? And why is it unreasonable to believe that a still growing population in France of six million largely unassimilated North African Muslims can change the French national character irrevocably? With one of Europe's lowest natality rates (together with that of Italy) and with multicultural doctrines being taught in schools and in the media, the European French population may be justified in feeling demographically and culturally threatened.[21] Aristotle notes in the *Politica* that a polity does not remain the same if one replaces all or most of its population. That remains the case even if the new population settles in the same location and bears the same name as its displaced predecessors.[22]

One problem French populism will have to face and that its critics have not addressed is the Front's appeal to contradictory politics. Quite often the National Front falls between two stools: social democracy and classical liberalism. Talk about "détatisation" and economic freedom may win some of the owners and captains of industry, but is not likely to create for the Front a permanent working-class constituency.[23] It attracts that constituency by taking a hard line on both crime and immigration and by demanding that employers have only French workforces. The Front has also advocated social measures—e.g., family-leave allowances—which approximate those elsewhere introduced under feminist auspices. Unlike the contemporary Left, the Front has taken this position to encourage natality and to rebuild the French population.[24]

What must be asked, however, is whether the Front can continue to call for social measures of this kind without forfeiting its claims to be an opponent of the modern administrative state and an advocate of a market economy. Undoubtedly immigration has been, for the Front and other European populists, the most reliable electoral issue. As Perrineau and Jérôme Jaffré demonstrate in detailed analyses, the Front can bring together social classes, as occurred in the presidential race of April 24, 1988, when anti-immigration sentiments are at their height. That happens whenever the government ignores the rising anxiety about crime and about alien cultures spreading in certain urban areas.[25] Immigration also produces further demands on the already stretched funds for social services, and all contemporary populist movements have been quick to turn this problem to their advantage. Whether Austrian and Italian regionalists or the supporters of Proposition 187 in California, populists have stoked electoral fires by pointing to the pressures being put on safety nets by immigrants, and particularly by illegal ones.

Behind this financial issue is a communitarian one. Because welfare programs and pensions and services to the elderly require transfers of income from the young and employed, it seems necessary here that a bond exist between the payers and payees.[26] Social programs can no longer be credibly presented as insurance measures. They are, for the most part, gifts of money being made by one sector of society to another. And people only consent to such gifts willingly on behalf of those whom they see as members of a family or nation. They oppose doing the same for an uninvited stranger. Liberal pluralists therefore have had to convince others that all humankind have a right to the growing taxes that national governments collect. The making of this argument has not been easy, and populists have taken advantage of the skepticism generated by pluralist "human rights" rhetoric.

But this particular issue has not created an electoral majority for populists in France, any more than it has for similar protest movements in the United States. Typically the National Front has done well in the initial phase of French presidential races and in elections for the European Parliament. It has been less successful in regional races and must usually concede its votes, according to a prior agreement, to the candidates of the right-center parties upon reaching the second round of elections. In 1988 and 1992, during its best showings, the Front managed to elect only a handful of deputies to the Assembly. Though it has made strides in municipal races, particularly in Marseilles, Nice, and other urban centers of Arab concentration, the Front has not been able to displace the Gaulliste Right-Center as the French Left's official opposition. Because of its being a target of media attack and because of its lack of a large patronage base, the Front has had difficulty fielding candidates of national stature. According to Perrineau, most of its votes are gestures of protest, cast on ballots that will not decisively change the national party structure.[27]

In this respect it resembles the populist Right in the United States, which has now coalesced around the presidential hopeful Patrick J. Buchanan. Like Le Pen, Buchanan has defiantly rattled left-liberal elites, called for restrictions on immigration, and attacked "big government," except when it acts in pursuit of the national interest. Like Le Pen, Buchanan has angered Zionist groups by thundering at their anti-Christian remarks, opposing the Gulf War, and questioning some aspects of the established account of the Holocaust. In all of these gestures Buchanan, like Le Pen, has made it clear that he will not play by the other side's rules. He will not accept "Christian guilt" for the sufferings of non-Christians or "white guilt" for the condition of nonwhites. Buchanan scorns the grievances directed by alleged victims of Western civilization against the majority culture, and he treats these complaints in the context of a cultural and political revolution against his own country and coreligionists.[28]

Like Le Pen, however, Buchanan and his followers grouped in the American Cause have launched a protest movement without the possibility of building a majority base. Though tens of millions agree with Buchanan's stances, at least an equal number oppose them vehemently. And like Le Pen, Buchanan looks to a vanishing past for his own electoral counterrevolutionary army. Whereas Le Pen appeals to a bourgeois nationalist electorate to effect *his* counterrevolution, Buchanan hopes to turn society around with his fellow ethnic Catholics and with Southern white conservatives.[29] Neither core constituency, however, can yield the votes necessary to alter *national* political life in France or in the United States. Moreover, the control of social programs by federal administrations provides for them vast leverage in dealing with populist challenges. In the battle between President Clinton and a Republican Congress in 1995 over raising premiums for entitlement programs and forcing public administration to live within its means, Republican majority opinion in the United States melted away within weeks. Between October and December 1995, Clinton's popularity soared, even among groups who disagreed with him on social questions.[30]

The identitarian politics and appeals to a cultural heritage that populists favor can only work among those who share a traditional communal identity. Populists will not likely be able to mount a majority opposition to the managerial state in any other situation. The populist movements with the broadest and greatest long-range strength are regionally based. They have also developed within countries whose administrative frameworks are not so deeply implanted as those of the United States or France. In Austria the Freiheitliche Partei has moved from its original regional base in Carinthia to win the votes of Austrian non-Carinthian decentralizers and immigration restrictionists.[31] Before the Austrian federal elections of December 17, 1994, the FP had commanded almost 23 percent of the Austrian vote, and though its share has fallen to 21.5 percent, it remains highly competitive with the center-left Austrian Socialists and center-right People's Party.[32] In Italy the Lega Lombarda, founded in Milan, became a major national political force in less than ten years, and an expanded alliance that it helped put together for all of Northern Italy, the Lega Nord, entered the federal government, with major cabinet posts, in April 1994.[33]

There is no need to ascribe organizational genius to the leader of either of these movements: to the photogenic fortyish bachelor-sportsman, Jörg Haider, who heads the Freiheitliche Partei, or to the Milanese politician, already notorious for his wheeling-dealing, Umberto Bossi, who directs the Lega Nord. Regionalist parties that invoke communal identity and demand the right to determine their own citizenry do well in particular circumstances: having a Catholic rather than Protestant population and central governments that are problematic for their peoples. Austria, for example, only became a country in 1919, out of the battered remnants of a once great empire. Its socialist founders, moreover, repudiated any link—and in fact insisted on the "discontinuity [*Unterbrechung*]"—between their own republic and the Habsburg empire, which had been defeated in war and subsequently overthrown.[34] For years afterwards a substantial minority, if not majority, of Austrians favored union with Germany.

The unification of Italy in 1870 was equally fraught with problems, in this case glaring economic disparities between the industrial North and rural South and a parliamentary regime driven by graft. Social critics and historians were outlining the political failures of the Italian Risorgimento almost from the time that Italy had undergone its *unificazione mancata.*[35] The chief theorist of the League and a distinguished professor of government at the Catholic University of Milan, Gianfranco Miglio, has spent forty years detailing the structural flaws of all Italian regimes from 1870 onward. In 1980 Miglio took over the directorship of the Gruppo di Milano, a group that was drafting a model federal constitution for a regionalized Italy. His reason for this involvement was the conviction that Italians could not function as an effective national state.[36] Modern Italy, says Miglio, is a "neofeudal arrangement" for collecting and distributing patronage. He describes Italy not as a sovereign state but as a people beset by parties and administrators.[37]

Miglio, among other spokesmen for the League, has stressed the Germanic and quasi-Protestant character of his region, which has been unnaturally joined, or so goes the received account, to the Latin South and its lawless spirit.[38] Despite these efforts to present the Italian North as part of the Protestant commercial world (which by now in Europe may be an anachronistic concept), the communal sense animating Lombard regionalists seems strongest in Catholic societies. Both Protestant individualism and Protestant obedience to "lawful" authorities have aided managerial regimes working to "modernize" social morals. In Catholic, particularly Latin-Catholic, societies, by contrast, the taking of social control by such government has generally gone slower, because of deeper and more extensive family ties and less respect for public administration.[39] (As an obvious illustration one need only compare the amount of tax evasion in Italy to that of the United States, Canada, and Sweden. Among Italians it has been estimated as being at least four times as great as among Protestant democracies. Nor do Italians outside of politics refer to the Roman administration as "our government.")

The League until now has not brought about a changed constitution for Italy. Shortly after the spring 1994 victory, Miglio broke with his former advisee Bossi, on account of what he called broken promises.[40] A similar stalling might have occurred on the part of leaders of the Freiheitliche Partei if the December 1994 election had turned out better for them. Haider might have had second thoughts about pressing forward with his plan to reconstruct Austria and might have accepted a major role for his party in a center-right coalition.[41]

119

More important, however, in the long view is that regional populists in Central Europe have made their own will matter. They have generated widespread discussion of issues that public administrators and most prestige newspapers would prefer to ignore, from immigration restrictions to regionally determined rights of citizenship. The *leghisti* delight in citing Article 33 of the Declaration of Rights, which precedes the current Italian constitution. In this article the Italian national assembly is given the power to alter fundamentally the constitution of its own government. Italian regionalists and their allies may eventually have the votes to bring about such a change.[42]

A certain similarity may be seen between European Catholic regionalists and the Québecois. Like European regionalists, the Québecois live in a problematic and, relatively speaking, recently devised federal structure, have an established regional identity, and insist on their right to rescind a political arrangement deemed as unsuitable for their culture. The former premier of Quebec and (former) head of the secessionist Parti Québecois, Jean Parizeau, has also complained of the "ethnic factor," that is, unwanted non-Francophone immigration into his province, which he blames on the federal government.[43] Without formally separating until now, the Québecois have extracted from the federal administration sizable concessions on linguistic and immigration questions.[44]

What does distinguish the Québecois separatists from Central European regionalists is ideological. The Québecois do not reject either managerial politics or social engineering. They seem happy with both, as long as they are practiced by Francophone administrators. By contrast, Austrian and Italian regionalists represent the bourgeois liberal politics of the nineteenth century, without a continued belief in the framework of the nation state. For them, central governments no longer seem to serve established societies. They are seen as predatory and intrusive, stripping peoples of their earnings and distributing them among strangers and politicians. In the face of this perceived degeneration of the nation state, European bourgeois regionalists feel they must look elsewhere for appropriate political forms.

These intended forms are at least partly based on a return to a market economy and to a fortified civil society. In a similar protest against administrative interference in communities and families, Le Pen has tried to resurrect the principle of "subsidarity." This, he explains, requires that barring an emergency, no more distant level of control be applied to problems that arise in a local or familial sphere than those authorities that already exist there. Allowing a central administration to interfere at will in the arrangements of families and regions undermines authority at every level, except for that exercised from the top. Far better, Le Pen maintains, to force the central state into acknowledging the legitimacy of other authorities than to concede its power as inevitable.[45] Miglio has examined the same theme from a constitutionalist angle. In a truly federalized Europe, he maintains, the central administrative state should continue to exist as an instrument of convenience. There one's deepest political loyalty, however, will be to a self-governing region possessing a distinctive cultural identity. Central governments may continue to provide for defense, though, as seen by Miglio, a European federal government can perform this function as well as an Italian national one for Lombardy, Liguria, and other Italian regions.[46]

Though devolution of power has become an issue in the United States as well, here it has not led to a tumultuous reconsideration of political structures. In the United States it has not posed a major threat to either the managerial state or its conception of democracy. For the most part, the call for devolution in the United States has been a barometer of periodic financial discontent. In *Investor's Business Daily* (15 November 1995), for example, we are made to think that "secession movements are alive and well in the U.S." and have erupted in New York, California, and Michigan. In all of these states, it is noted, there are widespread complaints about inattentive and distant governments that do not provide uniformly adequate services. The article cites economist Gordon Tullock, who believes that California "has simply grown too large to be governed as a simple entity and ought to be broken up."[47]

Investor's Business Daily calls attention to financial and managerial problems that are fueling "secessionist movements." But these movements are not about secession, and the comparison made in the piece between Catalan and Scottish separatists and the disgruntled residents of Upper Michigan and Staten Island is entirely misleading. Attempts in the United States to force the federal administration to give certain areas more public funding have nothing to do with regional secession. Regionalists predicate their claim to political sovereignty on cultural solidarity; the former, by contrast, is taking place among those without a cultural base or any real aspiration toward self-rule. In a country with an increasingly transitory population, it is becoming harder and harder to find families inhabiting the same locality from one generation to the next. In some areas deemed as secessionist-minded (e.g., California and Staten Island), demographic compositions change too rapidly to permit the growth of any long-standing identity between the majority population and a particular region.

The American populist-regionalist movement that may come closest to the European kind is the Southern League. Founded in Tuscaloosa, Alabama, in June 1994, it is directed by the Southern Presbyterian minister and history professor Michael Hill.[48] Both Hill and his advisor Thomas Fleming have established close ties to European regionalists and cite the Lega Nord as an organizational model for American Southerners. The American Constitution, they insist, was founded explicitly on the principle of dual federalism. Southern states are urged to reassert this principle to liberate their people from "government by fiat." In a manifesto published in the *Washington Post* (29 October 1995), Hill and Fleming present the South as a culturally distinct and profoundly Christian region. What the League seeks to do, they explain, is to cleanse their region of foreign administrative oppression: "After so many decades of strife, black and white Southerners of goodwill should be left alone to work out their destinies, avoiding, before it is too late, the urban hell that has been created by the lawyers, social engineers, and imperial bureaucrats."[49]

There is one truth that may embarrass the Southern League's founders but tells much about American political culture. While millions of Southerners, white and black, gave their votes to President Clinton and to an expanding federal administration, the Southern League, which claims to stand for an entire region, has only a membership of several thousand. The Italian Northern League, by contrast, has acquired a membership and electorate in the millions. Twelve years ago, more than a hundred thousand Lombard separatists gathered to celebrate the victory won at Legnano in 1176 by the *medieval* Lombard League against Holy Roman Emperor Frederick Barbarossa.[50]

Historical memories and cultural identities are weaker in the United States than in Europe. But equally noteworthy is the stunning success achieved by the American managerial state in neutralizing its opposition. Entitlement programs and media support for expanded social services have increased governmental power against by-now-waning opposition. Both Christopher Lasch and political sociologist Stanley Rothman comment on the link between the current American political class and the breakdown of America's Protestant bourgeois ethos. Social constraint, individual responsibility, and deferred gratification once provided the moral framework for constitutional government. These qualities were especially critical for a polity that stressed individual identity and whose religious underpinnings were Protestant and more individualistic than those of Catholic societies.

Lasch believes that cultural renewal and communal freedom are still possible in the United States because the lower middle class continues to resist wayward elites.[51] Lasch's pessimism is short-term, inasmuch as he looks to working-class decency to renew American society. Rothman, however, offers a gloomier prediction about freedom and community in the United States. With deep regret he declares that "it is still my expectation (or fear) that the future does lie with authoritarian bureaucratic societies, even if these are partly associated with the market and private property." One reason this seems likely, he suggests (with unmistakable moral anger), is that "the current decay of bourgeois standards is translating itself into escalating physical violence." This outburst of "the violence which was always breaking through the patina of civilization" will require repressive physical control, and Rothman does not believe that, without individual religious constraint, either the state or individuals can "restore or create a sense of personal responsibility."[52] Intellectuals will not likely tame human nature by devising humanistic or pluralist values. On this point Rothman is unsparingly harsh: "A renewal may occur in the society, or there may even be a shift in orientation on the basis of a new cultural understanding, but such a shift will not be initiated by secular intellectuals."[53]

Despite my general agreement with much of this analysis and its underlying concern, I would disagree respectfully with two of Rothman's points. One, it is not clear that culture was primary and politics secondary (as Rothman at least suggests, if not explicitly states) in the unraveling of bourgeois society. The managerial state played a steady and significant role in effecting that result. It created a public of individual claimants (and, finally, governmentally approved victims) for handouts and other administrative favors, and it set into operation a series of programs aimed at behavior modification that have been largely successful. As Paul Veyne reminds us in looking at life under the Roman Empire, most people at most times have been *apolides,* that is, not without a place of residence but without interest in their civic existence.[54] They have belonged to what Benjamin Ginsberg in another context calls the "captive public," those who allow government to do things for and to them.[55] Far from being an unusual situation, it is the one in which all people, save for sporadic and exceptional groups, have been willing to live. This truth was apparent to Plato, Aristotle, and Xenophon, who assumed that Greeks but few others had a disposition for civic affairs. Most non-Greeks might exist under stable regimes, but not under those that they constructed and oversaw.[56] Americans may have become like ancient Persians, more fit to be ruled than to rule themselves, but the reasons are political and not just moral and cultural. The managerial state has contributed to an entire way of life, and Americans, by embracing it, have also accepted its cultural accompaniments. Others have not made these adjustments with the same alacrity; and among Southern and Central Europeans premodern or early-modern institutions and attitudes have acted as a force of resistance.

Rothman also may be wrong to imagine that the present lack of moral self-discipline must result in a police state erected for the sake of public order. Behind this prediction can be glimpsed the shade of classical political theory. According to Plato and Aristotle, a decayed democracy produces licentious conduct, which becomes the seedbed of tyranny. Tyrants rise to power by fanning democratic disorder and by exploiting personal and political excesses.[57] But in postliberal societies such as ours, violence and intemperate conduct are behavioral and administrative problems. Criminals can be warehoused and treated therapeutically, while those with the means will get out of harm's way by relocating as far from inner cites or deteriorated suburbs as public transportation allows. Nor has the growth of the managerial state left the United States impoverished. GNP continues to grow, together with the size, reach, and financial needs of government.[58]

A process that has aided this managerial control of social behavior is the transformation of the family. Rothman notes this development, and Edward Shorter, in *The Making of the Modern Family*, treats it in some detail. A social historian, Shorter looks at the transition from the modern to the late modern family and singles out the distinguishing characteristics of this process: the ascendancy of peer group socialization in place of parental authority, the large-scale entry of women into the work force, and the growing dissociation of erotic activity from marriage.[59] Shorter explores the institutional changes that have affected the Western family in the twentieth century, and particularly in the last forty years. While undoubtedly connected to social, demographic, and cultural circumstances, the weakening of the bourgeois family, as examined by Shorter, is further correlated to a specific political occurrence: in the last seventy years the managerial state has become the dominant socializing force and accelerated those cultural changes of which it has approved.[60]

In *The Search for the American Right Wing*, William B. Hixson indicates how tightly the defense of bourgeois modernity has been tied to opposition to the managerial state: between 1955 and 1987 the one constant feature in the American grassroots Right was its increasingly archaic view of modern society. The Right, as seen by Hixson, combines a political idea with a social one, a premanagerial conception of the federal government that combines a belief in the nuclear family with well-defined gender roles. Unlike Hofstadter, who demonizes the populist Right, Hixson does not denigrate his subjects. Rather, he is struck by the apparent hopelessness of their restorationist dream. As an oppositional force the populism analyzed by Hixson faces insurmountable problems. It has had to build a political coalition that weds economic grievances to cultural stands.[61] But both of these positions are intrinsically difficult for a populist movement in late-twentieth-century America. Calls for communal or local control in moral and social matters will likely arouse suspicion from journalists and the media. Such demands typically bring forth damaging assaults on the "fascist" mindset behind them. And the types of long-term material concerns that an American populist movement must address are the ones the managerial state has already used to consolidate its power. Such a movement will not be electorally successful unless it offers itself as a material provider, but in so doing it may have to replicate the establishment that it claims to be opposing. This is doubly true for left-wing populists, who fail to give even the appearance of being independent of the state. The democratic socialist Alan Wolfe, for example, praises Scandinavian socialism, while inveighing against the market-driven government in his own country.[62] But, as Christopher Lasch rightly observes, despite Wolfe's fondness for populist tropes, he does not object to the political establishment, except to the extent that it tolerates a quasi-free market.[63]

In any case, appeals to a moral heritage have become divisive in our society. Talk about lawfulness and marital fidelity has angered civil rights and feminist activists looking for codewords for racism and repressive Victorian standards.[64] And "Judeo-Christian," a term invented by Christian traditionalists hoping to reach out to Jews, has aroused more peeve than acceptance. Jews polled on this usage do not want to be identified with an explicitly Christian ethic, while atheists, Muslims, and Buddhists resent the failure of Judeo-Christians to extend to them recognition of *their* moral cultures.[65]

In an even bolder search for value-unity, the self-described libertarian populist Bill Kauffman offers this recipe for the restoration of American localism: "Only when we restore to Americans their birthright—local self-government in prideful communities that respect the liberties of every dentist and Baptist and lesbian and socialist and hermit and auto parts dealer—will we remember what it means to an American first."[66] Though Kauffman makes a cogent case against the merits of an American empire spreading "global democracy," it is unclear how his own communitarian, localized America would work, even if the managerial state approved it. Culturally unified groups may conceivably include auto parts dealers and dentists and may even indulge a few hermits. But they are not likely to embrace traditional Baptists, lesbians, and socialists in "prideful communities." To whatever extent such groups do live together, it will be as a pluralist experiment overseen by political therapists, or as urban conglomerations without social or cultural unity.

An alternative vision of a posttherapeutic America with some communal elements can be discerned in a short book by John Gray, *In the Enlightenment's Wake* (1995). Gray would concede most of the argument of this chapter about the unbroken social and political power of the managerial state and about the dishonesty of its "liberal" self-image. Although by sentiment a classical liberal, Gray does not hide his belief that his own heritage is now obsolete.[67] Nonetheless, he believes that Western public administration may be introducing a new kind of society by promoting Third World immigration. Administrators and journalists have done this partly to render nation states more porous. But the immigrants who come in, Gray notes, are not socially isolated. They live in ethnic enclaves in which they are building an extensive communal life. These immigrants use their resources to erect mosques, support communal charities and services, and, like Eastern European Orthodox Jews, preserve distinctive cultures in settings that are both modern urban and ethnically heterogeneous.[68]

Gray's celebration of ethnic enclaves as the restorer of community in the West may be overly optimistic. He is celebrating not the return of *Western* community but the influx into Western countries of predominantly non-Western immigrants. Such a development, it may be argued, will produce cultural clashes and weaken even further the already fragile civilizational identities of the host countries. Communities, after all, are not simply interchangeable, and the arrival in France of millions of North African Muslims has alarmed French secular republicans as well as French Catholic nationalists. Incoming Muslims agitate to have their religious values taught in French schools, and they do not easily adapt, or so it is widely believed, to civil institutions that are not subject to ecclesiastical (by which is meant their own ecclesiastical) authorities.[69] There is also no guarantee that ethnic enclaves will throw their weight against the managerial state or its pluralist ideology. Generally, this has not been the case until now. In Canada, England, France, and Australia, Third World immigrant organizations and immigrant votes have supported parties and politicians who favor multicultural initiatives.[70] In-group cohesiveness among the immigrants has not caused them to rally to the threatened social traditions of their hosts.

Despite the objections that might be raised to Gray's expectations, he does present one undeniable truth: concentration of unassimilated communities of any kind in the West will bring the managerial state more difficulties than benefits. Administrators will have to deal with larger and larger numbers of people who feel no loyalty to their pluralist court religion or to its therapeutic projects. They will have to administer subjects whose home lives clash with their own public ideology and whose support will be purely perfunctory. American "moderate" conservatives (i.e., neoconservatives) have proposed ways of coping with this quandary. They have advocated generous immigration policies but stress the need to combine them with intensive public training in "democratic values." America should become the "first universal nation," but its steadily changing population should be made to appreciate the present political system and to carry on the crusade for "human rights."[71]

Unlike these relative moderates, however, administrators, social workers, and academics often romanticize the collective lifestyles of Third World immigrants. Whether as victims of the West or as imagined avatars of nonsexist and nonracist cultures, these groups are seen by the European and American Left as entitled to their differences. But it may be impossible for a managerial state to socialize those who have such a privilege or to check the balkanization which may result from its exercise. Proliferating alien cultures exercising a "right to difference" can, after all, subvert a host society. Though the resulting dilution of established ways of life may serve pluralist ends, it also prevents the forces of democratic progress from keeping a firm social grip. Shortly before his death, an English poet identified as a social democrat, Stephen Spender, complained of the difficulty of preserving "democracy" among those who "care nothing about it." Spender trembled for the political future if his London neighbors, mostly non-Western patriarchal theocrats, took over English society.[72] While this may never happen and while Spender's neighbors may continue to vote for Labour Party multiculturalists, their presence causes deviations from the behavioral norms that Western pluralists demand from mainstream citizens. This double standard is ultimately detrimental to the authority of the managerial state and its intellectual priesthood.

Equally important for the weakening of pluralist ideology is the ascendancy of postmodernism, though in the United States postmodernist ideas until now have had their strongest following on the intellectual Left. The postmodernism that is most familiar to Americans questions universal truths, treats science and logic as peculiarly Western inventions, and pleads for a "right to difference" among those allegedly victimized by Western institutions. Feminists, blacks, and gays have all appealed to a postmodernist Left to justify a distinctive form of self-expression for themselves and other reputed victims of Western hegemony.[73] Such appeals have been totally compatible with the reconstructionist designs of the managerial state. No less than multicultural social critics, the managerial state has emphasized the rights of accredited victims, and its own list of disadvantaged groups overlaps the one featured in postmodernist academic polemics.

But there is another side of postmodernism, already widely represented in Europe, that is explicitly opposed to the managerial pluralist conception of Progress. Basic to the European New Right, this postmodernism is associated with such controversial political theorists as Alain de Benoist, Marco Tarchi, and Alessandro Campi. Both Bossi and Le Pen have ties to this postmodernist Right, and the "differentialist form of argument [*argumentaire différencialiste*]" characteristic of regionalists and nationalists in Europe often betrays a postmodernist provenance for their ideas.[74] New Right theorists and feuilletonistes in France, Germany, and Italy deliver attacks on liberal universalism and consider "human rights" as a mere pretext for the expansion of the managerial state. Unhappily, these postmodernists confuse a late-twentieth-century development with the liberalism of the old bourgeoisie, while not paying enough attention to the differences between the world built and sustained by that class and contemporary mass democracy. Postmodernists of the Right sometimes also make the mistake of idealizing oppressive Third World regimes, because of the anti-Americanism that they and these governments share. And they persist in propagating simplistic negative views about the United States as the source of all the world's monetary, moral, and cultural evils, in the face of abundant counterevidence.[75]

But they also bring to their investigations a perspective limited to those who can survey political life from outside the present tolerated political conversation. They point out to what extent Right and Left in the West have become indistinguishable defenses of managerial power. Couched

in what seem arbitrarily formulated universals, these defenses of administrative manipulation, explains the postmodernist Right, are held to be
incontestable. Against the liberal managerial order and *its* list of human
rights, the postmodernist Right calls attention to its own alternative. It
speaks on behalf of the distinctiveness of peoples and regions and up-
holds their inalienable right not to be "culturally homogenized."

According to former New Leftists Paul Piccone and Russell Berman,
the appeal to political universals echoes a bourgeois culture that has
been appropriated by New Class operatives. The insistence that everyone
should follow the same political model, explain Piccone and Berman,
reflects the interests of state managers, now in alliance with multinational corporations and deluded or bribed intellectuals. All of these
groups are relentlessly opposed to human particularity and community,
conditions that obstruct the consolidation of their own power. Without
social planning as a human right, or so goes this postmodernist argument, families and regions in the United States would reaffirm their
identities and educate their young in accordance with ancestral wisdom.

This communitarian vision is open to criticism on several counts.
There is no evidence that most Americans are looking for roots, save as
a conversation piece or as a victimological asset. There also is no reason
to conclude that if people did organize themselves along traditional communal lines, they would thereby create a harmonious world. Communities have been hostile to each other throughout time, and it might be
asked whether the restoration in the United States of European ethnic
enclaves would lead to the happy interaction of American Serbs, American Croatians, and members of other groups bearing bitter memories
about historical enemies.

It is, furthermore, naive to believe that all communities will come to
view their own traditions as no better or worse than those of others. The
assumption of cultural superiority is not confined to global democratic
enthusiasts. It is equally characteristic of traditional religious and ethnic
communities, which have histories of treating each other unkindly. While
it may be possible to get most of these groups to live together, as they
were doing in the United States before a managerially directed pluralism, such coexistence will have to be built on the residual influence of
the Age of Reason. Postmodernists of the Right plainly detest this epoch;
nonetheless it was the Enlightenment belief in shared human Reason
that provided a basis for mutually respecting communities. Although the
Enlightenment also produced less fortunate legacies, particularly the
idea of "rational" world government, it did shape the prospect for com-

munities that can coexist in harmony. Defenders of that communal prospect, like Edmund Burke and Johann Gottfried Herder, also contributed
to the appreciation of national traditions and thereby to the flowering
of European romanticism. But there is nothing contradictory about an
organic traditionalism that tolerates and even finds some of itself in
other traditions. The considered tolerance of traditions shown by Burke
and other romantic precursors went beyond the outlook of a narrowly
sectarian or culturally closed society. Eighteenth- and nineteenth-century
cultural commentators assumed there were common features of thought
and habit in all civilized societies that made them more similar than
different. The attitude toward communities on the postmodernist Right
harks back to that modernist perspective more than it does to the exclusi-
vist sentiments of at least some pre- modern societies.

Another observation may be in order about the postmodernist Right.
Its defense of tradition has still not moved from a critical stance or a
shared demonology toward any workable alternative to the managerial
state. Although a source of hatred for the postmodernist Left (Jacques
Derrida, among other representatives of this side, has called for censor-
ing European New Right publications), the postmodernist Right has had
little direct political influence.[76] Its ideas remain entirely oppositional
and depend for their effect on being popularized by the European populist Right. Significantly, the intellectual and populist Rights both reveal
the same widening chasm between European regionalists like Alain de
Benoist and recycled nationalists like Le Pen. As Benoist has observed in
correspondence with me, it is only in the present "Manichean [intellec-
tual] universe" that he and Le Pen could be grouped together. In a less
controlled political culture, their differences would seem more obvious.
Unlike Le Pen, Benoist does not believe that cultural identity is fixed as
an "essentialist" attribute by "glorious historical points of reference."
Even less does he think, like members of the National Front, that the
"history of France stopped in the past."[77]

Despite high-placed enemies and internal divisions, the postmodernist
Right does continue to exercise a critical function. It has become the
other edge of the postmodernist sword. No longer do all attacks on bourgeois modernity come from either the academic scribes or the media
priesthood of the managerial state. The aggressive self-defensiveness of
human rights activists and engaged pluralists, moreover, suggests their
own intellectual limits. The pathologization of dissent and the calls for
government and media censorship that emanate from these groups un-
derscore their unwillingness to discuss openly what is now being chal-

lenged. Not only postmodernist intellectuals but European populists are accusing their opponents of hiding *obvious* truths. Thus Le Pen ridicules French journalists for "pretending" to believe what no thinking person could accept: that democracy means submission to administrators, that gender roles are social constructs, and that the French nation consists of populations wandering in and out of the historic French hexagon.[78] Despite the dismissive treatment given to such charges by the press, they do raise questions about the meaning of intellectual tolerance. Respectable journalists and academics do not invite discussion of what they no longer intend to treat as open questions. They expect that those whom they honor with academic and journalistic posts will know how to behave in ritualized dialogues. Those they induct into their circle will be sufficiently cowed or sensitized not to deviate from established therapeutic and globalist assumptions. This expectation may still be justified, but in a highly literate society with multiple information sources, it is hard to keep real political disagreement from being noticed.

Toward a Stripped-down Populism

An area in which the managerial state has been able to socialize easily is public education. Public school systems have been receptive to social psychologists and therapeutically inclined administrators; in much of the Western world public schools have functioned in the absence of serious competition. Ninety percent of American students attend public schools from kindergarten through high school, and in Italy, Sweden, Portugal, and Greece the percentage of students in pre-university public education is even higher.[79] In Italy and France, however, parents have organized to promote "liberty of instruction" and are now publishing nationwide reports on alternatives to public schools. Two plans for private education that have been touted in Europe are a Swedish program, first implemented in 1990, and the voucher proposal being introduced in some American states. Significantly, neither takes measures to keep the public sector out of private schools. In Sweden the government has tried to resurrect private education as a competitive alternative to the public system. By distributing subsidies the ministry of education has pushed the percentage of Swedish students attending private institutions from 1.1 to 5 percent. In the United States some states, for example, Michigan and Wisconsin, pay private schools, among others, a prearranged amount per registered student. This policy is presented as a means of increasing parental choice. But the Swedish and American plans leave the state, not private institutions, as the ultimate custodians of learning: the Swedes are rebuilding private education as a state-administered project, while Americans make public support for private schools dependent upon compliance with federal and state behavioral and admissions guidelines.[80]

Despite increasing public administration in the United States, some skepticism about its reach and purpose has set in. A changing attitude is present toward the ideas and class associated with governing. This attitude has gone from being affirmative in the 1950s, a time when the American "democratic faith" was most widely believed, to being overwhelmingly critical. Though Americans still want government to look after them, almost half of those polled fear the same government and do not believe it "represents" them.[81] The negative view of public education and the popular quest for private alternatives is a case in point. Although the state and its therapeutic administrators still hold the good cards in any plan now being considered to privatize education, more important, it would seem, is the demand itself. People are losing faith in the capacity of government to provide adequate educational services. Today the greatest faith in the American administrative regime is found among immigrants, a fact not likely to be lost on the political class and its defenders. Immigrants may feel grateful to a government that has encouraged them to come, in the face of popular resistance.[82]

One should not assume (like the American Political Science Association and columnist David Broder) that Americans, especially young ones, have turned cynical about government. "Cynical" refers to those who question the self-congratulation engaged in by the American political class. People may vote for whatever gray alternatives the system permits, but no longer find those alternatives especially appealing and define their relation to them in starkly utilitarian terms. Most Americans do not wish to rule themselves but are not happy with the governing that goes on. Thus they ask that power be turned over to regions and states whenever they sense that federal administration does not respond to their needs. Finally citizens are protesting more and more against the rule of judges. Whence the outcry at judicial tyranny in California after the passage of Proposition 187 and in Colorado when a state referendum was passed against the introduction of special bills protecting gay rights.[83] The move by judges to strike down these populist initiatives caused tempers to flare. Furthermore, judicial governance in the United States, which in Kansas and Illinois has resulted in taxes being raised for court-ordered school busing, has become an incendiary issue. Judicial remedies are now widely seen as excuses for the rule of social experts.

In 1995 several governors, most notably Pete Wilson of California and John Engler of Michigan, emphatically refused to pay for an unfunded mandate from Congress, the Motor Voter Act, which required the states to extend voting registration services to motor vehicle departments. Whereas most of the protesting governors stressed the unfair financial burden being inflicted, Wilson and Engler also brought up the populist constitutional issue, namely, that the federal government had no constitutional right to be interfering in the conduct of elections by the states.[84] As in his stand on Proposition 187 and his suspension of affirmative action programs in California, Wilson took the lead in marching under a populist banner. The citizens of states and their elected state officials, he indicated, were justified in resisting undue interference by federal administrators and unelected judges, or by Congress when it exceeded its enumerated powers.

Clearly Wilson, who rose politically as a liberal Republican, was trimming his sails to an electoral wind. His populist stands had brought him as a gubernatorial candidate in 1994 from more than twenty points behind his Democratic opponent to a decisive victory. In 1995 Wilson pushed his luck by trying to parlay his populist image into a presidential nomination. His lackluster personality kept this from happening, and thereafter Wilson returned to California to deal with judicial and administrative attempts to block his resistance to federal power.[85]

What is most striking about this populist adventure is its lack of a rightist ideological dimension. Unlike Buchanan and Le Pen, Wilson does not appeal to the ideals of bourgeois modernity or to Christian resistance to late modern lifestyles. He supports abortion rights, equivocates on gay issues, and generally gets poor grades from the Christian Right. He avoids cultural wars on most social issues in order to get to the heart of his agenda: the punishment of criminals, the restoration of power to the states, and tight control of borders against illegal immigrants.

In some of these stands Wilson resembles the Canadian populist Preston Manning, whose Reform Party in 1992 displaced the centrist Progressive-Conservatives as Canada's federal opposition on the right. Scion of a political dynasty from Alberta, where the elder Manning had been premier and head of the populist Social Credit Party, Preston Manning has continued a family tradition by opposing leftist elites. He has thundered against immigration expansionists and in Alberta was outspoken in support of the death penalty. Manning has called for a federal referendum

on the restoration of capital punishment and advocates the same democratic technique for other questions of national importance.[86]

For all of Manning's invocation of a Canadian *national* consciousness,
his party has distinctly regional and ethnic appeals. It picks up most of
its votes in the prairie and Western provinces. In 1992 Reform Party candidates won large pluralities in both these areas. The Reform Party has
also gained a stronghold in the British Protestant Canadian East, most
conspicuously around Uxbridge, Colburg, Newmarket, and Belleville.
There and elsewhere in Eastern Ontario, Manning's Anglophone Canadian nationalism enjoys exuberant support.[87] His party has opposed not
only Quebec-secessionism but the linguistic disabilities imposed on Quebec's Anglophone population by the ruling Parti Québecois. Manning
has thereby merged federalism and regionalism with British cultural
identity, though it is difficult to foresee what kind of change to the Canadian political structure he and his party would introduce once in power.

While it is not being argued that populism as a postliberal democratic
force can only prevail by avoiding divisive moral issues, this may be increasingly true of North American Anglophone societies. Without control of public administration, social programs, and the media, populists
must pick their issues with exceeding care. They will have to focus on
what is inoffensive to late modernist sensibilities but also on what captures electorates that fear violence and relative deprivation. Those whom
populists must attract belong to a Hobbesian world: driven by the quest
for commodity and the fear of violence, these electorates are capable of,
at most, provisional allegiances. They follow those who dispel their fears
and who convincingly promise to satisfy material needs.

But the convenient state that has resulted from this disposition and
from the ability of some to exploit it has at times acted imprudently. It
has tried to do what it should not, at the cost of its real but modest
mandate. The political class has forgotten that its subjects will serve it and
its court religion to whatever extent it goes on feeding and protecting. As
in Hobbes's Leviathan, though subjects are materially driven and fear-
obsessed, their loyalty is not unconditional. It is only there when their
needs are being met—or, more precisely, when people believe this is
happening. Fearful subjects have given up liberty for security, but they
may regret this choice if the sovereign loses their respect. This Hobbesian understanding of the nature and limits of authority goes back to the
dawn of modern political thought, and it throws light on the populist
insurgency that now confronts the managerial state.

✳ *Conclusion* ✳

THE PRECEDING study has been an exercise in what the sociologist Robert Merton called "specified ignorance."[1] No attempt has been made to chart any supposedly inevitable future for the managerial state. Nowhere is it claimed that this regime is collapsing or that existing opposition to it will succeed in changing its structure significantly. The arbitrary definitions of liberalism and an intrusive pluralism notwithstanding, the Western managerial state and its defenders may well survive their encounters with populist challengers. As long as public administration is viewed as a material provider, its subjects may continue to acquiesce in its control of social matters. One should not mistake intellectual arrogance or a vulnerable ideology for political weakness.

All that is being contended is that the current dispensation is under attack because of the gap between its democratic and liberal self-description and its imposed social policies. The efforts to justify these policies with archaic terminology or human rights rhetoric no longer elicit widespread belief. A populist resistance in Europe and to a lesser extent in North America, moreover, may indicate that liberal democracy as a concept and public administration as its practice are in trouble. But being in trouble is different from being mortally ill or about to be superseded. It is a political stage comparable to the "paradigm crisis" that Thomas Kuhn discusses in his history of science. The conceptual challenge posed to a particular cosmology may render it less and less credible and eventually precipitate a crisis in thought. But this will not necessarily lead to a new cosmology. Other conditions must exist for that to happen, most particularly the formulation of an acceptable new paradigm.[2]

To some, my observations about liberal democracy may seem captious. It may be objected that I do not appreciate the quest for social equality and a nondiscriminatory society undertaken by liberal democratic pluralist administrations. To this there are several possible rejoinders. First, I myself have not seen the evidence of an improved moral climate in my own profession. Universities today are less intellectually tolerant than when I entered college in 1959, and the advocates of openness and of governmental policies to promote openness in American education have, from where I stand, contributed heavily to that result.[3]

Second, my own bourgeois modernist sympathies, which are easy to guess, have not led me into self-delusion. I do not perceive any possibility of moving backward historically, a point repeatedly stated in this study. Lacking are the social presuppositions and political will for such a restoration or even for a mere approximation of one. The Whiggish liberalism of the nineteenth century, which stressed individual moral responsibility in a politically unreconstructed social space, operated with the aid of ascribed statuses. The values that liberalism exalted did not float in a vacuum but were closely related to gender and social ranks in a still partly aristocratic world. Manners and constraints were dictated by the demands of gentlemanly and ladylike behavior, and religion, particularly Protestantism, played a continuing role in shaping bourgeois character. These by now commonplace observations must be kept in mind to understand the difficulty of returning to the moral world of high liberalism from a postbourgeois managerial society. One simply cannot recreate the cultural benefits of the past, as one might its architecture or cuisine, through public projects or ad hoc committees. Values-education in schools may have positive or negative effects, depending on the critic's perspective, but is not likely to yield nineteenth-century ladies or gentlemen. Indeed, it is questionable whether value-traditionalists who speak of a decline in public morals desire to go back in any meaningful sense to the past. Rather, they seem interested in controlling predominantly underclass pathologies, such as teenage pregnancies, and getting adolescent boys to behave less riotously.

Third, those who may protest the acidic tone of my arguments should look more closely at the claims being made on the other side. Contemporary liberals are not applying old liberal doctrines by punishing homophobes and sexists or by trying to rearrange the income curve. They are pushing policies that cannot be traced to the bourgeois order that mass democracy and the managerial state helped to dislodge. Liberal-pluralist democrats may like their own politics better than the one embraced by an earlier generation of liberals. But their views and goals are different, and sometimes not even congruent, with what that generation understood as the social Good.

In a revealing but neglected essay for the *New Republic* in 1955, Deweyite Arthur Bestor admitted a great deal about the planning that he and his colleagues had done twenty years earlier. The philosophical approaches they had adopted, according to Bestor, were "social acids" intended to break down inherited belief systems: "The alliance between pragmation and liberalism was a fortuitous one, called forth by a particular historic situation. Pragmatism constituted in essence [a] sacred act of intellectual spoliation."[4] But it soon became apparent to Bestor and to other liberals that a pragmatism combining experimental methods with value-relativism is only a "dissolvant." It does not teach enough that is positive and betrays a "fundamental inadequacy" when applied to fighting fascism. It is therefore necessary to propagate a militant democratic religion through public education, an ambitious policy that Bestor and others pursued vigorously thereafter.

Fourth, despite my critical comments about its hypocrisies, my study treats respectfully the managerial state as an instrument of power. By now the managerial state may be comparable to what the sovereign state was in the time of Thomas Hobbes: an overshadowing presence that has forged its own forms of human association. It is also ringed with its own priesthood, which calls for the further consigning of social activities to administrative judgment. These extended reflections on the managerial regime draw upon the work on the sovereign state by Carl Schmitt (1888–1985). A legal theorist who studied the European state system, Schmitt regarded this arrangement as a unique and singularly effective source of international order. Out of an alliance of national sovereigns and enterprising jurists, Schmitt traced the conception of the nation-state, an entity monopolizing force within its own borders while engaging outside of them in diplomatic and military encounters.

Schmitt believed that intense conflict defined "the political," and the state that developed in early modern Europe had both channeled and subdued human contentiousness.[5] Through its monopoly of force and control of religious struggles, the sovereign state was able to minimize discord within its own frontiers. It turned violence, in the form of standing armies, against neighboring states with which it had territorial disputes. But these armed conflicts were limited to military encounters that only minimally affected civilians. An international protocol was worked out in the eighteenth century that provided for the management of what Emmerich de Vattel, the Swiss jurist, called "la guerre en forme." In Vattel's *Le droit des gens* (1758), Schmitt found a delineation of how the European state system worked, or at least was supposed to. Vattel makes no moral judgment about war; he simply lays out the legal procedure that sovereign states should follow in beginning and ending it. Vattel assumed that armed conflicts would culminate in diplomatic negotiations. They would not be fueled by religious or ideological passions and would leave the belligerents with the same governments as they had had before.

Schmitt listed reasons in his magnum opus, *Nomos der Ende im Völker-recht des ius publicum europaeum* (1950), why such a European order went from operating sporadically to breaking down. A politics of passion became increasingly prevalent from the French Revolution on, and by the nineteenth century Jacobinism nationalism and, finally, revolutionary socialism were significant political forces. Together with these destabilizing ideologies, technology also contributed to the undoing of an order of territorial states. Naval blockades, combat, and long-range weaponry made it difficult to spare civilians in warfare. They also made it hard to structure international relations around the discrete territorial units that had existed in the eighteenth century. Then too, modern nations, starting with revolutionary France, preferred total conflicts to old-fashioned orchestrated ones. These national struggles were typically fought under the banner of global ideals, and according to Schmitt, ideologically driven conscripted armies tended more and more to demonize their targets. Those who resisted the ideal embodied by one's nation were no longer viewed as human in thinking or in fact. Whence the uniquely savage character of twentieth-century warfare, which combines large armies and advanced technology with calls for total war.[6]

Faced by the breakdown of the European system of nation states and by the American-Soviet "bipolarity" during the Cold War, Schmitt raised the question of whether a new political order would take the place of the decayed *ius publicum europaeum*. His own quest for the glimpse of one led to speculation about the possibility of a world divided into spheres and controlled by regional powers.[7] Schmitt believed that American influence in the Western Hemisphere and postwar moves toward consolidating Europe economically and militarily were pointing in that direction. He did not foresee entirely, however, the liberal democratic managerial hegemony that reached full development in the postwar years and is now identified with "the end of history."[8] Under the rallying cry "free markets and democracy," American journalists and American politicians of almost all stripes call for renewed missionary efforts on behalf of the American model. This mission to redeem the unconverted has been realized more thoroughly than even its partisans may recognize. In North America, Western Europe, and Australasia, the managerial pluralist democracy discussed in this book remains dominant, even in the face of populist opposition. Supporters of this regime hope to maintain control by applying material incentives and, occasionally, political threats. And though the abuses to which "human rights" advocates react are sometimes brutal, the arguments made for an American mission of rights throughout the world are also open-ended. They can be and have been invoked to promote the privileged rights of journalists and other intellectuals, for whom Western governments have not been sufficiently moral. The morality in question is that of the advocate but rarely deviates from the expansionist interests of the managerial state.

In Western Europe and North America, this state rests its power upon a multitiered following: an underclass and now middle-class welfariate, a self-assertive public sector, and a vanguard of media and journalistic public defenders. Upon the basis of this following, the regime and its apologists have been able to marginalize their opposition. This is apparent on, among other places, the now respectable or moderate Right. There a tolerated opposition offers tepid criticism of the administrative state while warning against populist extremism. The religious Right does not oppose the administrative state, but hopes to have it implement "family values." What remains of an older Right, of mostly Catholic and Anglo-Catholic traditionalists, has even lost interest in the political causes for cultural changes. It has produced a vast literature on the spiritual and aesthetic crisis that has accompanied mass democracy, but treats the managerial state as incidental to a declining "moral imagination." Those in this group who notice structures of power usually break ranks after being scolded as "naturalists."[9] Unlike neoconservatives, who talk about politics as reflecting culture and imagine that both are correctable through social policy, the old Right confines its political discourse to the "state of the soul" and the corruption of imagination. At the same time, administrative democracy no longer faces a hostile Left of a kind that once treated political administration as an ally of corporate capitalism. Today's intellectual Left turns to public administrators in order to wage war on prejudice. Gay and gender issues and black and Hispanic self-esteem have replaced that focus on economic and political structures typical of the best leftist thought developed a generation ago. If the American intellectual Right has abandoned James Burnham and Robert Nisbet for William Bennett's *Book of Virtues*, the intellectual Left has declined even more precipitously, moving from the structural and cultural analysis of C. Wright Mills, Christopher Lasch, and Eugene Genovese to rote invectives against gender and homophobic insensitivity.[10]

Different kinds of ends may be upon us, an end of history or the "end of ideology" that social democrats of the 1960s maintained was then taking place. Less certain is whether any of these predicted ends will favor recognizable self-government or nonauthorized political debate. A managed therapeutic politics will not likely engender either of these conditions. Still, there is no reason to assume that such controls will prove intolerable. People may soon forget older liberal and democratic legacies in a thoroughly administered society that brings material security together with the assurance of psychic normality. This social planning will also attract the idealistic, at least those interested in combating newly discovered prejudice and instilling sensitive behavior. Moral crusades will not be lacking in such an arranged therapeutic future.

The consolidation of the managerial state and the imposition of its pluralist ideology have been the defining features of contemporary Western life. These trends may continue into the distant future and result in a more solidified international managerial order. But that order may confront obstacles, now only partly glimpsed, that will bring about disintegration and ultimately contribute to a new political configuration. Decentralizing, populist protest movements may yet overtake pluralist administration and undo the work of generations of social planners. If that happens, as unlikely as it now seems, Schmitt's quest for a political order to replace the Western system of nation states will reemerge as an unfinished task.

Whatever the future holds, Schmitt has been right in at least two of his interpretive assumptions. One is that liberalism and democracy belong to different epochs, one to the nineteenth century and the other to the twentieth. The putative merging of these ideas and movements into "liberal democracy" has brought forth not a true refinement of democratic practice but a garbling of political concepts. Once historically decontextualized, the terms "liberal" and "democratic" have surrendered a fixed conceptual meaning and any clear relation to what they signified a century ago.

Another Schmittian lesson that this book has tried to demonstrate is the recurrent "primacy of the political." We have looked at questions of power and the role of political elites in determining friends and enemies within the framework of the managerial state. This study has stressed the point that this regime, more than its liberal predecessor, requires the downplaying of genuine political differences. Predictably, its actors and defenders have ascribed unwelcome dissent to psychic abnormality or to scientific imprecision. In any case those who rule have not abandoned the practice of restricting disagreeable speech but are carrying it forward in the name of openness and combatting discrimination. Meanwhile, the administrative regime renders obsolete any attempt to draw lines between consensual and imposed authorities. Governing goes on in a blurred zone, between consent and nonaccountable control.[11] Unlike the Communist garrison-state or the Italian fascist "total state," the managerial state succeeds by denying that it exercises power.[12] Most fully developed in Northern Europe and North America, lands traditionally celebrating bourgeois liberties and Protestant individuality, managerial rule has consistently presented itself as collectively administered assistance. Rhetorically and propagandistically, it has been the helpmate of individuals set adrift in the industrial world, and administrators have claimed to enjoy "democratic" support because they have updated liberalism and infused it with social concern.

Behind this rhetoric, however, it is possible to discern other far-reaching projects, some of which this book has outlined. All of them have pertained to a specific form of rule and combined a public charge with generally ill-defined but expanding control. The administrative state, as it advances into its therapeutic phase, has refused to recognize its coercive reach or whatever advantages have accrued to it from those tasks it has gladly assumed. By concealing its operation in the language of caring, it has blinded us to the truths enunciated by Cicero, Hobbes, Weber, Schmitt and other past political analysts. *Potestas*, as Cicero explained, is given to increase one's dignity; it allows one to punish wrongdoers and to exercise magisterial authority, while becoming a means for preserving and securing a greater sufficiency of its own resources *(ad sua conservanda et alterius obtinenda idonearum rerum facultas)*.

Whether one takes these definitions or Hobbes's view that power is the means "to obtain some future apparent good," a discussion of government should be about control and the instruments available to its practitioners. It is understandable that the managerial state and its exponents should avoid discussing these themes in their formulations of social policy. The uninterrupted exercise of its power may depend upon not talking plainly about such unclean matters.[13] Yet, it is worth the effort to look beyond euphemism to see how political power is exercised. Behind the mission to sensitize and teach "human rights" lies the largely unacknowledged right to shape and reshape people's lives. Any serious appraisal of the managerial regime must consider first and foremost the extent of its control—and the relative powerlessness of its critics.

* *Notes* *

INTRODUCTION

1. *Gallup Poll Monthly* 367 (Spring 1996), 7–9; ibid., 368 (May 1996), 2–6.

2. Charles Krauthammer, "Don't Bail Out Clinton on Medicare!" syndicated in *Washington Post*, November 8, 1996, A2S.

3. *Gallup Poll Monthly* (April 1996), 7.

4. See Paul Craig Roberts, "Don't Look Now but the U.S. Ship Is Sinking," *Business Week*, November 1996, 22; and Jonathan Rauch's nonpartisan appeal to reduce budgets, "Self-inflicted Budget Woes," *U.S. News and World Report*, November 18, 1996, 94.

5. Maggie Gallagher, "It's Not Abortion, Stupid," syndicated in *New York Post*, November 8, 1996. Gallagher offers the entirely defensible view that the Republican appeal to "the self-sufficient man or woman" cannot attract socially isolated women; she shrewdly observes that "women voters hear the 'It takes a village' theme [of Hillary Clinton] not as a call to more government but as a call to community, unity, common ground." But what exactly can be done by opponents of big government to change this female tropism? For it is precisely "more government" and more intrusive government that women increasingly see as evidence of "community." Gallagher proves this point when she cites the reservations among women in regard to Republican plans to finance alternatives to public schools, now viewed as "the last remaining hub of vivid community life." Whatever the merits of this position, it does indicate, according to Gallagher, that women generally oppose any movement toward the privatization of education.

6. Mary Ann Glendon, *First Things* 69 (January 1997), 23. For a provocative attempt to contextualize the sensuous, materialist ethos of mass democracy at the end of the Cold War, see Panajotis Kondylis, "Marxismus, Kommunismus und die Geschichte des 20. Jahrhunderts," in *Der Marxismus in seinem Zeitalter* (Leipzig: Reclam Verlag, 1994), 14–36; and by the same author, "Die Antiquiertheit der politischen Begriffe," *Frankfurter Allgemeine Zeitung*, October 5, 1991; ibid., "Globale Mobilmachung," July 13, 1996.

7. Sigmund Knag, "The Almighty, Omnipotent State," *The Independent Review* 1, no. 3 (Winter 1997), 407–08; See also Robert A. Dahl and Edward Tufte, *Size and Democracy* (Stanford: Stanford University Press, 1973); Thomas Molnar, *Le Modèle défiguré, l'Amérique de Tocqueville à Carter* (Paris: Presses Universitaires de France, 1978); and by the same author, *L'hégémonie libérale* (Paris: L'Âge d'Homme, 1992). Needless to say, the view of the American government as a zone of combat among "neofeudal" interests is popular among European tradi-

tionalists for different reasons from those that recommend it to American social engineers. One group is looking back to the European confessional state; the other is looking forward to a thoroughly managed democracy which is still being created.

8. For a confident statement of the triumph of the liberal tradition throughout the current political spectrum, from the socialist Left to the free-market Right, see *The Economist*, December 21, 1996, 17–19.

CHAPTER ONE

1. Karl Loewenstein, "Militant Democracy and Fundamental Rights," *American Political Science Review* 31 (June 1937), 417–32; ibid. (August 1937), 638–58; and David Reisman, "Democracy and Dissent," *Columbia Law Review* 42 (1942), 729–80.

2. R. Alan Lawson, *The Failure of Independent Liberalism, 1930–1941* (New York: Putnam, 1971), especially 155–68; and Gary Bullert's angry but illuminating analysis of the value question in Dewey and his school, *The Politics of John Dewey* (Buffalo: Prometheus Books, 1983).

3. This subject is incisively treated in Christopher Lasch's *The True and Only Heaven: Progress and Its Critics* (New York: W. W. Norton, 1991), 430–50; also T. L. Haskell, *The Emergence of Professional Social Sciences* (Urbana: University of Illinois Press, 1977); and B. Sicherman, *The Quest for Mental Health in America 1880–1917* (New York: Arno Press, 1980).

4. *New Republic*, October 31, 1994, 4–6; see also Richard Herrnstein and Charles Murray, *The Bell Curve: Intelligence and Class Structure in American Life* (New York: Free Press, 1994).

5. *New Republic*, October 31, 1994, 25. According to Lind, "The crypto-nativist rationale for restricting high levels of immigration can only be strengthened by the fact that scholars as esteemed as Murray and Herrnstein fret over the danger posed by an immigrant population with low cognitive abilities. Not only must low I.Q. immigrants be kept out, according to Herrnstein, but low I.Q. native born Americans must be kept from reproducing." Moreover, "though the authors of *The Bell Curve* refuse to endorse eugenic measures . . . , the logic of their arguments points in the direction of sterilization." Since Murray and Herrnstein deny explicitly and repeatedly the moral and political wisdom of governmental policies of sterilization, Lind must rely on incriminating phrases about where the "logic of their arguments points." Having read this work myself, I find nothing there pointing in the ominous direction suggested by Lind.

6. Ibid.,18.

7. Ibid., 15–16.

8. Stephen Holmes, *The Anatomy of Antiliberalism* (Cambridge: Harvard University Press, 1993), xiv; also by the same author, "The Politics of Restoration," *The Economist*, December 24, 1994, 33–36.

9. Guido Ruggiero, *History of European Liberalism* trans. R. C. Collingwood (Boston: Beacon Press, 1959), especially 142 and 443 for Ruggiero's expressions of concern about the antiliberal tendencies of the modern democratic state.

10. Holmes, *Anatomy of Antiliberalism*, 238–39.

11. For characteristic statements of Locke's interest in property rights, see his *Two Treatises of Government*, ed. Peter Laslett (New York: Cambridge University Press, 1963), 286, 309, 347–348. Chapter 7, section 94 of the *Second Treatise* indicates that "Government has no other end but the preservation of property" (ibid., 347).

12. Holmes, *Anatomy of Antiliberalism*, 240. Holmes infers from Locke's refusal to grant an "hereditary privilege" to any member of the commonwealth as against any other a general "norm of equality" and a commitment to "universal education" and "universal suffrage." This inference is certainly open to question, seeing that Holmes's point of reference is Locke's defense of equal obligation among citizens of civil society. Locke neither universalizes citizenship nor makes an argument for political equality for everyone who resides in a particular territory.

13. This limitation on citizenship in Locke's conception of the social contract is well stated in Peter H. Schuck and Roger M. Smith, *Citizenship Without Consent* (New Haven: Yale University Press, 1985); also Paul Gottfried, "Anatomy of an Apology," *Telos* 97 (Fall 1993), 5–8.

14. J. Salwyn Schapiro, *Liberalism: Its Meaning and History* (Princeton: Van Nostrand, 1958), 4–6.

15. Norman Gash, *Aristocracy and People: Britain 1815–1865* (Cambridge: Harvard University Press, 1979).

16. Ludwig von Mises, *Die Gemeinwirtschaft. Untersuchungen über den Sozialismus* (1932; reprint, Munich: Philosophia Verlag, 1981), 473.

17. Ludwig von Mises, *Liberalismus* (Sankt Augustin: Akademia Verlag, 1993). See Hans-Hermann Hoppe's illuminating biography of Mises in the preface.

18. Ruggiero, *European Liberalism*, 442.

19. Ibid., 143–44.

20. Friedrich von Hayek, *The Road to Serfdom* (Chicago: University of Chicago Press, 1944), 12–14; also Hayek's article, "Tomorrow's World: Is It Going Left?" *New York Times Magazine*, June 24, 1945, 12.

21. *Hayek, Road to Serfdom*, 70–71.

22. See, for example, Ludwig von Mises, *Bureaucracy* (New Haven: Yale University Press, 1944).

23. Hermann Finer, *The Road to Reaction*, second edition (Chicago: Quadrangle Books, 1963), 114. Two historical errors in Finer's work are particularly glaring. On page 115 he confuses the recent mode of interpreting the Bill of Rights with its original reasons for existence.Thus he asserts that, contrary to the attempts of classical liberals to use a federal system to limit sovereignty in the United States, "it was the Bill of Rights that curbed the majority." In its origin and

well into the twentieth century, the Bill of Rights was seen as a bulwark against the expansion of national power at the expense of the states and their citizens. Finer also assumes that the social programs passed in Bismarckian Germany were intended to prepare the Germans for war. Almost all accounts known to this author attribute these programs to Bismarck's hope of neutralizing German socialism by having the Reichstag introduce social pensions. This action had nothing to do with militarism.

24. Ibid., 115.

25. Ibid., 37.

26. Ibid., 29.

27. George Dangerfield, *The Strange Death of Liberal England, 1910–1914* (New York: Capricorn Books, 1935), viii.

28. L. T. Hobhouse, *Liberalism*, ed. Alan P. Grimes (reprint, Oxford: Oxford University Press, 1971); also by the same author, *The Labour Movement* (reprint, New York: Macmillan, 1987).

29. This is the boldly stated and cogently developed argument of Arthur A. Ekirch Jr. in *Ideologies and Utopias: The Impact of the New Deal on American Thought* (Chicago: Quadrangle Books, 1969); also James Gilbert, *Designing the Industrial State: The Intellectual Pursuit of Collectivism in America, 1880–1940* (Chicago: Quadrangle Books, 1972).

30. Ekirch, *Ideologies and Utopias*, 327–40.

31. Ibid., 327.

32. John Dewey, "The Future of Liberalism," *Journal of Philosophy* 32 (April 1935), 230.

33. John Dewey, *A Common Faith* (New Haven: Yale University Press, 1934), 72–73.

34. Lewis Mumford, *Faith for Living* (New York: Harcourt, Brace, & Co., 1940), 330.

35. Ibid., 327.

36. Charles Austin Beard and Mary Beard, *The Rise of American Civilization* (New York: Macmillan, 1930); and Henry Steele Commager, *The American Mind* (New Haven: Yale University Press, 1950), 303–05.

37. Despite Charles Beard's progressive politics and materialist interpretation of the American founding, his nationalism and his opposition to America's entry into the two World Wars gained for this onetime follower of Dewey a certain sympathy on the isolationist Right. See George H. Nash, *The Conservative Intellectual Movement in America Since 1945* (New York: Basic Books, 1976).

38. Arthur M. Schlesinger Jr., *The Vital Center: The Politics of Freedom* (reprint, New York: Da Capo Press, 1988).

39. J. K. Galbraith, *The Liberal Hour* (Boston: Houghton Mifflin, 1960).

40. See J. S. Mill, *Autobiography* (reprint, New York: Columbia University Press, 1960); and the symposium on Mill's "liberalism" in *Political Science Reviewer* 24 (1995).

41. This perception about the ongoing reconstruction of the past is stressed in John Lukacs's *Historical Consciousness* (New York: Random House, 1968).

42. Elie Halévy, *The Growth of Philosophic Radicalism*, trans. Mary Morris Clanden (London: Faber & Faber, 1934).

43. On the liberal internationalism of World War Two isolationists, see Justus D. Doenecke's introduction to the papers of the America First Committee in *In Danger Undaunted* (Stanford: Hoover Institution Press, 1989), 2–51; and Cordell Hull, *The Memoirs of Cordell Hull* (New York: Macmillan, 1948), 1729–42. In the conclusion to his memoirs, Hull warns specifically against the erection of trade barriers as a hindrance to international peace.

44. See Paul Gottfried, *The Conservative Movement*, second edition (New York: Twayne-Macmillan, 1993), 162–65.

45. On the attraction of imperialism for Fabian socialists and for others on the English Left, see Bernard Semmel, *Imperialism and Social Reform* (London: Ashgate Publishing Co., 1993); on the globalist impulse in postwar American liberalism, see John Ehrman, *The Rise of Neoconservatism: Intellectuals and Foreign Affairs* (New Haven: Yale University Press, 1995).

46. See Theodore J. Lowi, *The End of Liberalism: Ideology, Policy, and the Crisis of Public Authority* (New York: W. W. Norton, 1969), 2–3; also Carl Schmitt, *The Concept of the Political*, trans. and intro. by George Schwab (New Brunswick: Rutgers University Press, 1976), 35–36.

47. See *Exporting Democracy*, ed. A. F. Lowenthal (Baltimore: Johns Hopkins University Press, 1991), 234.

48. See Lester Frank Ward, *Applied Sociology: A Treatise on the Conscious Improvement of Society by Society* (reprint, New York: Ayer, 1974); and *Planned Social Intervention*, ed. Louis A. Zurcher Jr. and Charles M. Bonjean (London: Chandler Publishing Co., 1970).

49. Friedrich von Hayek, *The Counter Revolution of Science* (1955; reprint, Indianapolis: Liberty Press, 1980), 168–88.

50. Dewey, *A Common Faith*, 82.

51. Lowenstein, "Militant Democracy," 657.

52. Ibid., 658.

53. Alonzo L. Hamby, *Liberalism and its Challengers* (New York: Oxford University Press, 1985).

54. See, for example, Thomas Pangle, *The Spirit of Modern Republicanism: The Moral Vision of the American Founders and the Philosophy of Locke* (Chicago: University of Chicago Press, 1988).

55. Thomas Molnar, *Le Modèle défiguré: l'Amérique de Tocqueville à Carter* (Paris: Presses Universitaires de France, 1978).

56. Lionel Trilling, *The Liberal Imagination: Essays on Literature and Society* (New York: Harcourt-Brace, 1991); and Louis Hartz, *The Liberal Tradition in America: An Interpretation of American Political Thought since the Revolution* (New York: Harcourt-Brace, 1991).

57. Hans Blumenberg, *The Legitimacy of the Modern Age* (Cambridge, Mass.: MIT Press, 1983), particularly 94–104.

58. William Galston, *Liberal Purposes: Goods, Virtues and Diversity in the Liberal State* (New York: Cambridge University Press, 1991), 304.

59. Ibid., 4–18.

60. John Rawls, *A Theory of Justice* (Cambridge, Mass.: Harvard University Press, 1971), 141.

61. Ibid., 60.

62. Ibid., 76–78.

63. Galston, *Liberal Purposes,* 272–73; also my review of *Liberal Purposes* in *Review of Metaphysics* 46 (September 1992), 153.

64. This remark comes from John Gray's review of Rawls's *Political Liberalism* in the *New York Times Book Review,* May 16, 1993, 35.

65. Rawls, *Theory of Justice,* 78, 102–112; Mises anticipates Rawls's argument in *Die Gemeinwirtschaft,* 432–35, by defending a capitalist economic organization as beneficial to the least favored. See also Léon Walras, *Elements of Pure Economics,* trans. William Jaffé (Homewood, Ill.: American Economic Association, 1954), 51–64.

66. Rawls, *A Theory of Justice,* 79.

67. Finer, *Road to Reaction,* 52–60.

68. Ibid., 38.

69. Friedrich von Hayek, *The Constitution of Liberty* (Chicago: University of Chicago Press, 1960), 248, 148, and 489.

70. Mises, *Liberalismus,* 35; and Gottfried Dietze, *Liberalism Proper and Proper Liberalism* (Baltimore: Johns Hopkins University Press, 1985).

71. Mises, *Liberalismus,* 36.

72. In *Bureaucracy* and in *Omnipotent Covenant: The Rise of the Total State and Total War* (New Haven: Yale University Press, 1944), Mises treats public administration as either a pernicious legacy from the preliberal past (as in the Prussian case) or an accompanying feature of otherwise different regimes. Unlike Max Weber and James Burnham, he seems to have been unaware of the political revolutionary character of modern administration. Except for his remarks about Prussia, Mises usually speaks kindly about *Berufsbeamte.*

73. Detailed figures on the growth of the English public sector are available in R. Rose's anthology *Public Employment in Western Nations (Cambridge: Cambridge University Press, 1985).* Table 2.12, compiled by Richard Parry, indicates that already ten years ago 56 percent of British disposable income came out of public sources.

74. Michael Novak, *The Spirit of Democratic Capitalism* (New York: Simon & Schuster, 1982), particularly 111–13, 253. One of Novak's favorite synthetic terms is "social welfare democratic capitalism," a concept whose problematic nature he fails to engage.

75. See Novak's remarks in his own publication, *Religion and Liberty* (January/February 1991), 6.

76. John Lukacs, "The Stirrings of History," *Harper's* 281 (August 1990), 48.

77. John Lukacs, *The End of the Twentieth Century and the End of the Modern Age* (New York: Ticknor & Fields, 1993), especially 6–9, 242–71.

78. *Nation*, April 6, 1927, 364.

CHAPTER TWO

1. James Fitzjames Stephen, *Liberty, Equality, Fraternity*, ed. Stuart D. Warner (Indianapolis: Liberty Classics, 1993), 156. For Weber's views on the growing relation between bureaucracy and modern democracy see *From Max Weber: Essays in Sociology*, ed. and trans. by Hans Gerth and C. Wright Mills (New York: Oxford University Press, 1958), 139; for Weber's suggestion in "Politics as Vocation" that modern democracy must choose between soulless officialdom and charismatic leadership, ibid., 113–114; and Max Weber, *Gesammelte Politische Schriften*, ed. Johannes Winklemann (Tübingen: J.C.B. Mohr, 1958), 532–33. For Joseph Schumpeter's arguments about the connections and differences betwen bourgeois liberalism and social democracy, see Joseph Schumpeter, "Sozialistische Möglichkeiten von heute," *Archiv für Sozialwissenschaft und Sozialpolitik* 48 (1922), 305–06; Francois Perroux, *La Pensée économique de Joseph Schumpeter: les dynamiques du capitalisme* (Geneva: Droz, 1965); and Schumpeter's study of the decline of bourgeois liberal society, *Capitalism, Socialism, and Democracy* (London: Unwin University Books, 1943), most particularly 81–87.

2. See Pierre Rosanvallon's intellectual biography of the famed liberal statesman, *Le Moment Guizot* (Paris: Gallimard, 1985), 75–86, 132–40.

3. Ibid., 95–104; and Guizot's address before the French Assembly on October 5, 1831, cited in *Histoire parlementaire de France: Recueil complet des discours prononcés dans les Chambres de 1819 à 1848 par Mr. Guizot* (Paris 1863–1864), 1: 316. Despite his reservations about popular rule, Guizot also praised France as "genuinely democratic" in ibid., 178. The statesman then went on to limit his definition of good democracy to the principle and operation of legal equality for French citizens.

4. William Lecky, *Democracy and Liberty* (reprint, Indianapolis: Liberty Press, 1981) 1: 303–04.

5. For a generally sympathetic, well-researched study of German socialism in English, see W. L. Guttsman, *The German Social Democratic Party 1875–1933* (London: Allen & Unwin, 1981).

6. Lecky, *Democracy and Liberty*, 1: 324. Also Donal McCartney, *W.E.H. Lecky: Historian and Politician 1839–1902* (Dublin: The Lilliput Press, 1994). A strength of McCartney's biography is his attempt to relate his subject's anxiety about democracy to Lecky's observation of Irish peasants and English factory workers. Lecky's upbringing in the British Ascendancy in Ireland contributed to his concern.

7. Panajotis Kondylis, *Der Niedergang der bürgerlichen Denk-und Lebensform. Die liberale Moderne und die massendemokratische Postmoderne* (Weinheim: Acta Humaniora, 1991), 188–207.

8. Ibid., 169–88.

9. Ibid., 238–67; See also Kondylis's analysis of the classical conservative, as opposed to classical liberal, worldview in *Konservatismus. Geschichtlicher Gehalt und Untergang* (Stuttgart: Klett, 1986).

10. See Hilton Kramer, *The Revenge of the Philistines: Art and Culture, 1972–1984* (New York: Free Press, 1985); also the anthologized essays from Kramer's magazine, *The New Criterion Reader: The First Five Years* (New York: Free Press, 1988).

11. Kondylis, *Der Niedergang der bürgerlichen Denk-und Lebensform,* 208–26.

12. See Albert Thibaudet's preface to Gustave Flaubert's *L'Education Sentimentale* (Paris: Gallimard, 1965). In one particularly revealing scene, following the February 1848 Revolution in Paris, Sénécal, Dussardier, and other republican zealots featured in Flaubert's novel exhort a crowd, without success, to accept lives of material austerity. One speaker, who speaks of the need to follow the primitive church, is shouted down by an alcohol vendor as a "calotin [religious fanatic]"; ibid., 323–33.

13. Quoted in *Washington Post,* September 9, 1995, A19.

14. Kondylis, *Der Niedergang der bürgerlichen Denk-und Lebensform,* 167–69.

15. Ibid., 21–49.

16. John Plamenatz, *Ideology* (London: Pall Mall Press, 1970), 21.

17. Rosanvallon, *Le Moment Guizot,* 53; and Robert Fossaert, "La Théorie des classes chez Guizot et Thierry," *La Pensée* (January/February 1955).

18. F. G. Bratton, *The Legacy of the Liberal Spirit* (Boston: Beacon Press, 1943), ix.

19. John Gray, *Liberalism* (Minneapolis: University of Minnesota Press, 1986), 2.

20. Paul A. Rahe, *Republics Ancient and Modern: Classical Republicanism and the American Revolution* (Chapel Hill: University of North Carolina Press, 1992); also my review essay on this book in *Modern Age* 37 (Spring 1995), 264–69; N. D. Fustel de Coulanges, *La Ville Antique* (Paris: Hachette, 1874), especially 131–265. Fustel notes (ibid., 238) that connubial restrictions were so severe in Greek city-states and in the early Roman republic that offspring were viewed as illegitimate if the parents were not from the same polity—or at least confederated ones. An Athenian law still in force as late as the fifth century B.C., and mentioned by Plutarch, declared that "nothos ho ek zenēs e pallakidos-hos an me eks astēs genētai nothon einai." One who sprang from a stranger or concubine was considered "nothegenēs [baseborn]."

21. Gray, *Liberalism,* xi.

22. Stephen, *Liberty, Equality, Fraternity,* 136; 137–164 passim.

23. Louis Dumont, *Essais sur L'individualisme* (Paris: Editions du Seuil, 1983), 33–133.

24. Ibid., also his *Homo aequalis, I: Genèse et épanouissement de l'idéologie économique* (Paris: Gallimand, 1977).

25. This tendency to overgeneralize about the Reformation roots of what seem aspects of late modernity is already present in Dumont's depiction of John Calvin; see *Essais sur l'individualisme,* 72–80. Dumont's association of individual self-sufficiency and a revolution against established hierarchy with Calvin's conception of predestined grace also bears a striking resemblance to French clericalist polemics against Protestant modernity. This theme dominates, for example, Jacques Maritain's *Trois Réformateurs: Luther, Descartes, Rousseau* (Paris: Plon-Nourrit, 1925), a work that also draws a provocative but not well-documented line from the Reformation to modern individualism.

26. Gertrude Himmelfarb, *The Idea of Poverty: England in the Early Industrial Age* (New York: Knopf, 1984).

27. James T. Kloppenberg: *Uncertain Victory: Social Democracy and Progressivism in European and American Thought, 1870–1920* (New York: Oxford University Press, 1986), 389.

28. Ibid., 387–88; also Walter Struve, *Elites Against Democracy: Leadership Ideals in Bourgeois Political Thought in Germany, 1890–1933* (Princeton: Princeton University Press, 1973).

29. See especially Lecky, *Democracy and Liberty,* 1: 350–65.

30. Stephen, *Liberty, Equality, Fraternity,* 156.

31. Lecky, *Democracy and Liberty,* 1:303.

32. Stephen, *Liberty, Equality, Fraternity,* 180; also B. E. Lippincott, *Victorian Critics of Democracy* (Minneapolis: University of Minnesota Press, 1938).

33. François Guizot, "De la démocratie dans les sociétés modernes," *Revue française* 3 (November 1937), 197–208; for a general discussion of the American political example as presented by Tocqueville on the French doctrinaires, see Pierre Manet, *Intellectual History of Liberalism,* trans. Rebecca Balinski (Princeton: Princeton University Press, 1994), 93–106.

34. Guizot, "De la démocratie," 197.

35. Two favorable biographical portraits are R. B. Nye, *George Bancroft* (New York: Knopf, 1944); and Lilian Handlin, *George Bancroft: The Intellectual as Democrat* (New York: Harper & Row, 1984).

36. George Bancroft, *History of the Formation of the Constitution of the United States* (New York: D. Appleton & Co., 1882), 2:366.

37. Ibid.

38. Alexis de Tocqueville, *Democracy in America,* trans. Henry Reeve (New York: Knopf, 1966), 2:31–32.

39. George Bancroft, *History of the United States* (Boston: Little, Brown, & Co., 1872), 10:592.

40. The debate about extending the suffrage in early and mid-nineteenth-century Europe centered on differing opinions concerning the political capacity of the working class and the advance of human consciousness. Without know-

ingly being part of that debate, Bancroft took a position in regard to it. Moreover, in Europe such democratizing views were associated generally with political centralization and eventually, with the adoption of social policy. See Jacques Droz, *Réaction et suffrage universel en France et en Allemagne* (Paris: Société d'histoire de la révolution de 1848, 1963). Rosanvallon aptly notes in *Le Moment Guizot* that a democratic franchise was seen in the mid-nineteenth century as an "anticipated recognition of a popular capacity more than as a consequence of the principle of civil equality" (136–37). Underlying it was the anticipation of continued human progress, which would result from an expanding human intelligence.

41. Gray, conversation with the author, June 25, 1993; also Herbert W. Schneider, *Making the Fascist State* (New York: Oxford University Press, 1928), 101–3; and Franz Borkenau, *Pareto* (New York: John Wiley & Sons, 1936), 18–21.

42. Luigi Einaudi, *La condotta economica e gli effetti sociali della guerra italiana* (Bari: Laterza, 1933); and Renzo De Felice, *Mussolini* (Turin: Einaudi, 1965), especially 1:419–544.

43. Vilfredo Pareto, *Le trasformazioni della democrazia*, ed. Mario Missiroli (Milan: Capelli Editore, 1964), 111–12.

44. Ibid., 113.

45. Ibid., 162.

46. Ibid., 169–70.

47. See Missiroli's preface to *Le trasformazioni*, 9–31; W. Rex Crawford, "Representative Italian Contributions to Sociology: Pareto, Loria, Vaccaro, and Sichele," in *An Introduction to the History of Sociology*, ed. H. E. Barnes (Chicago: University of Chicago Press, 1948); and Paolo Maria Arcani, *Socialismo e democrazia nel pensiero di Vifredo Pareto* (Rome: Volipe, 1966).

48. The *Trattato* was translated as *The Mind and Society: A Treatise on General Sociology* by Andrew Bongiorno and Arthur Livingston in 1935. See reprint (New York: AMS Press, 1983), especially 2458–72.

49. These last two written works by Pareto are attached to Missiroli's edition of *Le trasformazioni*, 161–73. It should be stressed that we are here dealing with *Pareto's* view of Italian fascism. Though Renzo De Felice may be right in treating the Italian fascist movement as a modernizing force associated with the historical Left, Pareto perceived it differently, namely, as a possible safeguard for the achievements of bourgeois civilization. See De Felice's by now widely accepted view of the Italian fascist movement in *Interpretations of Fascism*, trans. Brenda Huff Everett (Cambridge: Harvard University Press, 1977).

50. Pareto, *Le trasformazioni*, 109.

51. Charles Krauthammer, "Jones Beach and the Decline of Liberalism," *Time*, September 5, 1994, 82.

52. Maurice Cowling, *Mill and Liberalism* (Cambridge: Cambridge University Press, 1963), 87–88; and J. S. Mill, *Three Essays on Religion* (reprint, New York: Aris Press, 1995), 110.

53. Cowling insists that Mill's conviction, as stated in *Utilitarianism,* that general happiness can best be advanced by making everyone rational and free of religious prejudice, undergirds his entire ethic. See Cowling, *Mill and Liberalism,* 52–53; and Mill's *Utilitarianism* (reprint, New York: American Classical College Press, 1988), 192–93.

54. Cowling, *Mill and Liberalism,* 145.

55. Two of Weber's extended observations on the need for plebiscitary authority in modern democracy to circumvent bureaucratic tyranny are found in *Economy and Society,* ed. Guenther Roth and Claus Wittich, trans. Ephraim Fischoll (reprint, Berkeley: University of California Press, 1978), 1:268–69; and in Marianne Weber, *Max Weber: A Biography,* trans. Harry Lohn (New York: John Wiley & Sons, 1975), 653.

56. Quoted in Wolfgang Mommsen, *The Age of Bureaucracy: Perspectives on the Political Sociology of Max Weber* (New York: Harper & Row, 1974), 87.

57. Max Weber, "Speech for Austrian Officers in Vienna," *The Interpretation of Social Reality,* ed. J.E.T. Eldridge (New York: Scribner's, 1971), 197. See also Roslyn Wallach Bologh, "Max Weber and the Dilemma of Nationality," in *Max Weber's Political Sociology,* ed. Ronald M. Glassman and Vatro Murvar (Westport, Conn.: Greenwood Press, 1984), 175–86.

CHAPTER THREE

1. On the connection between the new monarchies and the *novi homines,* see Wallace Ferguson, "Toward the Modern State," in *The Renaissance* (New York: Harper & Row, 1953), 1–27; Arnaud d'Herbomez, "Le fonctionarisme en France à la fin du moyen âge," *Revue des questions historiques,* 85 (1903); and Gianfranco Miglio's informative essay on the early modern foundations of the bureaucratic nation state, "Genesi e trasformazioni del termine-concetto 'stato,' " included in Miglio's *Le regolarità della politica* (Milan: Giuffrè Editore, 1988), 2: 799–832.

2. Alexis de Tocqueville, *The Old Regime and the French Revolution,* trans. Stuart Gilbert (Garden City: Doubleday, 1955), particularly 32–87.

3. G.W.F. Hegel, *Werke in zwanzig Bänden,* vol. 7 (Frankfurt: Suhrkamp, 1970), sections 310, 473.

4. Rosanvallon, *Le Moment Guizot,* 124–31; reasons for the opposition from the democratic Left to the enfranchisement of French public officials in 1831 are given in Odilen Barrot's *Mémoires* (Paris: Plon, 1875), 1:252–57.

5. James Burnham, *The Managerial Revolution* (reprint, Westport, Conn.: Greenwood Press, 1972); and Samuel T. Francis's unfairly neglected monograph on Burnham, *Power and History: The Political Thought of James Burnham* (Lanham, Md.: University Press of America, 1984).

6. See John P. Diggins, *Mussolini and Fascism: The View from America* (Princeton: Princeton University Press, 1972); and John Lukacs, *The Last European War, September 1939/December 1941* (Garden City: Anchor Press, 1976).

7. See Arnold J. Heidenheimer, ed., *Comparative Public Policy*, second edition (New York: St. Martin's Press, 1983), 176–81. On the difficulty of funding continental welfare states *à coups de déplafonnements*, by steadily raising the ceiling on payments for social programs, see A. Joubert, "L'assiette des cotisations sociales," *Droit social* (June 1993); the contributions to the theme "La crise du financement du régime général," *Espace social européen*, April 9, 1993; and Pierre Rosanvallon, *La crise de l'état-providence* (Paris: Seuil, 1981).

8. Karl Hardach, *Political Economy of Germany in the Twentieth Century* (Berkeley: Unviersity of California Press, 1980); and Eric Owen Smith, *Third Party Involvement in Industrial Disputes: A Comparative Study of West Germany and Britain* (Brookfield, Vt.: Ashgate, 1989).

9. Richard Rose, *Politics in England*, fifth edition (Boston: Little, Brown & Co., 1989), 8–19; idem, *The Emergence of the Welfare State in Britain and Germany*, ed. W. J. Mommsen (London: Croom-Helm, 1981), particularly 343–83; and Hugh Heclo, *Modern Social Politics in Britain and Sweden* (New Haven: Yale University Press, 1974), 141–47, 254–72.

10. On the personal and political ties between Macmillan and Wilson, see Leslie Smith's biography *Harold Wilson* (New York: Charles Scribner's Sons, 1964), especially 75–76; and Kenneth O. Morgan, *The People's Peace: British History, 1945–1989* (New York: Oxford University Press, 1990), 358–433.

11. Harry Schwartz, "Health Care in America: A Heretical Diagnosis," *Saturday Review*, August 14, 1971, 14–17.

12. Richard Rose and Rei Shiratori, eds., *The Welfare State East and West* (New York: Oxford University Press, 1986), particularly 3–37; and Phyllis Moen, *Working Parents: Transformation in Gender Roles and Public Politics in Sweden* (Madison: University of Wisconsin Press, 1989), 21–23.

13. U. S. Council of Economic Advisors, *Annual Report* (Washington, D.C.: U.S. Government Printing Office, 1993–1995), tables on 232–33.

14. Robert Higgs, *Crisis and Leviathan: Critical Episodes in the Growth of Government* (New York: Oxford Unversity Press, 1987), 20–27.

15. James T. Bennett and Thomas DiLorenzo, *Underground Government: The Off-Budget Public Sector* (Washington, D. C.: Cato Institute, 1983); and idem, "How the Government Evades Taxes," *Policy Review* (Winter 1982), 71–89.

16. *The American Enterprise* (July/August 1995), 35.

17. Cf. Robert Higgs, *The Transformation of the American Economy, 1865–1914* (New York: Wiley & Sons, 1971); and idem, "Eighteen Problematic Propositions on the Analysis of the Growth of Government," *Review of Austrian Economics* 5, no. 1 (1991), 3–40.

18. *The American Enterprise* (July/August 1995), 41.

19. L. T. Hobhouse, *Liberalism*, 25.

20. John Dewey, *Liberalism and Social Action* (New York: Capricorn Books, 1963), 32.

21. Ibid., 90.

22. Ibid., 83.

23. Hobhouse, *Liberalism,* 25, 66.

24. Allan Carlson, *The Swedish Experiment in Family Politics: The Myrdals and the Interwar Population Crisis* (New Brunswick: Transaction Publishers, 1989); Roland Huntford, *The New Totalitarians* (New York: Stein & Day, 1980), particularly 62–64; and Nicolaj-Klaus Kreitor, "The Conservative Revolution in Sweden," *Telos* 98–99 (Winter 1993/Spring 1994), 249–54.

25. Rosanvallon, *Le Moment Guizot,* 25–46; and L. Trénard, "L'enseignement sous la monarchie de Juillet," *Revue d'histoire moderne et contemporaine* 12 (1965).

26. David P. Conradt, "West Germany: A Remade Political Culture," *Comparative Political Studies* 7, no. 2 (July 1974), 222–38.

27. *Time,* May 7, 1945; "A Problem in Global Penology," *Saturday Review* July 28, 1945, 7–12; H. Eulau, "Germans Have No Rights," *New Republic,* July 16, 1945, 62; and J. Katz, "Germany Can Be Re-educated," *American Scholar* 14, no. 3 (July 1945), 381–82. See also Herbert Ammon, "Antifaschismus, im Wandel?" in *Die Schatten der Vergangenheit,* ed. Uwe Backes, Eckhard Jesse, and Rainer Zitelmann (Frankfurt and Berlin: Propyläen, 1990), 568–94.

28. Dwight D. Murphey, *Liberalism in Contemporary America* (McLean, Virginia: Council for Social and Economic Studies, 1992), 131–32.

29. Dewey, *Liberalism and Social Action,* 72–73.

30. Robert B. Westbrook, *John Dewey and American Democracy* (Ithaca: Cornell University Press, 1991), 545.

31. Herbert Croly, *Progressive Democracy* (New York: Macmillan, 1914); on the profound effect of Croly's work on the American Progressive Party and its political leaders, see J. T. Kloppenberg, *Uncertain Victory: Social Democracy and Progressivism in European and American Thought, 1870–1920* (New York: Oxford University Press, 1988), 314–16. Herbert's father, David, was a leading American exponent of Comtean positivism and sought to raise his son on this blend of social planning with faith in historical Progress. See David W. Levy, *Herbert Croly of the New Republic* (Princeton: Princeton University Press, 1985).

32. Herbert Croly, *The Promise of American Life* (New York: Macmillan, 1909), 454.

33. Walter Weyl, *The New Democracy* (New York: Macmillan, 1912), 327–28.

34. Ibid., 329.

35. Croly, *The Promise of American Life,* 409, 413.

36. Horace M. Kallen, *The Liberal Spirit: Essays on the Problems of Freedom in the Modern World* (New York and Ithaca: Cornell University Press, 1948), 190; 91–127.

37. Ibid. 47–67; see also *The Future of Peace* (Chicago: University of Chicago Press, 1941).

38. Kallen, *The Liberal Spirit,* 218.

39. Ibid., 220. Kallen moves easily between apparently contradictory positions in his philosophic as well as social writings. Thus in "The Need for a Recovery of

Philosophy," published in *Creative Intelligence: A Recovery of Philosophy*, ed. John Dewey (New York: Henry Holt & Co., 1917), 409–67, Kallen insists that values are both subjective and irrational but are also guides for social progress. Some of these "interests," which are "relations, responses, attitudes subjectively obvious and irrational," can be transformed into "expressive ideas" and, most importantly, into the vision of experimental science. While this argument may be demonstrable, it is not clear that Kallen proves it in either this particular essay or his discursive observations about cognition in *Journal of Philosophy, Psychology, and Scientific Method* 9, (1915–16), 252–55.

40. Arthur Champagne and Stuart Nagel, "Minimizing Discrimination Based on Race and Sex," *Nationalizing Government*, ed. Theodore Lowi and Alan Stone (Beverly Hills: Sage, 1978), 334–35.

41. James Weinstein, *The Corporate Ideal in the Liberal State, 1900–1918* (Boston: Beacon Press, 1968); and C. Wright Mills, *The Power Elite* (New York: Oxford University Press, 1956).

42. Samuel T. Francis, *Beautiful Losers: Essays on the Failure of American Conservatism* (Columbia: University of Missouri Press, 1993), particularly 60–87, 95–117; and for another penetrating attack on the corporate state from the Old Right, see Murray N. Rothbard, "War Collectivism in World War I," in *A New History of Leviathan*, ed. Ronald Radosh and Murray Rothbard (New York: E. P. Dutton, 1976), 66–110.

43. That managerial states are not ideologically interchangeable is a point that has not received sufficient attention, from Bruno Rizzi's pioneering study of the Soviets onward. See *The Bureaucratization of the World*, trans. Adam Westoby (New York: Free Press, 1985).

44. See, for example, *Wall Street Journal*, January 26, 1990, A14; March 16, 1990, A14; April 30, 1990, A1; and *New York Times*, October 20, 1990, A20; December 9, 1991, A16; June 20, 1991, A22. All of these commentaries call for expanding Third World immigration and for broadening the right of asylum. Cf. also F. Fukuyama, "Immigrants and Family Values," *Commentary* 96 (August 1993), 2.

45. *Newsweek*, August 9, 1993, 16–23.

46. See Congressman Armey's remarks and the positive response to them in *Wall Street Journal*, May 24, 1995, A16.

47. Arthur S. Link, *Woodrow Wilson and the Progressive Era, 1910–1917* (New York: Harper & Row, 1954), 19.

48. Herbert Croly's editorial note in *New Republic*, November 21, 1914, 7.

49. Link, *Woodrow Wilson and the Progressive Era*, 239.

50. Raymond Moley, *The First New Deal*, foreword by Frank Freidel (New York: Harcourt, Brace & Co., 1966), 355–60; Basil Rauch, *The History of the New Deal, 1933–1938*, fourth impression (New York: Capricorn Books, 1963).

51. Allan Brinkley, *The End of Reform: New Deal Liberalism in Recession and War* (New York: Knopf, 1995), 15–65, 86–174, 201–26, and 265–72. Brinkley is particularly thorough in demonstrating the almost hand-to-mouth redefinition of liber-

alism that went on during the New Deal. He recognizes the connection between American ideas about social planning in the interwar period and the "new liberal" legacy left by earlier Progressives and by European social democrats. Despite his obvious sympathy for New Deal liberals, Brinkley does not hide the disjunction between their views of government and society and those of traditional liberals.

52. *New Republic,* January 21, 1931, 259.

53. See Kallen's endorsement of the Italian way in *New Republic,* January 12, 1927, 207–13; the rest of this issue, including the fulsome editorial note of Croly, is devoted to an "Apology for Fascism." Such apologies do not prove that Kallen and Croly were fascists, any more than Tugwell, Dewey, and Dewey's disciple Sidney Hook, all of whom were then celebrating the "Soviet experiment," were Stalinists. These social planners were still shopping for models that might be applied to an American "liberal" managerial state. The *New Republic* in the late twenties characteristically stressed the merits of both the fascist and Soviet efforts at social reconstruction. See John Dewey's series of six articles about his visit to Soviet Russia in *New Republic,* November 14, 1928; November 21, 1928; December 5, 1928; December 12, 1928; and December 19, 1928.

54. Higgs, *Crisis and Leviathan,* 1–19, 258–62.

55. Ibid., 256.

56. Gary S. Lawson, "The Rise of the Administrative State," *Harvard Law Review* 107 (1994), 1231.

57. Bruce Ackerman, "Constitutional Politics/Constitutional Law," *Yale Law Review* 99 (1989), 510–15.

58. Lawson, "The Rise of the Administrative State," 1253.

59. Kevin Phillips, *The Politics of Rich and Poor* (New York: Knopf, 1995); and "It's the Republicans' Turn to Go Too Far," *Philadelphia Inquirer,* October 12, 1995, A7.

60. See, for example, John Ward Studebaker, "Salvaging Democracy through Education," *Parents Magazine,* November 1934, 10; idem, "The Education of Free Men in American Democracy," *School Life* 27, no. 1 (October 1941), 5–7; and Studebaker's John Adams Lecture at U.C.L.A. on March 18, 1948, "Education and the Fate of Democracy." The author also had access to a detailed but still unpublished essay on the educational thought of John Ward Studebaker by Stephen J. Sniegoski, a historian of the U.S. Department of Education.

61. David Fromkin, *In the Time of the Americans: F.D.R., Truman, Eisenhower, Marshall, and MacArthur* (New York: Knopf, 1995), preface.

62. Paul Piccone and Gary Ulmen, "Rethinking Federalism," *Telos* 100 (Summer 1994), 12–14.

63. Christopher Lasch, "The Revolt of the Elites," *Harper's* (November 1994), 40.

64. Pierre Rosanvallon, "Repenser la Gauche," *L'Express,* March 25, 1993, 116.

CHAPTER FOUR

1. Christopher Lasch, *The Revolt of the Elites and the Betrayal of Democracy* (New York: W. W. Norton, 1995).

2. See, for example, Elizabeth Fox-Genovese, *Feminism without Illusions: A Critique of Individualism* (Chapel Hill: University of North Carolina Press, 1991); Jean Bethke-Elshtain, *Democracy on Trial* (New York: Basic Books, 1995); and the symposium on the "National Prospect," in *Commentary* 100 (November 1995).

3. See Irving Kristol, *Two Cheers for Capitalism* (New York: Basic Books, 1978); idem, "Libertarian and Bourgeois Freedoms," *National Review,* December 5, 1975, 1338–39; idem, "Countercultures," *Commentary* 98 (December 1994), 35–39; and Mark Gerson's "Reflections of a Neoconservative Disciple," in *The Neoconservative Imagination,* ed. Christopher DeMuth and William Kristol (Washington: American Enterprise Institute, 1995). 165–72.

4. Jürgen Habermas, *Die Moderne: Ein unvollendetes Projekt,* third edition (Leipzig: Reclam Verlag, 1994), 75–85.

5. Karl Mannheim, *Ideology and Utopia,* trans. L. Wirth (Boston and New York: Beacon Press, 1936), 208.

6. See, for example, R. J. Neuhaus, "Democratic Conservatism," *First Things* 1 (March 1990), 65–67; Ben Wattenberg, "Back to Our Prime Mission," syndicated in *Washington Times,* March 9, 1989; Gregory Fossedal, *Exporting Democratic Revolution* (New York: Basic Books, 1989); and Paul Gottfried, "At Sea with the Global Democrats," *Wall Street Journal,* January 19, 1989.

7. S. M. Lipset, *Political Man* (New York: Doubleday, 1960), 403.

8. *American Enterprise* (July/August 1995), 31. See also Ben Wattenberg, *The First Universal Nation: Leading Indicators and Ideas about the Surge of America in the 1990s* (New York: Free Press, 1991). An already archaic testimony to Cold War perceptions is Paul Hollander's *Anti-Americanism: Critiques at Home and Abroad* (New York: Oxford University Press, 1992).

9. This reconciliation of the American capitalist Right with social democracy is the *idée-maîtresse* of my work, *The Conservative Movement,* revised edition (New York: Twayne-Macmillan, 1992).

10. For two critical treatments of this development, see Claes G. Ryn, *The New Jacobinism* (Washington: National Humanities Institute, 1991); and Christopher Lasch, "The Obsolescence of Left and Right," *New Oxford Review* 56 (April 1989), 6–15.

11. Wolfgang H. Mommsen, "Wandlungen der nationalen Identität," in *Die Identität der Deutschen,* ed. Werner Weidenfeld (Bonn: Bundeszentrale für politische Bildung, 1983), 177. See also Ralph Giordano's best-selling (in Germany) consideration of the burdens of German history, *Die zweite Schuld oder von der Last Deutscher zu sein* (Hamburg: Nasch & Rohring, 1987).

12. Jürgen Habermas, "Recht und Gewalt-ein deutsches Trauma," *Merkur* 1 (1984); see also Stephen Eisel, *Minimalkonsens und freiheitliche Demokratie* (Paderborn: Schoningh, 1986), 50–182, 228–58.

13. Ben Wattenberg, "Is the Republican Contract with America All That Conservative?" syndicated in *Washington Times*, February 22, 1995.

14. This view is presented from different angles in Steven E. Ambrose, *Rise to Globalism*, sixth edition (New York: Penguin Books, 1991); Alonzo L. Hamby, *Liberalism and its Challengers* (New York: Oxford University Press, 1985); Carl Gershman, "Democracy as the Wave of the Future," *Current* 312 (May 1989), 18–25; and Claes G. Ryn, "The Democracy Boosters," *National Review* March 24, 1989, 31–32.

15. See the feature stories on Patrick J. Buchanan in *Time*, November 6, 1995, and in *Newsweek*, March 4, 1996, 24–29.

16. For a politically sympathetic but methodologically critical treatment of Boas and the Boasians, see Carl Degler, *In Search of Human Nature* (New York: Oxford University Press, 1991), 61–78; for a meticulously collected bibliography of critical writings on Boas and the Boasians, see the notes for chapter 4 of Dinesh D'Souza's *The End of Racism* (New York: Free Press, 1995), 592–606.

17. Two books by the Swedish social planner Alva Myrdal can be seen as transitional works located between nineteenth-century eugenicism and Deweyite Progressivism: *Kris i befolkningsfrågan*, fifth edition (Stockholm: Bonniers, 1935); and *Nation and Family: The Swedish Experiment in Democratic Family and Population Policy* (Cambridge: MIT Press, 1968).

18. J. C. Burnham, "Psychiatry, Psychology, and the Progressive Movement," *American Quarterly* 29 (1960), 457–65; idem, "Medical Specialists and Movements toward Social Control in the Progressive Era," in *Building the Organizational Society*, ed. J. Israel (New York: Free Press, 1972); and idem, *Psychoanalysis and American Medicine 1894–1918: Medicine Science and Culture* (Madison, Conn.: International Universities Press, 1967).

19. H. A. Bruce, "Is Our National Vigor in Danger?" *Delineator* 93 (1918), 53.

20. Paul M. Dennis, "Psychology's First Publicist: H. Addington Bruce and the Popularization of the Subconscious and Power of Suggestion Before World War I," *Psychological Reports* 68 (1991), 755.

21. Thomas Szasz, *Law, Liberty and Psychiatry* (New York: Macmillan, 1963), 5, 39–71; see also his, *The Myth of Mental Illness* (New York: Harper & Row, 1961), and his *Psychiatric Justice* (New York: Macmillan, 1965).

22. *The International Covenants on Human Rights* (New York: U.N. Office of Public Information, 1976), 2–4.

23. Lasch, *True and Only Heaven*, 452.

24. Theodor W. Adorno (with Else Frenkel-Brunswick, Daniel J. Levinson, R. N. Sanford), *The Authoritarian Personality* (New York: Harper & Brothers, 1950), 269.

25. The advent of McCarthyism is made into a justification for the *Studies in Prejudice* series in the anthology *The Radical Right*, ed. Daniel Bell (New York: Doubleday, 1963); see especially Richard Hofstadter, "Pseudo-Conservative Revolt," 75–97.

26. Lasch, *True and Only Heaven*, 460–61; also Lipset's remarks on "Working Class Authoritariansim" in *American Sociological Review* 24 (1959), 482–501. For a critique of the Lipset-Adorno view of the working class, see S. M. Miller and Frank Riessman, " 'Working Class Authoritarianism' : A Critique of Lipset," *British Journal of Sociology* 12 (1961), 263–76.

27. Lasch, *True and Only Heaven*, 456–7; also Richard Hofstadter, *The Paranoid Style in American Politics* (New York: Knopf, 1965).

28. Walter Lippmann, *The Public Philosophy* (Boston: New American Library, 1955), 19.

29. Ibid., 106–7.

30. Ibid., 136.

31. Ibid., 137.

32. E. Beesley, "Why I Am a Liberal" (pamphlet published by the Liberal Party, London, 1885).

33. Lippman, *The Public Philosophy*, 136.

34. John H. Hallowell, *Moral Foundations of Democracy* (reprint, Chicago: University of Chicago Press, 1973). See also Charles Wellborn, *Twentieth Century Pilgrimage: Walter Lippmann and the Public Philosophy* (Baton Rouge: Louisiana State University Press, 1969). An engaged Christian disciple of Hallowell and then, like Hallowell, a professor of politics at Duke University, Wellborn presents the author of *The Public Philosophy* as a pilgrim whose spiritual journey is continuing.

35. Reinhart Koselleck, *Kritik and Krise. Eine Studie zur Parthogenese der bürgerlichen Welt* (Frankfurt am Main: Suhrkamp, 1973).

36. Horace M. Kallen, "Values and Existence in Philosophy, Art, and Religion," in *Creative Intelligence: Essays in the Pragmatic Attitude* (New York: H. Holt & Co., 1917), 461–62, and 408-67 passim.

37. Theodor J. Lowi, *The End of the Republican Era* (Narvon, Okla.: University of Oklahoma Press, 1995), 190.

38. Ibid., 238; for a detailed critical treatment of Lowi's book, see Wayne Allen, "Therapeutic Liberalism," in *The World and I* 9 (October 1995), 265–69.

39. See Dumont, *Essais sur L'individualisme*, 11–32.

40. John Dewey, *Experience and Nature* (La Salle: Open Court Press, 1926), 408; and Hilary Putnam, *Renewing Philosophy* (Cambridge, Mass.: Harvard University Press, 1992), 180–200.

41. Putnam, *Renewing Philosophy*, 135.

42. Ronald Dworkin, *Taking Rights Seriously* (Cambridge: Harvard University Press, 1977), 238–39.

43. Ibid., 232.

44. Max Weber, "Kritische Studien auf dem Gebiet der kulturwissen-schaftichen Logik," in *Gesammelte Aufsätze zur Wissenschaftslehre*, third edition (Tubingen: Mohr, 1968), 215–90. This originally Weberian notion is most fully developed in Carl Schmitt's controversial essay "Die Tyrannei der Werte," in *Die Tyrannei der Werte*, ed. Carl Schmitt, Eberhard Jungel, and Sepp Schelz (Hamburg: Lutherisches Verlagshaus, 1979), 31–40.

45. See Robert P. George, *Making Men Moral: Civil Liberties and Public Morality* (Oxford: Clarendon Press, 1993), 94–109; John Gray, *Enlightenment's Wake* (New York and London: Routledge, 1995), 74, 120–24; and the critical observations about Dworkin's notions of right and democracy in Joseph Raz's "Professor Dworkin's Theory of Rights," in *Political Studies* 26 (1978), 123–35.

46. Gray, *Enlightenment's Wake*, 129.

47. Ibid., 74–75, 120; and Dworkin, *Taking Rights*.

48. Amy Gutmann's editorial commentary in *Multiculturalism and 'The Politics of Recognition,'* ed. Charles Taylor (Princeton: Princeton University Press, 1992), 17.

49. Ibid., 23.

50. Ibid., 22.

51. Ibid., 43–44.

52. Peter Gabel, "Affirmative Action and Racial Harmony," *Tikkun* (May/June 1995), 33.

53. Ibid., 34; Michael Lerner, *Tikkun: To Heal, Repair, and Transform the World* (Oakland: Institute for Labor and Mental Health, 1992); and Mary Lefkowitz, "Jews and Blacks: Let the Healing Begin," *TLS*, June 9, 1995, 15.

54. On manipulated identities and designated victims and on the practice of the administrative state in raising "particular values to the level of universality," while pretending to be "value-neutral," see Paul Piccone, "The Crisis of Liberalism and the Emergence of Federal Populism," *Telos* 89 (Fall 1991), 3–14.

55. Adorno, *The Authoritarian Personality*, 7, 10.

56. *Ibid.*, vii.

57. Ibid., 57.

58. Ibid., 36, 41–43.

59. Ibid., 50.

60. Ibid., 36, 44–47.

61. See T. W. Adorno and Max Horkheimer, *The Dialectic of the Enlightenment*, trans. John Cumming (New York: Continuum, 1975). For a study emphasizing the contributions of Adorno, Horkheimer, and Arendt as critics of political modernity, see Russell Berman, *Modern Culture and Critical Theory: Art, Politics and the Legacy of the Frankfurt School* (Madison: University of Wisconsin, 1989).

62. Adorno, *The Authoritarian Personality*, 442–61; 474–84.

63. Ibid., 685–86.

64. Ibid., 676, 680–81.

65. Ibid., 788–820. For a perceptive methodological and substantive criticism of *The Authoritarian Personality*, see Tamotsu Shibutani, *American Journal of Sociology* 57 (1952), 527–29; and Joseph H. Bunzel, *American Sociological Review* 15 (1950), 571–73. Christopher Lasch (in *The True and Only Heaven*, 560) was right to notice how few of the reviewers criticize the study's crude psychological reductionism. Many of them in fact share its cosmological premises.

66. On the political culture of Cold War liberalism, see Alexander Bloom, *Prodigal Sons* (New York: Oxford University Press, 1986), 209–73.

67. For a recent restatement of this "vital center" position on foreign policy, see Arthur Schlesinger Jr., "Back to the Womb?" *Foreign Affairs* (July/August 1995), 2–7.

68. Chilton Williamson Jr., *The Immigration Mystique* (New York: Basic Books, 1996), 69–70.

69. Ibid.; and A. P. Maingot, "Ideology, Politics, and Citizenship in the American Debate about Immigration Policy: Beyond Consensus," in *U.S. Immigration and Refugee Policy*, ed. Mary M. Kritz (Lexington, Mass.: Lexington Books, 1983), 29–30.

70. Peter Brimelow, *Alien Nation: Common Sense about America's Immigration Disaster* (New York: Random House, 1995), 95–96.

71. Ibid., 109.

72. Deborah Sontag, "Calls to Restrict Immigration from Many Quarters," *New York Times*, December 13, 1992.

73. Julian Simon, *Economic Consequences of Immigration* (Cambridge, Mass.: Basil Blackwell, 1989), 45–46.

74. Earl Raab, *Jewish Bulletin*, February 19, 1993, 23.

75. Shikha Dalmia, "Cultural Purity Drives Anti-Immigration Cause," *Detroit News*, October 11, 1995, A9.

76. See Wayne Lutton and John Tanton, *The Immigration Invasion* (Petoskey, Mich.; Social Contract Press, 1994) particularly 94–104. Indicative of what Brimelow calls "America's one-way immigration debate" is that informed advocates of a more restricted immigration (e.g., Lutton and Lawrence Auster) can have their heavily documented books published only by small institutes. Until last year, Brimelow was the single exception to this rule. Immigration expansionists, by contrast, have works published by leading commercial presses, which are then favorably reviewed in the *New York Times, Washington Post*, and *Wall Street Journal*. As Brimelow notes, the often problematic statistics cited by Julian Simon and other pro-immigration publicists receive indulgent treatment in mass publications.

77. *The Federalist Papers* (New York: The New American Library, 1961), 38. A work that shows the novel nature of the expansionist approach to immigration proposed by Dahmia, Simon, and the libertarian Cato Institute is Lawrence Auster's *The Path to National Suicide: An Essay in Immigration and Multiculturalism* (Monterey, Va: AICF, 1990). For the same observations about Australia, see Kath-

NOTES TO CHAPTER 4

erine Bett's *Ideology and Immigration: Australia 1976 to 1987* (Melbourne: Melbourne University Press, 1988).

78. Stephen Brooks, "How Ottawa Bends: Plastic Words and the Politics of Social Morality," in *How Ottawa Spends 1994–95* ed. Susan D. Phillips (Ottawa: Carleton University Press, 1994), 71.

79. Ibid., 77.

80. Ibid., 87; also Uwe Pörksen: *Plastikwörter. Die Sprache einer internationalen Diktatur* (Stuttgart: Klett-Cotta, 1989).

81. Maurice Cowling, *Mill and Liberalism*, 157.

82. Pat Shipman, *The Evolution of Racism* (New York: Simon & Schuster, 1994), 191.

83. Cited in Degler, *In Search of Human Nature*, 194.

84. See Gunnar Myrdal, *An American Dilemma: The Negro Problem and Modern Democracy* (New York: Harper & Brothers, 1962), 75–76, 106–16, 145–48; and David Southern, *Gunnar Myrdal and Black-White Relations* (Baton Rouge: Louisana State University Press, 1987).

85. See Degler, *In Search of Human Nature*, 210–20.

86. Gordon W. Allport, *The Nature of Prejudice* (Reading, Mass.: Addison-Wesley, 1979), 6–8, 25–28; and Steven Goldberg, *When Wish Replaces Thought* (Buffalo: Prometheus Books, 1991).

87. See Herbert Andrew Deane, *The Political Ideas of Harold J.Laski* (New York: Columbia University Press, 1955), 13–33.

88. Isaac Kramnick and Barry Sheerman, *Harold Laski: A Life on the Left* (New York: Allen Lane/Peguin Press, 1993), 227.

89. Westbrook, *John Dewey and American Democracy*, 304.

90. John Dewey, *Lectures In China*, ed. R. W. Clapton and Tsuin-chen Ou (Honolulu: University of Hawaii Press, 1973), 43–44.

91. On the transformational opportunities provided by the First World War for Dewey and other Progressivist intellectuals, see James Gilbert, *Designing the Industrial State: The Intellectual Pursuit of Collectivism in America 1880–1940* (Chicago: Quadrangle Books, 1972), 232–34; Charles Hirschfeld, "Nationalist Progressivism and World War I," *Mid-America* 45 (July 1963); and Murray N. Rothbard, "World War I as Fulfillment: Power and the Intellectuals," *Journal of Libertarian Studies* 9, no. 1 (Winter 1989), 95–98.

92. Habermas, *Die Moderne*, 103.

93. Ibid., 103, 32–54.

94. Aristotle, *Constitution of Athens* Oxford Classical Texts (Oxford: Oxford University Press, 1957), sections 26.4, 27.1.

95. Paul Veyne, *Le Pain et Le cirque: Sociologie d'un pluralisme politique* (Paris: Seuil, 1976), 87–92; 106–8.

96. The text of the Ontario Human Rights Code is available in English and French in the *Canadian Human Rights Reporter* (March 1992); the additions which

were passed two years later can be seen in the *[Toronto] Globe and Mail,* January 15, 1994.

97. See Saul Bellow's response in the *Globe and Mail,* March 15, 1994; Jonathan Rauch, *Kindly Inquisitors: The New Attacks on Free Thought* (Chicago: University of Chicago Press, 1993); and Barbara Kulaszka, *The Hate Crime Laws in Canada 1970–1994* (Ebticoke, Ont.: Canadian Association for Free Expression, 1994).

98. This law, no. 72–546, passed by the National Assembly, is reproduced in *Le Monde,* June 8, 1972.

99. Note Charrière's remarks in *Le Quotidien de Paris,* September 23, 1988, 32; the account of his legal problems in Eric Delcroix, *La Francophobie: Crimes et délits idéologigues en droit français* (Paris: Editions Libres Opinions, 1993), 47–48; and Luc Rosenzweig's discussion of LICRA in *Libération,* July 5, 1983, 7.

100. Achille-Fould's remarks dealing with race consciousness can be read in the National Assembly's *Journal Officiel des Débats,* June 7, 1972, 2281.

101. See Delcroix, *La Francophobie,* 40–41; and the *Racismes/Antiracismes,* ed. Pierre-André Taguieff et al. (Paris: Librairie des Méridiens, 1986), 309–13.

102. An impassioned but informative treatment of such anti–hate speech laws in Europe is Eric Delcroix, *La Police de la Pensée contre le Révisionnisme* (Paris: Diffusion, 1994).

103. Ibid., 25–43.

104. *Le Figaro,* May 25, 1993.

105. See Annie Kriegel's extended criticism of *l'affaire-Notin* in ibid., April 2, 1990, especially 2.

106. Ibid., June 27, 1994; the apparent support given to these *vigies* by the World Zionist Organization is reported in the *Daily News,* September 19, 1993, 34.

107. The citations from Madame Boulouque are taken from *Le Monde*'s editorial on January 14, 1994. In this commentary, the paper defends criminal laws passed against the expression of racist or Holocaust-revisionist opinions as necessary to "prevent the transgression of our values of tolerance and universalism."

108. See *Federal Register* 59, no. 47 (March 10, 1994), 11448–50.

109. Any comment about the family resemblance between themselves and the multiculturalists is one that "moderate" pluralists vigorously resist. Thus the anti-Communist and social democrat Deweyite Sidney Hook in his autobiography, *Out of Step: An Unquiet Life in the Twentieth Century* (New York: Harper & Row, 1987), attacks affirmative action as the "immoral practice of reverse discrimination" (350). Hook overlooks the historical development from the socioeconomic interventionism that he favored, including his adhesion to various humanist manifestoes, to a degree of administrative control he now finds excessive.

110. Quoted In Robert Detlefsen, *Civil Rights under Reagan* (San Francisco: ISC Press, 1991), 141–42.

111. For the by now conventional criticism of affirmative action, see Nathan Glazer, *Affirmative Discrimination: Ethnic Inequality and Public Policy* (Cambridge: Harvard University Press, 1987).

112. For an analysis of affirmative action's politically totalizing effect, see Nicholas Capaldi, *Out of Order: Affirmative Action and the Crisis of Doctrinaire Liberalism* (Buffalo: Prometheus Books, 1985); and on the judicial activism that has driven these programs, see P. C. Roberts and Lawrence Stratton, *The New Color Line: How Quotas and Privilege Destroy Democracy* (Washington, D.C.: Regnery, 1995). The Italian-American social theorist Paul Piccone is particularly effective in demonstrating the "rationality" of New Class therapeutic initiatives. In looking at the Canadian welfare state, Piccone stresses the pursuit of power in the way administrators create a "politically homogeneous community by reducing a normally recalcitrant population marked by group particularities to a clientele of abstract, manipulable individuals dependent on the state." See Paul Piccone, "Riforma o secessione: il caso canadese," in *Ideazione* 3, no. 4 (July/August 1996), 60. The only observation to be added is that once having finished this transformational task, the therapeutic-managerial state exercises further power by reassigning "abstract individuals" to concocted ethnicities.

113. *U.S. Commission on Civil Rights Newsletter* (January 1995); and Herbert I. London, "When Civil Rights Protagonists Demand a Dictatorial Regime," in *Measure* 128 (April/May 1995), 8. For observations on the connection between affirmative action directives and the enforcement on campuses of "politically correct" speech and behavior, see Lino A. Graglia, " 'Hate Speech' Codes and 'Political Correctness': Fruit of 'Affirmative Action'," *Northern Kentucky Law Review* 23, no. 3 (1996), 505–14; idem, "'Affirmative Action,' Past, Present, and Future," *Ohio Northern University Law Review*, 22–4 (196), 1207–25; and idem, "*Podberesky, Hopwood*, and *Adorand*: Implications for the Future of Race-Based Programs," *Northern Ilinois University Law Review* 16, no. 2 (Spring 1996), 287–93. Although Graglia denies any legal or political link between civil rights legislation through 1964 and the abuses he attacks, he is relentless in searching out the administrative path going from the efforts of the EEOC to ban "discrimination" to the current applications of "political correctness."

CHAPTER FIVE

1. On the essential liberalism of Hegel's constitutional theory of the state, see Karl Rosenkranz, *Hegel als deutscher Nationalphilosoph* (Leipzig, 1870); Paul Gottfried, *The Search for Historical Meaning*, 3–19; and Steven B. Smith, *Hegel's Critique of Liberalism* (Chicago: University of Chicago, 1989), particularly 98–149.

2. Rosanvallon, *Le Moment Guizot*, 246; and Guizot's own justification for his plan of public instruction in "Rapport du Roi sur l'exécution de la loi de 28 juin 1833" (Paris, 1834).

3. John D. Hicks, *The Populist Revolt: A History of the Farmers' Alliance and the People's Party* (1931; reprint, Lincoln: University of Nebraska Press, 1961), especially 261–71.

4. See Lasch, *Revolt of the Elites*, 92–114.

5. Jean-Marie Le Pen, *Pour la France: Programme du Front National* (Paris: Editions Albatros, 1985), 10.

6. For a composite picture of the electorate and ideology associated with the National Front, see inter alia Jean-Christian Petitfils, *L'Extrême Droite en France* (Paris: PUF, 1983); Pierre-André Taguieff, *Le national populisme* (Paris: Le Seuil, 1989); Anne Tristan, *Au Front* (Paris: Gallimard, 1987); Christopher Bourseiller, *Extrême Droite* (Paris: Editions François Bourin, 1991); and Guy Birenbaum, "Front national: Les mutations d'un groupuscule," *Intervention* (March 15, 1988), 25–32.

7. On the electoral differences between the lepénistes and earlier postwar populist movements of the Right, see D. Drouin and Marc Pons de Vincent, *Analyse comparative de l'émergence électorale de deux forces d'extrême droite: le mouvement poujadiste et le Front National* (Univerité de Lyons III, 1986); *Le Front National à découvert*, ed. Nonna Mayer and Pascal Perrimeau (Paris: Presses de la Fondation Nationale des Sciences Politiques, 1989), 37–52; and François Platone, "Histoire de l'électorat Le Pen," *Le Journal des élections* (April/May 1988), 23–24. On the differences between interwar fascist sympathizers and supporters of today's European populist Right, see Wolfgang Kowalsky's informative essay, "Die Vergangenheit als Crux der Linken," in *Die Schatten der Vergangenheit* (Frankfurt and Berlin: Propyläen, 1990), 595–613.

8. Mayer and Perrimeau, *Le Front National*, 56–58.

9. See Le Pen, *Pour la France*, 18–19.

10. For an account of this incident, see *La République menacée: Dix ans d'effet Le Pen*, ed. Edwy Plenel and Alain Rollat (Paris: Le Monde, 1992), 69–78. The defector in question, Jean Marcilly, had been responsible for the view of the FN president, still prevalent in some quarters, as a devout Catholic. In *Le Pen sans bandeau*, Marcilly creates a biographical portrait intended for Le Pen's supporters on the Catholic Right. To this day French bookstores and French book distributors specializing in devotional literature sell copies of Le Pen's defenses of Catholic social morality. In a revisionist portrait, *Le Pen revu et corrigé*, however, Marcilly tries to erase his earlier image-making by presenting Le Pen as a cynic who posed as *catholique bon teint* for electoral reasons. By 1991 the biographer-journalist had broken with his boss and gone off to live with Le Pen's alienated wife Pierrette.

11. Le Pen, *Pour la France*, 54–85.

12. Ibid.; 20–21, 46.

13. Bourseiller, *Extrême Droite*, 80, 87, 104–5.

14. Typical of these proliferating invectives tracing Le Pen's ideas and electorate to Nazi sources and sympathizers are Joseph Algazy, *L'Extrême Droite en France* (Paris: L'Harmattan, 1989); *L'Extrême Droite en questions* (Paris: Cercle Condorcet,

Ligue des Droits de L'Homme, 1991); René Monzat, *Enquêtes sur l'extrême droite* (Paris: Le Monde Editions, 1992); and Harvey G. Simmons, *The French National Front: The Extremist Challenge to Democracy* (New York: Westview, 1996)

15. Quoted in *Le Monde*, September 13, 1987; and commented on by Patrick Jarreau in ibid., September 20–21, 1987.

16. In an extended interview with Alain Rollat that appeared in a condensed form in *Le Monde*, June 8, 1984, Le Pen attacks the French Left for not being evenhanded in its condemnation of Communist and Nazi mass murder. He also complains of the tendency of intellectuals "to stamp all over the old Nazi wolfskin when there are no longer Nazis inside. Nazism belonged to a historical epoch; it is not something existing in perpetuity."

17. On the general lack of interest in civil liberties among French Jews and their representative argumentations, see Anne Kriegel, "Le leurre de l'antisémitisme," *Le Figaro*, April 2, 1990; Paul Gottfried, "Crimes of Opinion," *Insight*, June 10, 1996; and a provocative study of Jewish political behavior in relation to outside groups, Kevin B. MacDonald, *A People that Shall Dwell Alone: Judaism as an Evolutionary Group Strategy* (Westport, Conn.; Praeger, 1994). See also Pierre Birnbaum, *Anti-Semitism in France: A Political History from Léon Blum to the Present* (Oxford: Blackwell, 1992); and Norman Ravitch, "Your People, My People; Your God, My God," *The French Review* 70, no. 4 (March 1997), 515–27.

Though the FN leadership has shown inexcusably bad taste in joking about Jewish critics, *Le Monde* has not demonstrated that Le Pen is in fact a Holocaust-denier. All it can prove is that during interviews on September 13 and 18, 1987, Le Pen lumped together Nazi atrocities against Jews with other Nazi crimes committed against "gypsies, Christians, and patriots, as a detail of the Second World War." His remarks about the French Left's unwillingness to come to terms with the sordid history of Communism in France as well as in Eastern Europe has obviously hit a raw nerve, because they are *entirely* correct. *Le République menacée*, published by *Le Monde*, disparages the attempt to call attention to Soviet crimes or the fact that French Communists collaborated with the Nazis during the fall of France. The self-evident truth, however, is that Le Pen and his critics are equally guilty of sweeping aside the embarrassing details of the past, that is, the past anti-Semitism of the French nationalist Right.

18. See Franklin Hugh Adler, "The Decline of the French Left," *Telos* 103 (Spring 1995), 191; and Pierre-André Taguieff, "Political Science Confronts Populism," ibid., especially 18–20.

19. See, for example, P. A. Taguieff, "L'identité francaise et ses ennemis: le traitement de l'immigration dans le national racisme français contemporain," *L'homme et la société* 77–78 (December 1985), 187–200; Michel Winock, "Les flambées du nationalisme francais," *L'Histoire* 73 (December 1984), 11–25; Jean-Paul Honoré, "Jean-Marie Le Pen et le front national," *Les temps modernes* 41 (April 1985), 1843–71; and the FN view of French history by Jean Madiran, 'De millénaire capétien à la bataille de France," *Itinéraires* (Winter 1987). On disconti-

nuities between interwar fascist constituences and the electoral base of the FN, see Wolfgang Kowalsky, "Die Vergangenheit als Crux der Linken" in *Die Schatten der Vergangenheit*, 595–613.

20. Typical of the journalistic response to Le Pen's identitarian argument is the view stated in *La république menacée*, 303–19, that the presence of (by now) more than three million North African Muslims in France is a "challenge [*défi*]" that requires a redefinition of the state's role in dealing with citizenship. Henceforth the French administration should solve the "contradictory mixture" of a state-conferred citizenship based on "abstract universality" and a civil society which continues to make cultural and economic distinctions. The state is therefore invited to assume a therapeutic as well as redistributionist function in rendering the "social system more open and more flexible."

21. For a detailed study of the antinatal trends in Western, and particularly European, countries, see *Are World Population Trends a Problem?*, ed. Ben Wattenberg and Karl Zinsmeister (Washington, D.C.: American Enterprise Institute, 1983).

22. Aristotle, *Politica*, Oxford Classical Texts (Oxford: Oxford University Press, 1957), Section 1276a: 34–40.

23. In a study of FN voters in the suburbs of Paris between 1984 and 1988, Nonna Mayer finds an overrepresentation of professionals and business owners until 1986; from 1986 on, however, the Front managed to attract less educated voters, including unemployed workers. According to Mayer, disaffection with the political class remains a drawing card for the FN, which has not had to take sides decisively in social confrontations, except against non-European immigrants (see *Le Front National*, 249–63). François Platone and Henri Rey, who have done research on the Communist-leaning Parisian suburb of Seine-Saint-Denis, note that "a growing proletarianistation" of the Front votes has taken place (see ibid., 268–81). See also Henry Roy, "Quelques réflexions sur l'évolution électorale d'un département de la banlieue parisienne: la Seine Saint-Denis," *Hérodote* 43 (1986), 6–38.

24. On the pivotal importance of anti-immigration sentiment among the FN electorate, see the studies by Serge Etchebarne and Jean Viand in *Le Front National*, 284–321; and P. A. Taguieff, "La rhétorique du national populisme, les règles élémentaires de la propagande xénophobe," *Mots* 9 (October 1984), 113–38. An argument that needs further development but seems highly plausible is the one made by Franklin Adler in *Telos*, cited above, that the present electoral surge of the FN betokens not the ascendancy of "rightwing extremism" but the decline of the French Left. Like Taguieff, Adler questions whether "extrême droite" is a useful analytic term and whether it is accurate to portray the FN as unalterably procapitalist. According to Adler, both the insolvency of the French welfare state and the French Left's lack of political credibility have caused French workers increasingly to turn to the FN for leadership and solutions. This in turn has led the Front into adopting the slogans of a European workers' party.

25. Mayer and Perrimeau, *Le Front National*, 49–52; Jérôme Jaffré, "Le Pen ou le vote exutoire," *Le Monde*, April 12, 1988.

26. Pierre Rosanvallon, *La nouvelle question sociale* (Paris: Editions Du Seuil, 1995), 36–44, 69–75.

27. Mayer and Perrimeau *Le Front National*, 54–57; Pascal Perrineau, "Quel avenir pour le front national?" *Intervention*, March 15, 1986, 33–41.

28. See Patrick J. Buchanan's statement of personal belief in his autobiographical *Right from the Beginning* (Boston and New York: Little, Brown & Co. 1988), 58–79, 96–99, and 337–59. For his views on immigration, crime, and welfare, see "Dialogue is not for Hoodlums," *New York Post*, May 11, 1991, 13; "D.C.: A Liberal Wasteland," ibid., January 24, 1990, 17; and "Manitoba, USA?" ibid., April 14, 1990, 13. For a learned defense of Buchananite populism, see S. T. Francis, "The Buchanan Revolution," *Chronicles* (July 1991), 12–13; for a critical but sympathetic treatment of the same phenomenon, see Paul Gottfried, *The Conservative Movement*, 159–66; Scott McConnell's commentary "Buchanan: After the Flameout," *New York Post*, March 13, 1996; and Edward Luttwak, "Buchanan vuol dir no a Gates," *L'Espresso*, March 8, 1996, 92–98. For a negative assessment of Buchananite conservative nationalism, see David Frum, *Dead Right* (New York: Basic Books, 1994), 124–58. For Buchanan's most extensive statement of his isolationist foreign policy, see "American First—and Second and Third," *National Interest* 19 (Spring 1990), 77–82. And on the presumed natural limits of Buchanan's cultural stands, see *Wall Street Journal*, February 22, 1996, A16.

29. On the predominantly Catholic ethnic core of Buchananite populism, see my essay "Populism and Neoconservatism," *Telos* 90 (Winter 1991–92), 184–88; the sarcastic identification of Buchanan with the Catholic Right in Charles Lane's "Daddy Boy" in *The New Republic*, January 22, 1996, 15–19; and Michael Lind's commentary "Buchanan, Conservatism's Ugly Face," *New York Times*, August 19, 1992.

30. See the polling information for Clinton and his Republican congressional opposition in *New York Times*, December 3, 1995, 31; ibid., December 14, 1995, 1; and Thomas Edsall's comments in *Washington Post*, December 17, 1995, 12.

31. See the comments on the FP in the *New York Times*, October 13 and December 17, 1995; and Paul Hockenos, "Jörg Haider: Austria's Far Right Wunderkind," *World Policy Journal* 12, no. 3 (Fall 1995), 75–76.

32. See the detailed analysis of the FP's electoral setback in December 1995 in *Corriere della Sera*, December 18, 1995, 7–8. Despite my repeated attempts to get in touch with the FP's leaders in Vienna, I have received no response until now. Almost all my information on this subject was taken from the late Donald I. Warren, who was doing a biography of Jörg Haider at the time of his death.

33. For an overview of the League, see Ivo Diamanti, *La Lega. Geografia, storia, e sociologia di uno nuovo soggetto politico* (Rome: Donzelli, 1993); and the special issue on "The Leagues in Italy," *Telos* 90 (Winter 1991–92).

34. See William Bluhm, *Building an Austrian Nation: The Political Integration of a Western State* (New Haven: Yale University Press, 1973), especially 12–46.

35. Books in English that highlight the problematic nature of Italian state-building are Joseph LaPalombara, *Interest Groups in Italian Politics* (Princeton: Princeton University Press, 1964); and P. A. Allum, *Italy—Republic Without Government?* (New York: W. W. Norton, 1973).

36. See Alessandro Campi, "Beyond the State: Gianfranco Miglio's Challenge," trans. Paul Piccone, *Telos* 100 (Summer 1994), 103–22; and the contributions by Miglio and his collaborators in *Verso una nuova costituzione* (Milan: Giuffré, 1994).

37. See Miglio, *Le regolarità*, 447–49, 901–26.

38. Ibid., 1095–98. According to sociologist Roberto Biorcio, Northern Italian "laboriosità" has become a sustaining myth in the Lombard quest for regional self-identity, in the absence of other viable cultural legacies. See Renato Mannheimer, ed., *La Lega Lombarda* (Milan: Feltrinelli, 1991), 68–72.

39. See Ivo Diamanti's essay "Una tipologia dei simpatizzanti della Lega," in Mannheimer, *Lega Lombarda*, 159–95. Despite Diamanti's gratuitous value judgments about the ignorance and bigotry of the League's voters, he is correct to stress its continuing dependence upon a rural electorate which until recently embodied Catholic as well as localist sentiments.

40. See Umberto Bossi, *Io, Bossi, e la Lega: Diario segreto dei miei quattro anni sul carroccio* (Milan: Mondadori, 1994).

41. Cf. the unflattering but detailed portrait of Haider in *New York Times Magazine*, April 21, 1996, 42.

42. Miglio, *Le regolarità*, 877–941; and Giorgio Ferrari, *Gianfranco Miglio: Un giacobino nordista* (Milan: Liber, 1993).

43. See *New York Times*, October 31, 1995, A12; and J. Parizeau, "The Case for a Sovereign Quebec," *Foreign Policy* 99 (Summer 1995), 69–77.

44. Peter Brimelow, "Canadian Roulette," *Forbes*, September 25, 1995, 46–48.

45. Le Pen, *Pour la France*, 10, 34–35, 125–34, 144–45.

46. See Gianfranco Miglio, *Una costituzione per i prossimi trenta anni* (Bari: Laterza, 1990); and Campi, *Miglio's Challenge*, 118–20.

47. *Investor's Business Daily*, November 15, 1995, 1.

48. See Christopher Shea's "Defending Dixie," in *Chronicle of Higher Education*, November 10, 1995, A9, A17; and Hill's responses in *Southern Patriot* 26 (December 1995), 1–2. A social theorist claimed by the League is former Marxist-Leninist historian Eugene D. Genovese. Though still a self-described socialist (albeit social reactionary), Genovese sympathetically outlines the League's critique of the "more disquieting features of the modern world" in *The Southern Tradition* (Cambridge, Mass.: Harvard University Press, 1994).

49. *Washington Post*, October 29, 1995, C3.

50. On this quest by the Lombard League for a shared regional history, see D. Vimercati, *I Lombardi alla nuova crociata* (Milan: Mursia, 1990).

51. Lasch, *Revolt of the Elites*, 25–49; clearly Lasch's harshest invectives are directed against the upper middle class as opposed to the lower middle and working classes.

52. Stanley Rothman, "The Decline of Bourgeois America," *Society* (January/February 1996), 16.

53. Ibid., 16–17.

54. Veyne, *Le pain et le cirque*, 87–89.

55. Benjamin Ginsberg, *The Captive Public* (New York: Basic Books, 1986).

56. On the cultural and genetic presuppositions for citizenship in classical republics and democracies, see the provocative chapter "Athens's Illiberal Democracy," in Paul Rahe's *Republics Ancient and Modern*, 186–218, and Ian Contiades, "Exthros kai Polemios eis tēn sugxronon politikēn theorian kai tēn hellenikēn arxaiotēta," published by the Griechische Humanistische Gesellschaft (Athens, 1969). Contiades's essay, which unfortunately has never been translated into English, underlines the centrality of the outsider in defining ancient political identities.

57. Aristotle, *Politica*, sections 1310b: 7–40, 1313a: 1–15; and Plato, *Res Publica*, Oxford Classical Texts, Book 9 (Oxford: Oxford University Press, 1965), sections 564–67.

58. See the essay "If the GNP Is Up, Why Is America Down?" by C. W. Cobb and others in *Atlantic Monthly* 276 (October 1995), 59–60; and the Bureau of Labor Statistics projections in *Occupational Outlook Quarterly* 39 (Fall 1995), 6–7.

59. Edward Shorter, *The Making of the Modern Family* (New York: Basic Books, 1975).

60. Ibid., particularly 5–21, 255–80; and Edward Shorter, "Illegitimacy, Sexual Revolution, and Social Change in Modern Europe," *Journal of Interdisciplinary History* 2 (1971), 237–72.

61. William B. Hixson, *The Search for the American Right Wing* (Princeton: Princeton Unviersity Press, 1992), particularly 351–57.

62. Alan Wolfe, *Whose Keeper? Social Science and Moral Obligation* (Berkeley: University of California Press, 1989). See my review of Wolfe's book in *Society* 27 (July/August 1990), 95–96.

63. Lasch, *Revolt of the Elites*, 102–4.

64. This argument is underlying or explicit in such feminist works as Andrea Dworkin, *Letters from a War Zone* (reprint, Chicago: L. Hill Books, 1992); Wendy Brown, *States of Injury: Power and Freedom in Late Modernity* (Princeton: Princeton University Press, 1995); and Shulamith Firestone, *The Dialectic of Sex: The Case for Feminist Revolution* (New York: Morrow, 1993).

65. For indignant denunciations of the usage "Judeo-Christian," see Alan M. Dershowitz, *Chutzpah* (New York: Simon & Schuster, 1991), 216–19.

66. Bill Kauffman, *America First* (Amherst, N.Y.: Prometheus Books, 1995), 231.

67. Gray, *Enlightenment's Wake*, especially 144–87.

68. Ibid., 18–30; and John Gray, *Beyond the New Right: Markets, Government and the Common Environment* (London and New York: Routledge, 1993).

69. See *L'Express*, November 3, 1989, 6–9; and *Le Monde Diplomatique* (December 1989), 1, 22.

70. On the alliance between Third World immigrants and the social Left in various Western societies, see Katherine Bett, *Ideology and Immigration: Australia 1976 to 1987*, 157–72; Peter Brimelow, *Alien Nation*, 146–51; Catherine Wihtol de Wenden, *Les immigrés et la politique* (Paris: Presses de FNSP, 1988); W. A. Cornelius, P. L. Martin, and J. F. Hollifeld, eds., *Controlling Immigration* (Stanford: Stanford University Press, 1994), 143–76; Wayne Lutton and John Tanton, *The Immigration Invasion*, 48–59; Leon Bouvier et al., "Shaping Florida: The Effects of Immigration," (pamphlet, Center for Immigration Studies, 1995); and André Lebon, "Immigration en France, données, perspectives," *Revue françaises des affaires sociales* (December 1992). The correlation being made does not involve a negative judgment. It merely challenges an assertion frequently heard among neoliberal and neoconservative immigration expansionists, like Ben Wattenberg, Francis Fukayama, and Julian Simon, that Third World immigration produces politically and culturally stabilizing effects. Despite Asian and Cuban exceptions, such immigration favors and reflects the ascendancy of social engineering and serves to encourage government efforts to enforce intrusive standards of tolerance. In the United States it has created a new clientele for affirmative action programs; see Frederick R. Lynch, *Invisible Victims: White Males and the Crisis of Affirmative Action* (New York: Praeger Books, 1991); and Peter Skerry, "Borders and Quotas: Immigration and the Affirmative Action State," *The Public Interest* 96 (Summer 1989), 88–89. Ira Mehlman (of the Federation for American Immigration Reform in Los Angeles) is currently working on a book dealing with the electoral support for expanded public administration from Third World immigrants in the United States.

71. See Francis Fukuyama, "Immigrants and Family Values," *Commentary* 95 (May 1993), 26–32.

72. Quoted in Leon Wieseltier, "Abracadabrant," *New Republic*, January 6, 1992, 28.

73. Illustrative of the alliance between postmodernism and the alleged victims of Western values are Catherine Belsey and Jane Moore Clenden, eds., *The Feminist Reader. Essays in Gender and the Politics of Literary Criticism* (New York: Macmillan, 1989); Leonard Lentricchia, *Criticism and Social Change* (Chicago: University of Chicago, 1984); and Stanley E. Fish, *Political Change* (New York: Clarendon Press, 1995).

74. See Franklin H. Adler, "Racism, Difference and the Right in France," in *Modern and Contemporary France*, NS 3.4 (1995), 439–51; and P. A. Taguieff, "From Race to Culture: The New Right's View of European Identity," *Telos* (Winter 1993/Spring 1994).

75. See Alain de Benoist's *Europe, tiers monde, même combat* (Paris: Laffont, 1986) as an affirmation of support for the Third World against the American Empire and Benoist's diatribe against American materialism and puritanical morality, "L'ennemi principal," *Eléments* 41 (March/April 1982), 37–40.

76. This and related topics are treated in a special issue of *Telos*, "The French New Right," 97–98 (Winter 1993/Spring 1994).

77. From a letter to the author from Alain de Benoist (July 27, 1996); see also Alain de Benoist, *L'Empire Intérieur* (Paris: Editions du Labyrinthe, 1996) for a multinational reconfiguration of European political life.

78. Cf. the portraits of European populist leaders in *Cosmopolitique* 18 (February 1991); Roberto Biorcio, "The Rebirth of Populism in Italy and France," *Telos* 90 (Winter 1991/92), 43–56; André Bejin's critical observations about "antiracist ideology" in *Racismes/Antiracismes* (Paris: Librairie des Méridiens, 1989); and P.-A. Taguieff, *Les fins de l'antiracisme* (Paris: Librarie des Méridiens, 1995).

79. See the dossier on European education in *Ideazione* 3, no. 4 (July 1996) 131–94, especially 158–71.

80. One of the few studies that treat the snares of state-supported privatization of education is Jeffrey Tucker's *The Voucher Reader* (Auburn, Ala.: Ludwig von Mises Institute, 1995).

81. See Richard Morin and Dan Balz, "Americans Losing Trust in Each Other and Their Institutions," *Washington Post*, January 28, 1996, A1; and *The Gallup Poll* (Wilmington, Delaware: Scholarly Resources, 1994), 32. Gallup polls indicate that whereas in January 1958, 73 percent of Americans "always or almost always" trusted their government, this figure by January 1994 had shrunk to 19 percent.

82. See the Roper survey figures on the attitudes of immigrants toward American society and life in *The American Enterprise* 104 (March/April 1995), 102–3.

83. On the Colorado amendment, see *Wall Street Journal*, May 21, 1996, B1; *New York Times*, May 21, 1996, A1; *Human Events*, October 20, 1995, 2–3; *U.S. News and World Report*, October 2, 1995, 2 and 7; and Lino A. Graglia, "*Romer v. Evans*: The People Foiled Again by the Constitution," *University of Colorado Law Review* 68, no. 2 (Spring 1997), 409–28. On Proposition 187, see *Economist*, May 3, 1995, 58; *New York Times*, September 2, 1992; and the cover story in *U. S. News and World Report*, September 25, 1995, 4–5.

84. See H. Fineman, "Riding the Wave," in *Newsweek*, May 22, 1995, 18–21; and H. Johnson, "Blowing in the Wind," *National Review*, May 15, 1995, 46–47.

85. See Sid Blumenthal's acidic observations about Wilson the populist, following his generally poor showing as a presidential candidate, in *New Yorker*, October 30, 1995, 46–50.

86. Although most Canadian political intellectuals resemble their American counterparts in supporting a large managerial state committed to social engineering, some have combined distaste for Manning with earnest attempts to understand his protest politics. See, for example, L. Fischer's "Learning Tough Po-

litical Lessons," *Maclean's*, April 25, 1994, 14–15; K. Whyte's "Cluster Bomb," *Saturday Night* 109 (October 1994), 8–9; and idem, "Pols in a Pod," *Saturday Night* 110 (March 1995), 10–12.

87. See the commentaries on Manning in *Maclean's*, October 11, 1993, 16–19; October 18, 1993, 17; and October 25, 1993, 14–17.

Conclusion

1. Robert Merton, *Sociological Ambivalence*, (New York: Free Press, 1976).

2. Thomas Kuhn, *The Structure of Scientific Revolutions* (Chicago: University of Chicago Press, 1970).

3. Among books that make and document this point are Roger Kimball, *Tenured Radicals: How Politics Has Corrupted Our Higher Education* (New York: Harper & Row, 1990); George Marsden, *The Soul of the American University: From Protestant Establishment to Established Non-Belief* (New York: Oxford University Press, 1994); and Thomas Sowell, *Inside American Education* (New York: Free Press, 1992). See also my own remarks in *Insight*, October 16, 1995, 18–20; and in "Postmodernism and Academic Discontents," *Academic Questions* 9, no. 3 (Summer 1996), 58–67.

4. *New Republic*, August 29, 1955, 18; also the detailed critical study of the moral and scientific claims made by Dewey and his disciples in John Patrick Diggins's *The Promise of Pragmatism: The Crisis of Knowledge and Authority* (Chicago: University of Chicago Press, 1995).

5. See Carl Schmitt, *The Concept of the Political*, trans. and intro. by George Schwab (New Brunswick: Rutgers University Press, 1976); and Paul Gottfried, *Carl Schmitt: Politics and Theory* (Westport, Conn.: Greenwood Press, 1990), especially 57–82.

6. Carl Schmitt, *Nomos der Erde im Völkerrecht des Ius Publicum Europaeum*, second edition (Berlin: Duncker & Humblet, 1974), 220–60.

7. Ibid., 167–219, 290–98.

8. See the essay by Francis Fukuyama, "The End of History?" *The National Interest* 16 (Summer 1989), 4.

9. The political irrelevance of the "archaic Right" is a recurrent theme in Samuel T. Francis's *Beautiful Losers: Essays on the Failure of American Conservatism* (Columbia: University of Missouri Press, 1993); for a dispassionate treatment of the major forces and conflicts on the contemporary American Right, see George H. Nash, *The Conservative Intellectual Movement in America*, second edition (Wilmington, Del.: Intercollegiate Studies Institute, 1996), 278–341.

10. An essay that broke ground in pointing to the intended vacuity of contemporary ideological debate is Christopher Lasch's "The Obsolescence of Left and Right," *New Oxford Review* 56 (April 1989), 5–15. See also Marco Tarchi, "In Search of Right and Left," trans. Franco Sacchi, *Telos* 103 (Spring 1995), 181–88; and Thomas Molnar's penetrating comments on American political character in

Du mal moderne: Symptomes et antidotes (Cité de Québec: Beffroi, 1996), 83–91, 122–33.

11. On the connection in the United States between administrative consolidation and federally organized "crusades," see Robert Nisbet's *The Present Age* (New York: Harper & Row, 1988), particularly 20–40.

12. A reading of Renzo De Felice's multivolume study of Italian fascism, particularly the second volume, *Mussolini il fascista: L'organizzazione dello stato fascista. 1925–1929* (Turin: Einaudi, 1968), suggests the inchoate nature of the Italian national revolutionary attempt to structure a modern managerial state. De Felice depicts Mussolini as engaged primarily in a balancing act throughout the late twenties, trying to maintain civil peace between *sindicalisti* and *industriali* and between laicists and clericalists. Mussolini's success in this period was not in laying the foundations of a "total state" (however much fascist theorists seized on that term) but in integrating rival groups into a political nation. Mussolini had to come to terms with a Catholic authoritarian presence that formed a state within his own. See De Felice's discussion of that problem in ibid., 382- 436.

13. Still the best work by an American, even after seventy years, on the hypocritical priggish attitude toward power among "public servants" is Irving Babbitt's *Democracy and Leadership* (1924; reprint, Indianapolis: Liberty Classics, 1979), particularly 274–78. For related opinions by an exponent of Babbitt, see Claes Ryn's introductory essay to the new edition of Babbitt's *Rousseau and Romanticism* (New Brunswick, N. J., and London: Transaction Publishers, 1991). After reading through textbooks on public administration by authors who obviously admired it, my student assistant Bill Patch compared the attitude toward power among his sources to the "unwillingness of some sex offenders to talk about human sexuality." More interesting may be to speculate why public administrators and their advocates feign this innocence of power—or, will not identify any regime they favor with force. In contrast to authoritarian and theocratic regimes, caring administrative states are thought to enforce "human rights" and "fairness" without imposing their will at the expense of others.

One possible criticism of the preceding study is methodological. It may be objected that too much has been made about considerations of power but not enough about other causal explanations for the modern state. An international economy, high tech industries and a mobile work force are at least as responsible for cultural and political changes as the expansion of public administration (or so critics of my position might argue in pointing to a changing economic landscape). But in fact I do take into account industrialization and urbanization as preconditions for both democracy and the rise of the managerial state. These circumstances contributed to a political dynamic that has shaped the surrounding society. It is also possible for a highly advanced economy to coexist, as in Switzerland, with strong local government. Being tied to a large economy does not necessitate an equally large administration. Nor do educated professionals have to side with an expanding administrative state or with therapeutic politics.

Much of the base for European populist movements, particularly the Lega Nord, comes from those associated with an urban economy and possessing university training.

There are features of the managerial therapeutic state that cannot be plausibly interpreted as mere responses to economic growth. Having the state interpose itself with increasing frequency between spouses and between parents and children, having government officials monitor conversations among employees of large firms and industries for actionable hate speech, and attaching to applicants for schools and jobs governmentally imposed victim and nonvictim statuses are not entirely nor primarily explainable as policies determined by economic change. Though the government and media both cite the overall material advantages of Third World immigration, detailed studies, such as Roy Beck's *The Case Against Immigration* (New York: W. W. Norton, 1996), prove exactly the opposite. Brimelow, Beck, Edward Luttwak, and other analysts show that the present immigration, because of its character and level, impacts negatively on wages and damages particularly the employment opportunities of the underclass. Here as in other cases the political class pursues economically questionable practices for ideological reasons and social control. It then makes economic arguments to justify its course of action. Despite some overstatement, a useful corrective study dealing with the dubious connection between material well-being and political administrative centralization is Hans-Hermann Hoppe's *A Theory of Socialism and Capitalism* (Boston: Kluwer Academic Publishers, 1989).

* Index *

Abelard, Peter, 7
abortion, vii–viii, 143n.5
Achille-Fould, Aymar, 105
Ackerman, Bruce, 68
Adler, Franklin, 114, 168n.24
Adorno, Theodor, 4, 480, 91–94
After Virtue (MacIntyre), 95
Aid to Dependent Children, 55
Alien Nation (Brimelow), 96
Allport, Gordon, 100
American Cause, 117
American Enterprise, 54
American Jewish Committee, 80, 94
American Political Science Association, 132
American Political Science Review, 3
American Psychiatric Association, 79
Anatomy of Antiliberalism (Holmes), 5
Ancient City, The (Coulanges), 37
Annual Report (U.S. Council of Economic Advisors), 54
anti-Semitism, 80, 89, 92–94, 109, 113–14; exaggerated re the French National Front, 113–14, 167n.17; overestimated in postwar U.S., 89, 92
Arendt, Hannah, 93
Argentina, 111
Aristotle, 88, 103, 115, 123–24
Armey, Dick, 64, 77
Athens, ancient, 103, 150n.20
Atlee, Clement, 53
Augustine, St., 36
Auster, Lawrence, 97
Australia, ix, 104, 127, 162–63n.77
Austria, ix, 50, 105, 118–20
Authoritarian Personality, The (Adorno and Horkeimer), 4, 19, 80–81, 91–94
authoritarian personality, attributed to German males, 58

Babbitt, Irving, 81, 110
Bancroft, George, 41–43

Beard, Charles, 15, 146n.37
Beard, Mary, 15
Beauvoir, Simone de, 88
Beesley, Edward, 83
Bell Curve, The (Herrnstein and Murray), 4–5, 144n.5
Bennett, William, 71, 139
Benoist, Alain de, 113, 128, 130
Berle, Adolph, 65–66
Berman, Russell, 129
Berry, Mary Frances, 107
Bestor, Arthur, 59, 136–37
Bethke-Elshtain, Jean, 72
Bettelheim, Bruno, 80
"Beveridge Report on Social Life" (in England), 53
Bingham, Hiram, 14
Bismarck, Otto von, 7, 11
Blanqui, Louise Auguste, 34
Blumenberg, Hans, 21
Boas, Franc, 78, 99
Boasians, 100
Bobbio, Norberto, x
Book of Virtues (Bennett), 139
Borah, William, 16
Bosanquet, Bernard, 13
Bossi, Umberto, 118, 128
bourgeoisie, 45, 136. *See also* liberalism
Brandeis, Louis, 7
Bratton, F. G., 36
Brazil, 111
Bright, John, 15, 26
Brimelow, Peter, 96–97, 162n.76
Brinkley, Allan, 65, 156–57n.51
Broder, David, 132
Brooks, Stephen, 98–99
Bruce, H. Addington, 79
Buchanan, Patrick J., xiii, 16, 63, 77, 117, 133
Burke, Edmund, 17, 130
Burnham, James, 50, 63, 66, 139
Burnham, John C., 78

177

Campi, Alessandro, 128

Canada, ix, 7–9, 25, 98–99, 104, 114, 119–20, 127, 133–34. *See also* populism

Canadian Panel on Violence against Women, 99

Canadian Reform Party, xiii, 133–34

capitalism, 10, 51; bureaucratic control of society compatible with, 93; "democratic," 27, 148n.74; and the welfare state, 27–28

Carlson, Allan, 57

Catéchisme Socialiste (Guesde) 31

Cato Institute, 98

Champagne, Anthony, 62

Charlemagne, 115

Charrièhristian, 105

Chirac, Jacques, 113

Christian Century, 96

Cicero, Marcus Tullius, xiv, 141

citizenship, limited, 98, 103, 171n.56

Clinton, Bill, vii–viii, 74, 118, 122

Clinton, Hillary, 90

Cobden, Richard, 15

Columbia Law Review, 3

Commentary, 95

Commerce Clause (U.S. Constitution), 67

Common Faith, A (Dewey), 14

Common Sense, 14

Communism, Communists, 10, 51, 56; Soviet, 50

communitarians, 72

Comte, August 10, 14, 17–18, 75

Congress for Cultural Freedom, 81

Congressional Budget and Impoundment Control Act, 54

Congressional Budget Office, 54

Conradt, David, 58

Considerations on Representative Government (Mill), 10

Constitution of Athens (Aristotle), 103

Constitution of Liberty, The (Hayek), 26

constitutional liberty, 6

Coulanges, N. D. Fustel de, 37, 150n.20

Council of Europe, 106

Counter Revolution of Science, The (Hayek), 18

Cowling, Maurice, 47, 99, 153n.53

Crisis and Leviathan (Higgs), 67

Croly, Herbert, 59–60, 64–66, 157n.53

custom, "despotism" of, 83

Dahl, Robert A., x, 59

Dahmia, Sikha, 98

Dahrendorff, Ralf, 76

Dangerfield, George, 12

Defunis v. Odegaard, 86–87

Delcroix, Eric, 106

democracy, 304, 6, 11, 19, 24–27, 149n.3; administered, xii–xiv, 9, 26; cultural and ethnic identities in, 32; decline of, ix–x, 48, 59, 69, 81; German, 76; and hedonism, 34, 49; ideology of liberal variant as a U.S. export, 68–69; in industrialized societies, 61–63; liberal, ix–x, 8, 18, 27–28, 30, 38, 47, 49–109 passim; vs. liberalism, 30–48; mass, 30, 32–34, 48, 73, 81, 110–34; modern and premodern, 32, 103; and pluralism, 69–109 passim; right to, 74; social, 9, 11–120, 27, 37, 39–40, 46; totalitarian, 81; and the welfare state, 26, 49–71, 75

Democracy and Leadership (Babbitt), 81

Democracy and Liberty (Lecky), 31

Democratic Party, Democrats, viii, 29

Denmark, 54

Dennis, Paul M., 79

Derrida, Jacques, 130

Detroit Free Press, 98

Dewey, John, 3, 13–14, 18, 22, 36–37, 55–60, 66, 68, 75, 83, 86, 101–2, 107

Dialectic of the Enlightenment, The (Adorno), 93

Dietze, Gottfried, 26

Diggins, John P., 37, 51

DiLornzo, Thomas, 54

discrimination, social and gender, 62

Dole, Robert, vii–viii

droit des gens, Le (Vattel), 137

Dumont, Louis, 37–38, 86, 151n.25

Durkheim, Emile, 55

Dworkin, Ronald, 86–88

Economic Consequences of Immigration (Simon), 97

Education sentimentale, L' (Flaubert), 34
education and socialization, 28, 131–32
Eisel, Stephan, 76
Eisenhower, Dwight, 69
Ekirch, Arthur A., 13, 28
elections, 1996 U.S., vii, viii, xiii
Emerson, Ralph Waldo, 88
End of Liberalism, The (Lowi), 17
End of the Republican Era, The (Lowi), 85
England, 24–25, 31, 39, 46–47, 50, 52–53,
    65, 74, 98, 101, 104, 127. *See also* immi-
    gration; welfare state
Engler, John, 133
English Fabians, 17
Enlightenment, 5, 33, 129
Enlightenment's Wake, In the (Gray), 126
entitlement programs, entitlements, vii–xi,
    122
environmentalism, 100
Equal Employment Opportunities Commis-
    sion, 25
Erasmus, 7
Europe, vii–ix, 41, 58, 104, 139. *See also spe-
    cific countries*
European Commission against Racism and
    Intolerance, 106
Express, L', 70

*Failure of Independent Liberalism, 1930–41,
    The* (Lawson), 3
Family Leave bill, vii
family values, vii
fascism, fascists, 14, 31, 51, 56, 66; attrac-
    tiveness to American Progressives and
    New Dealers, 66, 157n.53; German, 51;
    Italian version as attempt to safeguard
    bourgeois civilization, 44–46, 152n.49,
    175n.12; Latin, 51
Federal Reserve Board, 64
Federal Trade Commission, 64
Federalist Papers, The (Hamilton, Jay, Madi-
    son), 98
Felice, Renzo De, 5, 175n.12
Finer, Hermann, 11–12, 19, 24–25, 145–
    46n.23
Fish, Hamilton, 16
Flaubert, Gustave, 34, 150n.12

Fleming, Thomas, 122
Flowerman, S. H., 92
Forbes, 96
Fox-Genovese, Elizabeth, 72
France, viii, 25, 30, 39, 41, 49–50, 52–53,
    84, 104–7, 110–18, 126–27, 130–31; plu-
    ralist persecution of "insensitive" writers
    in, 105. *See also* immigration; National
    Front; populism franchise, expanded
    electoral, 49–50, 151–52n.40
Francis, Samuel T., 63
Franco, Francisco, 61
Frankfurter Allegemeine Zeitung, 76
Frederick Barbarossa, 122
free market, 3, 7, 8, 11–12, 16, 37, 147n.43
freedom, individual, 35–38, 59, 151n.25
Freiheitliche Partei (Austria), viii, 118–19
French Ministry of Interior, 107
French *philosophes,* 5
French Radicals, 17
French Revolution (1789), 41–42, 49–50,
    84
French Revolution (1848), 40, 150n.12
Fromkin, David, 69

Gabel, Peter, 90
Galbraith, John Kenneth, 15
Gallagher, Maggie, vii–viii, 143n.5
Gallup Polls, vii
Galston, William, 21, 23, 25
Garvey, Marcus, 51
gay rights, xi, 132
Gemeinwirtschaft, Die (Mises), 9
General Agreement on Tariffs and Trade,
    16
Genovese, Eugene, 139
George, Robert, 87–88
German Polity, The (Conradt), 58
Germany, 3–4, 31, 39, 46, 52–53, 58, 63,
    66, 76, 105, 118; reconstruction of post-
    war society in, 76, 102–3
Gingrich, Newt, 54
Ginsbert, Benjamin, 123
Giolitti, Giovanni, 44
Gladstone, William, 8
Glazer, Nathan, 5
Glendon, Mary Ann, ix–x

Goldberg, Stephen, 100
government: "big," 117; as a broker among competing interests, x, 143n.7; bureaucratic, 110; democratization of, 30–40, 49–50, 151–52n.40; identified with social planning, 73; instability of democratic, 40–41, 110; as instrument of a political class, xi–xiv, 72–73, 123, 132; interventionist, 101; and people who allow it to do things for and to them, 123, 132; as provider of social therapy, 79; and public sentiment to reduce size of, vii. *See also* public administration; state; welfare state
Grammar of Politics, A (Laski), 101
Gramsci, Antonio, 63
Gray, John, 23, 36–37, 43, 87–88, 126–27
Greece (modern), 131
Green, T. H., 13
Guesde, Jules, 31
Guizot, François, 30–31, 35, 37, 40–42, 50, 58, 100, 149n.3
Gutmann, Amy, 88–89

Habermas, Jürgen, ix, 73, 76, 102–3
Haider, J., 118–19
Halévy, Elie, 16
Hallowell, John H., 83–84
Hamby, Alonzo L., 20
Hardach, Karl, 52
Harper's, 28
Hartz, Louis, 9, 20
hate, hatred: crimes manifesting, xii; racial, 93; in speech, 89
Hayek, Friedrich, 10–12, 18–19, 24–26, 28
Hegel, G.W.H., 13, 41, 50, 59, 110
Hegel's Philosophy of the State and History: An Exposition (Morris), 13
Herder, Johann Gottfried, 130
Herrnstein, Richard, 4–5
Higgs, Robert, 54, 67–68
Hill, Michael, 122
Himmelfarb, Gertrude, 38
History of British India (Mill), 16
History of European Liberalism (Ruggiero), 5
History of the Formation of the Constitution of the Untied States (Bancroft), 42

History of the United States (Bancroft), 41–42
Hitler, Adolph, 4, 25, 51, 63, 94
Hixson, William B., 124–25
Hobbes, Thomas, 28, 134, 137, 141
Hobhouse, L. T., 13, 56, 57
Hofstadter, Richard, 81, 125
Holland, 53–54
Holmes, Stephen, 5–7, 145n.12
Homo Aequalis (Dumont), 37
Hook, Sidney, 101, 164n.109
Horkheimer, Max, 4, 80, 92–93
Hull, Cordell, 16, 147n.43
human right(s), 98, 130; codes of, 104; to democracy, 74; as an excuse for U.S. intervention abroad, 138–39; to mental soundness, inculcated by government, 79; newly discovered, 88; to social planning, 129
Hume, David, 6, 23

Ickes, Harold, 65
immigration, viii–xiii, 14–15, 63–64, 96–98, 112, 162–63nn.76 and 77; to Australia, 127, 162–63n.77; its benefits for the managerial state, 127, 132, 172n.70; to Canada, 127; and cultural heterogeneity in host country, 97; to England, 53, 127; to France, 112–16, 126–27, 168nn.23 and 24; to Germany, 76; from Mexico, 64; to Quebec, 120; from Third World, 53, 64, 96, 112–16, 126–27; to U.S., 64, 77, 133
Immigration and Nationality Act (U.S.), 96
Institute for Jewish Advocacy, 97
intelligence, influence of heredity on, 4–5, 144n.5
International Covenant on Economic, Cultural and Social Rights, 79
Investor's Business Daily, 121
Italy, 51–52, 118–22, 131; historical relation of democracy to liberalism in, 43–46

Jaffré, Jérôme, 116
Jay, John, 98
Jefferson, Thomas, 6

Journal of Philosophy, 14
Judis, John, 4–5, 55

Kallen, Horace, 60–61,66, 75, 84–86,
    101–2, 107, 155–56n.39, 157n.53
Kant, Immanuel, 23
Kauffman, Bill, 125–26
Kennedy, Edward, 96
Kennedy, John F., 75–96
Kennedy, Robert, 96
King, Martin Luther, Jr., 96
Klineberg, Otto, 100
Kloppenberg, James, 39
Knag, Sigmund, x–xi
Kondylis, Panajotis, 32–35
Koselleck, Reinhart, 84
Kramer, Hilton, 33
Kramnick, Isaac, 101
Krauthammer, Charles, vii, 47
Kreitor, Nikolaj-Klaus von, 57
Kriegel, Annie, 106
Kristol, Irving, 72
Kuhn, Thomas 135

Lasch, Christopher, 5, 37, 70, 72, 80, 95,
    111, 122–23, 125, 139
Laski, Harold, 101, 107
Lawson, Gary S., 67–69
Lawson, R. Alan, 3
Lazarfeld, Paul, 80
Lecky, William, 31, 39–40
Le Gallou, Jean-Yves, 113
Le Pen, Jean-Marie, 111–15, 117, 120–21,
    128, 130–31, 133, 166n.10, 167nn.16
    and 17, 168n.20
Lega Lombarda (Lombard League, mod-
    ern Italy), 118
Lega Nord (Northern league, modern
    Italy), 118–19, 122
Legacy of the Liberal Spirit, The (Bratton), 36
Legitimität der Neuzeit, Die (Blumenberg),
    21
Lerner, Michael, 90–91
Levinson, Daniel J., 92
liberalism: authoritarianism in J. S. Mill's
    version of, 47–48; and the bourgeoisie,
    30–33, 35, 38–40; bureaucratic govern-
ment not incompatible with old version
of, 44–46, 110; changed meaning of, ix,
xi, 3–6, 29, 156–57n.51; and constitutional liberty, 6; and constitutional monarchy, 35–36; continuity of in U.S. history alleged, 19–29; decontextualization
of, 36–39, 69; vs. democracy, 30–48; and
the Democratic Party (U.S.), 29; European, 10, 43; vs. fascism, Nazism, 304,
14, 18–19; German, 103; and internationalism, 16–19, 61, 72–109; misidenti-
fied with pluralism and liberal democracy, 72–109 passim; and neoconservatives, 29; new and old, 12, 29,
33; polemical sense of, 305; "progressive" character of, 13–19; and property
rights, 6; semantic problems with, 3–29;
universal values alleged for, 6
Liberalism (Gray), 36
Liberalism (Hobhouse), 13
Liberalism (Mises), 26
Liberalism: Its Meaning and History
    (Schapiro), 7
Liberalism in Contemporary America (Mur-
    phey), 58
Liberalism and Its Challenges (Hamby), 20
Liberalism and Social Action (Dewey), 56
Liberty, On (Mill), 83
*Ligue Internationale Contre le Racisme et l'Anti-
    semitisme*, 105
Linda, Michael, 4–5
Link, Arthur S., 4–66
Lippmann, Walter, 66, 81–84, 110
Lipset, S. M., 59, 74–75, 81, 94
Locke, John, 5–7, 23, 27, 37–38, 145n.12
Loewenstein, Karl, 3, 18–19
Loewenthal, Leo, 80
Loi Gayssot (France), 106
Lombard league (medieval Italy), 122
Lowenthal, Richard, 76
Lukacs, John, 28, 51
Lutton, Wayne, 97

Machiavelli, Niccolò, 45
MacIntyre, Alasdair, 37, 95
Macmillan, Harold, 53
Maistre, Joseph de, 5

Making of the Modern Family, The (Shorter), 124

Managerial Revolution, The (Burnham), 50

Manchester Guardian, 13

Mannheim, Karl, 74

Manning, Preston, xiii, 133–34

Martel, Charles, 115

Marx, Karl, 17, 55

Matteoti, Giacomo, 51

McCarthy, Joseph, 80

Mead, Margaret, 78, 102

Medicare, vii

Merton, Robert, 135

Mexico, 64, 96

Michels, Robert, 48

Miglio, Gianfranco, 25, 119, 121

"Militant Democracy and Fundamental Rights" (Loewenstein), 3, 17–18

Mill, James, 12, 15–16, 26

Mill, John Stuart, 10, 12, 15–16, 18, 30, 37, 40, 47–48, 75, 83, 99, 153n.53

Mills, C. Wright, 63, 139

minorities, ix, 86, 90; classification of in U.S., 108; quotas for, xi, 25, 63

Mises, Ludwig von, 9–11, 24, 26, 148n.72

Moley, Raymond, 65

Molnar, Thomas, x, 20

Mommsen, Wolfgang, 76

Monde, Le, 106, 113–14

Montagu, Ashley, 100

Montesquieu, Charles de Secondat, 23

Morris, George Sylvester, 3

Morrison, Toni, 88

Mugabe, Robert, 34

multiculturalism, 88–91, 114, 164n.109; and the British Labour Party, 127; in France, 114

Mumford, Lewis, 3, 14–15

Murphey, Dwight D., 58

Murray, Charles, 4–5

Mussolini, Benito, 44, 51, 66, 175n.12

Myrdal, Alva, 57

Myrdal, Gunnar, 57, 100

Nagel, Stuart, 62

Nation, 14

National Front (France), viii, 111–17, 130, 168nn.23 and 24

National Labor Relations Act, 65

National Labor Relations Board, 65

National Recovery act, 65

National Review, 75

National Socialism, 50

nationalism, 10, 16, 44, 46, 134

Nature of Prejudice, The (Allport), 100

Nazis, Nazism, 3, 10, 63, 66; American 97; French neo-, 113–14; as label of opprobrium used by pluralist ideologues, 77, 167n.16

neoconservatives, 29, 72–73, 139

New Class, 72–73, 129

New Deal, 65–70, 94–95; historiography of, 31

New Democratic Party (Canada), 7

New Republic, 4–5, 14, 51, 55, 59–60, 64–66, 82, 96, 136

New Right, 128–30

New School for Social Research, 60

New York Times, 64, 96–97

New Zealand, ix

Newsweek, 64

Nisbet, Robert, 139

Nomos der Ende im Völkerrecht des ius publicum europaeum (Schmitt), 138

Norwar, 54

Notrin, Bernard, 106

Novak, Michael, 27, 148n.74

Officiis, DE (Cicero), xiv

Ontario Human Rights Code, 104

Origen, 36

Ortega y Gasset, José, 81, 110

O'Sullivan, John, 75

Palmerston, Henry John Temple, 8, 15

Pangle, Thomas, 20

Pareto, Vilfredo, 24, 39, 43–46, 48, 152n.49

Parizeau, Jean, 120

Parks, Rosa, 96

Peel, Robert, 8

Peirce, Charles Sanders, 102

Pericles, 36, 103

Peron, Juan, 111

Perrineau, Pascal, 112, 116

Phillips, Kevin, 68

Philosophical Radicals, 16

Philosophy of Right (Hegel), 13, 50; not an invitation to social engineering, 110

Piccone, Paul, 69, 129, 165n.112

Plamenatz, John, 35

Plato, 36, 88, 90, 123–24

pluralism, x, 69–71, as behavioral coercion, 85; critics thereof alleged to be socially diseased, 95; vs. custom, 83; dissent against stifled, 102–9; and environmentalism, 100; globalist ideology of, 74, 95–102, 138–39; and human rights, newly discovered, 88; and liberal democracy, 71–109; and multiculturalism, 88–91, 164n.109; vs. objectivity in scholarship, 90; and postmodernism, 128–30; and public administration, 90, 107; as public philosophy, 83–95; scientific pretensions of, 86, 100; and sensitivity to the disadvantaged, 85–87, 95; vs. settled beliefs, 82–84; universalist pretensions of, 84; value-relativity of, 83–88

Politica (Aristotle), 115

Political Man (Lipset), 74

populism, populists, ix, xii; in Anglophone Canada, xiii, 133–34; in Austria, viii, 118–20; and the avoidance of devisive moral issues, 131–34; in California, 132–33; in France, 111–17, 120, 130–31; in Italy, 118–22; in Latin America, 111; and the New Right, 128–30; as a postliberal democratic force, 110–34; in Quebec, 120; and regionalism, 118–22; strength greatest in Latin-Catholic societies, 119; in the U.S., xiii, 117–18, 121–26, 132–33; weakness of 135, 138, 141

Pörksen, Uwe, 99

Portugal, 131

postmodernism, 128–29

Poujade, Pierre, 112

Price of Freedom, The (Lippmann), 81

Princeton University Center for Human Values, 88

Progressive Democracy (Croly), 59

Progressives (U.S.), 66, 77–79, 82; espousal of racial segregation by, 77; and fascism, 66, 157n53

Promise of American Life, The (Croly), 59, 64

property rights, 6, 48, 67

Prussia, 50, 57

public administration, xii, xiv, 11, 19, 24–28, 39, 148n.72; vs. both capitalism and socialism, 51; democracy intertwined with, 48; effect of greater on aggregations on individuals than traditional communities, 107; equality of esteem as social policy of, 62; and ethnic inclusiveness, 23–25; expansion of not a necessary consequence of economic growth, 175–76n.13; and immigration, 127, 172n.70; as a material provider, 135; popular government identified with, 19; and science, 10, 56; spiritual transformation of passive citizens as aim of, 90; and the welfare state, 49–71. *See also* democracy, liberal

Public Philosophy, The (Lippmann), 81–83

Putnam, Hilary, 86

Quebec, 120

Quotidien de Paris, 105

Raab, Earl, 97

racial integration, 5–6

racism, 80, 89, 105–6, 109

Rae, Bob, 7

Rahe, Paul, 37

Rauch, Basil, 65

Rawls, John, 21–24, 37, 88

Reader's Digest, 10

Reagan, Ronald, 74

redistribution of income, wealth, 10, 19, 21–26, 30, 38, 46–47, 73

Reisman, David, 3

Rémusat, Charles, 40–41

Republic (Plato), 90

Republicans (U.S.), vii

Republics Ancient and Modern (Rahe), 37

Revolt of the Elites, The (Lasch), 72

Revolt of the Masses (Ortega y Gassett), 8

Rise of American Civilization, The (Beard and Beard), 15
Rizzi, Bruno, 66
Road to Reaction, The (Finer), 11, 145–46n.23
Road to Serfdom, The (Hayek), 10, 25
Roberts, Paul Crag, vii
Roepke, Wilhelm von, 113
Roosevelt, Eleanor, 78
Roosevelt, Franklin D., 65, 69, 75, 93
Roosevelt, Theodore, 64–65
Rosanvallon, Pierre, 70
Rothman, Stanley, 122–24
Rousseau, Jean Jacques, 34
Ruggiero, Guido, 6, 10
Russia, 50, 66

Sartre, J. P., 83
Scandinavia, 46–47
Schapiro, J. Salwyn, 7, 12
Schlesinger, Arthur Jr., 15, 95
Schmitt, Carl, x, 17, 68, 137–38, 140–41
Schumpeter, Joseph, 32
Schwartz, Harry, 53
Search for the American Right Wing, The (Hixon), 124
Second Treatise of Government, The (Locke), 6
Sheerman, Barry, 101
Shorter, Edward, 124
Simon, Julian, 97
Smith, Adam, 7, 27, 37
Smith, Eric Owen, 52
social engineering. *See* social planning
social planning, xi–xiv, 5, 13–16, 19–20, 25–28, 30; German, 59; government identified with, 73; as a human right, 129; vs. inherited belief systems, 136
social sciences: as instrument of indoctrination, 80; politicization of, 79–80
socialism, 9–10, 12, 24, 31, 46, 51; its decline misleading, 55; Scandinavian, 66, 125; and scientific planning, 99
socialization, 55–62, 124; democratic, ix, xiv, 4, 17–19, 77–78; educational, 28, 131–32
Socrates, 7, 82

Sombart, Werner, 9
Sontag, Deborah, 97
Southern League (U.S.), 122
Soviet Union, 98
Spain, 50, 61
Spender, Stephen, 127
Spirit of Democratic Capitalism, The (Novak), 27
state: administrative, 67–68, 139–41; ideologies of, 156n.43; as instrument of power, 137, 175–76n.13; instrumentalist, 85; managerial, 85, 123, 125–27, 135–41; socialist, 101; therapeutic, 79, 85; undemocratic character of modern type of, 69. *See also* welfare state
Stein, Dan, 97
Stephen, James Fitzjames, 30, 37, 40, 47–48
Stephen, Leslie, 48
Sterilization Act (Sweden), 57
Stimson, Henry, 16
Strange Death of Liberal England, 1910–1914, The (Dangerfield), 12
Strauss, Leo, 20
Studebaker, John Ward, 68
Studies in Prejudice (Horkheimer and Flowerman), 90–91, 94
suffrage, universal, 6
Sweden, 57, 65, 119, 131–32
Szasz, Thomas, 79

Taguieff, Pierre André, 114
Tarchi, Alessandro, 128
tax evasion, 119
Taylor, Charles, 72, 89
Thatcher, Margaret, 27–28, 53, 74, 113
Theory of Justice, A (Rawls), 21–23
Thucydides, 36
Tikkun, 90
Time of the Americans: F.D.R., Truman, Eisenhower, Marshall, and MacArthur, In the (Fromkin), 67–68
Tixier-Vignancour, Jean-Louis, 112
Tocqueville, Alexis de, 41–42, 48, 50
Tönnies, Ferdinand, 38
Trasformazioni della Democrazia (Pareto), 43
Trattato di Sociologia generale (Pareto), 45

Treitschke, Heinrich, 7
Trilling, Lionel, 20
True and Only Heaven, The (Lasch), 80
Truman, Harry, 69
Tugwell, Rexford, 28, 65–66

Ulmen, Gary, 69
UNESCO, 99–100
universal nation, 76–77; U.S. identified as, 95
U.S. Commission on Civil Rights, 107–8
U.S. Council of Economic Advisors, 54
U.S. Department of Education, 107

Valdès-Boulouque, Martine, 106–7
Vargas, Getulio, 111
Vattel, Emmerich de, 137
Veblen, Thorstein, 18
Veyne, Paul, 103, 123
Voltaire, 7
voters: female, vii–viii; gender gap among, viii. *See also* franchise; suffrage

Wagner, Robert, 65
Wall Street Journal, 64, 75, 77
Walras, Leon, 24
Ward, Lester Frank, 18

Washington Post, 122
Watson, J. B., 78
Wattenberg, Ben, 77
Weber, Max, 26, 30, 32, 39, 48, 74, 87, 141
Weinstein, James, 63
welfare state, vii–xiii, 7, 12, 26; Canadian, 165n.112; and cultural diversity, 60–62; democratic, 26, 49–71, 72, 75; English, 27, 52–53; national, 62; popular demand for, 49, 62, 68; as public administration's achievement, 49–71; reversal of unlikely, 54–55, 68; and transfers of income, 49–50
Westbrook, Robert B., 59, 101
Weyl, Walter, 60, 66
Whitehead, Laurence, 17
Williamson, Chilton, Jr., 96
Wilson, Harold, 53
Wilson, Pete, xiii, 133
Wilson, Woodrow, 17, 20, 64–66, 69, 75, 77, 101
Wolfe, Alan, 125

Xenophon, 123

Zionists, 51

NEW FORUM BOOKS

New Forum Books makes available to general readers outstanding original inter-disciplinary scholarship with a special focus on the juncture of culture, law, and politics. New Forum Books is guided by the conviction that law and politics not only reflect culture but help to shape it. Authors include leading political scientists, sociologists, legal scholars, philosophers, theologians, historians, and economists writing for nonspecialist readers and scholars across a range of fields. Looking at questions such as political equality, the concept of rights, the problem of virtue in liberal politics, crime and punishment, population, poverty, economic development, and the international legal and political order, New Forum Books seeks to explain—not explain away—the difficult issues we face today.

Paul Edward Gottfried, *After Liberalism:*
Mass Democracy in the Managerial State

Peter Berkowitz, *Virtue and the Making of*
Modern Liberalism

John E. Coons and Patrick M. Brennan, *By Nature Equal:*
The Anatomy of a Western Insight